90 DAYS TO SUCCESS IN FUNDRAISING

Timothy Kachinske

Course Technology PTR

A part of Cengage Learning

COURSE TECHNOLOGY
CENGAGE Learning™

Australia, Brazil, Japan, Korea, Mexico, Singapore, Spain, United Kingdom, United States

COURSE TECHNOLOGY
CENGAGE Learning™

**90 Days to Success in
Fundraising**
Timothy Kachinske

**Publisher and General Manager,
Course Technology PTR:**
Stacy L. Hiquet

**Associate Director of
Marketing:**
Sarah Panella

Manager of Editorial Services:
Heather Talbot

Marketing Manager:
Mark Hughes

Acquisitions Editor:
Mitzi Koontz

Project Editor/Copy Editor:
Cathleen D. Small

Editorial Services Coordinator:
Jen Blaney

Interior Layout Tech:
Bill Hartman

Cover Designer:
Luke Fletcher

Indexer:
Sharon Shock

Proofreader:
Sandi Wilson

For product information and technology assistance,
contact us at **Cengage Learning Customer &
Sales Support, 1-800-354-9706**

For permission to use material from this text or product,
submit all requests online at **cengage.com/permissions**
Further permissions questions can be e-mailed to
permissionrequest@cengage.com.

All trademarks are the property of their respective owners.

Library of Congress Control Number: 2008935220

ISBN-13: 978-1-59863-876-9

ISBN-10: 1-59863-876-9

Course Technology, a part of Cengage Learning
20 Channel Center Street
Boston, MA 02210
USA

Cengage Learning is a leading provider of customized learning solutions with office locations around the globe, including Singapore, the United Kingdom, Australia, Mexico, Brazil, and Japan. Locate your local office at: **international.cengage.com/region**.

Cengage Learning products are represented in Canada by Nelson Education, Ltd.

For your lifelong learning solutions, visit **courseptr.com**.

Visit our corporate Web site at **cengage.com**.

Printed in Canada
1 2 3 4 5 6 7 11 10 09

For Edward and Frances

About the Author

Timothy Kachinske has extensive experience in developing and managing fundraising programs. Over a period of 17 years, he has served as a development officer at a private liberal arts college, a research university, an international science organization, a social service agency, an overseas American college, and an independent school. At these organizations he has had responsibilities directly related to annual funds, special events, corporate and foundation fundraising, major gifts, planned giving, and capital campaigns.

Tim holds a B.A. from the University of Minnesota, Duluth, and an M.A. from the University of Minnesota. He is a Microsoft Certified Professional with core competency in Microsoft Dynamics CRM 4.0, and he holds multiple certifications from Sage Software. He is a veteran of the US Army with 16 months overseas duty.

Tim lives in a suburb near Washington, D.C., where he currently works as a consultant.

About the Technical Editors

David Williams

David Williams is Vice Chancellor for University Advancement and Marketing at the University of Wisconsin-Stout. He previously served as Vice President for University Advancement at Minnesota State University and Vice President for Development at Ripon College.

Farrand McDonald O'Donoghue

Farrand McDonald O'Donoghue is Development Director at the Bishop John T. Walker School for Boys. She has previously served as a development officer at The Smithsonian Institution, the United States Navy Memorial, and The Catholic University of America.

John Abodeely

John Abodeely is the Arts Education Manager for Americans for the Arts, the nation's leading nonprofit organization for advancing arts in America. John leads the Arts Education Network, a national network of 5,000 individuals and groups.

Edward Kachinske

Edward Kachinske is the author of more than 24 titles in the Customer Relationship Management industry, including *Maximizing Your Sales with Microsoft Dynamics CRM 4.0* and *Maximizing Your Sales with Salesforce.com*.

Contents

Chapter 3
Special Events 59

Chapter 5
Corporate Relations 153

Chapter 6
Major Gifts, Planned Giving, and Endowment . . 177

Chapter 7
Capital Campaigns. **203**

Chapter 8
Fundraising Software 217

Introduction

Fundraising is the word broadly used to refer to the solicitation of money for a charitable purpose. In the nonprofit sector, fundraising refers to the collection of charitable contributions from donors who may receive a tax deduction as a result. Professionals who work for nonprofit organizations and are engaged in the planning and soliciting of contributions are called *fundraisers*. Every nonprofit organization in the United States depends on fundraising for its survival. No nonprofit organization can survive, much less flourish, without dedicated employees engaged in fundraising.

The terms *development* and *advancement* are often used in the nonprofit world as synonyms for fundraising. Professionals working in fundraising positions at nonprofit organizations may be called *development officers*. The name *development office* refers to a department in which everyone is primarily engaged in managing or supporting the fundraising effort of the organization. The term *advancement* is used commonly in education circles (colleges, universities, and independent schools) in connection with fundraising. *Advancement* also encompasses areas and positions not primarily engaged in fundraising, such as college relations, school relations, community relations, parent relations, alumni relations, and public relations.

This book is intended to be of assistance to anyone interested in fundraising. Chapter 1 will take you through the job search, application, and interview process. Chapters 2 through 5 cover the four areas of competence in fundraising that are the most common entry points for professionals: annual fund, special events, foundation relations, and corporate relations. Hopefully, each of these chapters contains enough information and advice to ensure success in your first 90 days on the job.

In Chapters 6 and 7, you will read about major gift fundraising, planned giving, endowments, and capital campaigns. Professional positions in these areas normally require prior fundraising experience. However, it is possible in some cases for professionals to make a career change into these areas so long as they have other appropriate transferable experience. Even if you are not directly engaged in these major gift roles at the beginning of your fundraising career, you will need to understand what they involve.

The final two chapters provide a discussion of fundraising software and the vast, new possibilities of fundraising on the Internet.

The best advice in this book is contained in the interviews with "seasoned fundraisers." Each one of these individuals is a highly respected, successful professional with many years of experience in development work. Each one has made the world a better place. Enjoy their insights and take their counsel!

Best of luck for success in your first 90 days as a fundraiser.

—Tim Kachinske

Chapter 1

Finding and Securing a Position

- Searching for a Position
- Interviewing for a Position

No one ever grows up thinking, "I want to be a fundraiser." However, countless people engaged in fundraising professions look back over their careers with gratitude and pride, thankful that life took them in that direction and proud of the contributions they have been able to make through their work. Fundraising nourishes and sustains the nonprofit sector of American society. It is absolutely vital to the network of educational, medical, religious, environmental, and social organizations that Americans depend on in so many ways.

Everyone in this great country has been served, and served well, by nonprofit organizations. You may have been born in a nonprofit hospital. At some point in your youth, you may have benefited from a community athletic organization or the local branch of a national youth organization, such as Boy Scouts or Girl Scouts. You may have checked books out of a Carnegie library. Perhaps you attended an independent or parochial school. Perhaps your family was helped through a difficult time, such as a fire or a natural disaster. If you start thinking about your life, your education, and the lives of people you know, you will undoubtedly find instances when you have been touched in very important ways by nonprofit organizations.

Most successful fundraising professionals working for nonprofit organizations have found their calling in ways that seem logical in retrospect but could never have been predicted. In recent years, several academic degree programs in fundraising have sprouted up, but such programs have not been able to satisfy the nonprofit sector's constant need for new fundraising professionals. The majority of successful fundraisers still do not enter the profession through a professional school. Many, but by no means all, have had a liberal arts education. However, the one factor that unites all successful fundraising professionals is not their background. It is their passion for the work.

DIALOGUE WITH A PROFESSIONAL: MSGR. DENNIS MAHON

Monsignor Dennis Mahon has served in executive or administrative positions in a variety of educational and social service organizations over the past two decades. Presently, he is serving on the senior graduate faculty of communications at Seton Hall University. He has previously served as Vice President for Development at The Catholic University of America, Executive Director of Catholic Community Services (Newark, NJ), and Vice Chancellor of Seton Hall University.

At The Catholic University of America in Washington, DC, a comprehensive research institution enrolling more than 5,000 undergraduate and graduate students, Msgr. Mahon supervised a 40-plus person advancement staff. He served as the university's chief major gifts officer and also had responsibilities to retool the undergraduate student marketing and admissions effort.

At Catholic Community Services, the largest social welfare agency in the state of New Jersey, Msgr. Mahon led a staff of 1,100 employees and an annual budget of $72 million. Mahon led CCS's first annual gala dinner in 1998, achieving more than $1 million in pledges. The fundraising efforts of Catholic Community Services support a vast array of social welfare programs, impacting the lives of more than 80,000 adults and children annually.

Msgr. Mahon earned a Ph.D. in mass communication from Syracuse University. He earned his B.A. in classical languages at Seton Hall University and completed seminary studies at Immaculate Conception Seminary. Ordained in 1970, Msgr. Mahon was honored by Pope John Paul II in 1989 with the designation of Private Chaplain to His Holiness.

How did you first get interested in fundraising, and what was your first development role?

I was first interested in fundraising in 1990, while Vice President for Planning at Seton Hall, and I had the opportunity to speak with Board of Regents members about the details of the new library we had on the development track. I asked about an in-kind donation of 200 fire extinguishers from an alum and new Board member whose company manufactured such equipment.

The Board member said, "Sure, what else do you need?" Taking a gamble, I pointed to the $400,000 item for the internal sprinkler system, and he said, "I can do that too, and will also contribute $500,000." Obviously, this fundraising stuff looked very interesting.

How could a younger person or someone re-entering the workforce get development experience?

Fundraising is something so necessary to educational and nonprofit organizations that even before formally applying for a position, an interested person can volunteer to help with fundraising, ranging from calling your college classmates to helping the local Rotary toy drive. The need for help is universal to these groups, and the fundraising is perfectly genuine.

What kind of an educational background might be good for a recent graduate who is interested in a fundraising position at an educational organization or a social service agency?

A general liberal arts background will serve as well as any more specialized program of study. You basically need only recognize that the group you are volunteering or working for serves a philanthropic purpose and that the people you will be soliciting one way or another are capable of remarkable generosity.

What special skills are useful for someone interested in a fundraising position?

The best advice I ever received was from a wily and successful fundraising veteran. His advice was simplicity itself. If you can be the person who says, "Fred, only you know the answer to this question, but you could help Catholic Charities immensely if you could give us $250,000 a year for the next four years. Can you do it?"

If you have the moxie or chutzpah or courage or passion to be the person who directly asks such questions, you will have and will always have a place in a fundraising organization.

What kind of experience might be useful for someone who is thinking about a career change and is looking at a position in fundraising?

As I mentioned, there are infinite opportunities on a small scale to volunteer your help to so many organizations, whether you're calling your college classmates or helping with a local charity drive. You can try fundraising in practically a "no harm, no foul, no lose" situation. Just try out for the part of the person who can do the asking.

You've interviewed probably hundreds of people. What would be important for someone planning to interview for a development position?

When it comes down to interviewing for a remunerated position, clearly all the volunteering and testing should already be done, and you should have several experiences that you came to fully enjoy. The most important thing to keep in mind is that organizations absolutely need help in this area. There are no casual or conditional positions. They really need you. Show them that you are the person to do what they need done.

What have you found most rewarding in your various roles in fundraising?

Even with the best preparation, even with a straightforward "ask," people are still going to have to reply, more often than not, "I can't at this time." So, after you have put in all the effort, the gifts that come "effortlessly" are the ones you remember most.

We had asked a Catholic University alum for a $1,000,000 donation twice, at one-year intervals. It turned out that we should have been asking his wife. He regarded her interests more than his own. At the end of that second year, however, an attorney called from Florida and inquired whether CUA administered trusts. He was put in direct touch with University counsel, and two weeks later a $1.6 million donation was signed and sealed.

Have there been any challenges?

The challenges arise from the seeming nature of philanthropic and educational institutions. Their needs are usually so expansive that they succumb to the ultimately self-defeating bad habit of making up any projected annual budget shortfalls by simply "covering" the budget "gap" by hiking the fundraising goals for the next budget year. Not realistic, but such an inbred response that the national average duration for middle and upper fundraising professionals is two years.

You've been involved in raising gifts and grants for everything from churches to large universities and social service organizations. Are there great differences among these organizations from an applicant's point of view?

Not surprisingly, I'm going to say that the basic function of fundraising for churches, colleges and universities, or social service organizations is identical. Someone has to "ask." Having said that, experience will give you a better feel for who the major donors are, by name, in the three named areas.

Searching for a Position

There a numerous ways to look for a job in fundraising. If you are serious about pursuing a position, you should be looking at all of them. Because new positions crop up weekly, you want to know about all possible job search venues and return to them frequently. There is no single source of information about fundraising jobs; on the contrary, there are many sources for you to explore.

Online Search Engines

The process of finding out about job openings in fundraising (often called *development* or *advancement*) has been simplified greatly by online search engines. A few major newspapers, *The Washington Post* among them, still host job searches locally. Most, however, provide links to search engines that allow the job seeker the option of searching not only local, but national listings as well. For example, *The New York Times* and *The Boston Globe* link to Monster.com (see Figure 1.1).

The *Miami Herald*, the *Chicago Tribune*, and the *Los Angeles Times* all link to CareerBuilder.com (see Figure 1.2).

The Dallas Morning News, the *Atlanta Journal Constitution*, and the *St. Louis Post Dispatch* link to Yahoo! HotJobs (see Figure 1.3).

All of these job search engines allow you to do keyword searches to narrow down your search by type of job and location. Generally speaking, the keyword "fundraising" generates better results than "development." "Fundraising" pulls up the development jobs but does not usually return all of the different types of positions—business development, for example—that have the word "development" in the title or job description. These search engines allow you to post your resume, track your searches, and register to receive e-mail alerts when new jobs meeting your search criteria are posted. They also provide advice on a variety of topics, such as resume writing.

Meta search engines are very helpful because they pull job postings from a variety of sources, such as newspapers, nonprofit websites, and other search engines. Typically, they will state where each posting comes from and provide a link to the original advertisement. Indeed.com sweeps a huge range of sources and includes forums, a blog, and advice on job-related topics (see Figure 1.4).

Figure 1.1 *Monster.com.*

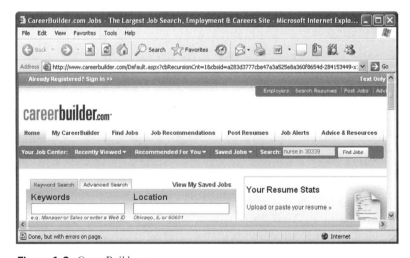

Figure 1.2 *CareerBuilder.com.*

Figure 1.3 *Yahoo! HotJobs.*

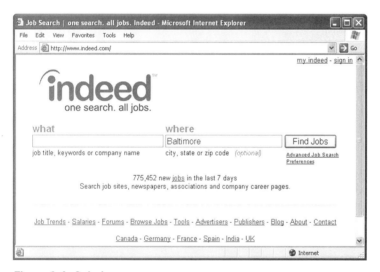

Figure 1.4 *Indeed.com.*

Juju.com, an updated descendent of the first job search engine site on the web, provides similar resources and is perhaps the easiest to use of all (see Figure 1.5). Just type in "fundraising" and your zip code, and a list of available positions will pop right up on the screen.

All of these search engines can be used at no cost. You may need to register in order to take advantage of some features, such as RSS feeds and e-mail alerts. Check them all out.

Figure 1.5 *Juju.com.*

Sites Oriented to the Nonprofit and Fundraising World

There are a number of helpful websites devoted specifically to the nonprofit world that can assist you in finding the development job that is right for you. Familiarize yourself with the most important sites and visit them frequently. Because these sites are maintained by entities that have a singular focus on fundraising, they are likely to yield possibilities that may not come to your attention by other means.

The Chronicle of Philanthropy

First on your list should be *The Chronicle of Philanthropy*, a biweekly national newspaper devoted to issues of interest to professional fundraisers. Many nonprofits advertise fundraising positions in *The Chronicle's* print edition and separately on its website. Every week hundreds of jobs are listed. It will cost you nothing to access *The Chronicle of Philanthropy's* website Jobs section and online search service (see Figure 1.6). Nevertheless, you should subscribe to the print newspaper to read the country's main newspaper for nonprofit management and to access to other useful tools on the

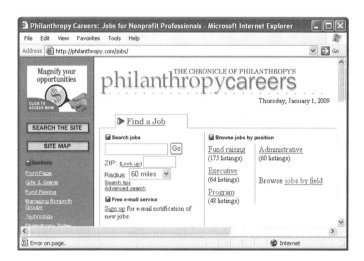

Figure 1.6
The Chronicle of Philanthropy's *job search page*.

website. Job listings in *The Chronicle* are paid for by advertisers and may not be snagged by meta-searches done by commercial job search engines. Often you will find position openings in *The Chronicle* that you won't see elsewhere.

Your can search *The Chronicle* by keyword, such as "fundraising," and you can narrow your search to within 30, 60, 90, or 120 miles of a zip code. You can, of course, omit the zip code filter if you are willing to relocate for your new job. The results of your search will produce a list of positions available that can be sorted by date posted, organization name, state, position (annual fund, capital campaigns, corporate and foundation relations, and so on), and field (advocacy, arts, community development, education, and so on). You can also do an advanced search and filter for specific development positions (annual fund, corporate and foundation relations, capital campaigns, and so on), for specific fields (advocacy, animal protection, community development, education, international, and so on) or by state or region of the U.S. The great advantage to *The Chronicle's* search engine is that it is indexed and maintained by people who know fundraising, and their expertise will help you to find precisely what you are looking for.

You can automate your search of *The Chronicle's* Philanthropy Careers by creating a search agent based on your most recent search criteria. This will enable you to receive e-mail messages alerting you to new jobs that match your search. This is a free service. To stop it or to change the search criteria, you simply cancel your previous search agent and create a new one.

In addition to Philanthropy Careers, *The Chronicle* has a web page called Regeneration that offers articles, resources, and links for seasoned private-sector professionals and people re-entering the workforce who are considering a career change in the nonprofit sector.

Association of Fundraising Professionals

The website of the Association of Fundraising Professionals (AFP) has a Jobs search site that is free to job seekers (see Figure 1.7). You can browse currently posted jobs in fundraising with a click of the mouse. You can also do advanced searches by state, job level, and a variety of specific categories of fundraising. These categories are the most detailed and specific available on any online search for fundraising jobs. You are likely to get very accurate and specific search results on this site. Sign up for a free account and create a search agent that will send you e-mail alerts of new jobs posted according to your criteria. After you familiarize yourself with the Jobs page and services, you should begin studying the other services of AFP. If you are successful in your job search, you will probably want to join AFP and its 30,000 members.

Figure 1.7
AFP's job search page.

Foundation Center

The Foundation Center's Job Corner lists fulltime job openings at U.S. foundations and nonprofit organizations (see Figure 1.8). Nonprofit advertisers pay a modest fee to post position openings. Searches for applicants are free and easy to filter by employer in two relevant employer categories (Educational Institutions or Nonprofit Organizations). You can also filter for positions by fundraising position categories (Development/Fundraising or Grantwriting), and by state. The Foundation Center search filters are reliable, and you don't need to have an account to use this site.

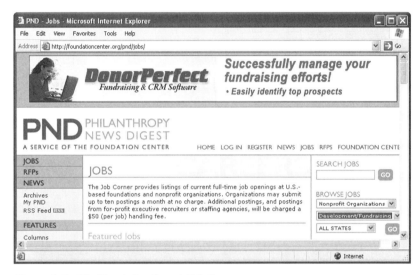

Figure 1.8 *The Foundation Center's Job Corner.*

Idealist.org

Idealist.org is a site maintained by the nonprofit Action Without Borders (see Figure 1.9). Among its many features for people working in the nonprofit world is its Nonprofit Jobs search engine. This is an internationally oriented site that enables you to filter job searches by country, state, city, area of focus (Art, Education, Health and Medicine, and so on), as well as a broad job category (Fundraising & Development). You can do searches without signing up, but to see the detailed postings of the lists returned on your searches, you will need to sign up for a free account. This is one of the largest nonprofit sites available, and it features blogs, repositories of information, and other resources for people in the nonprofit world.

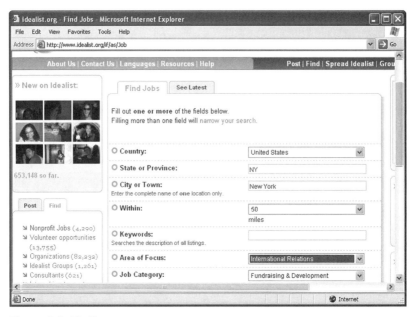

Figure 1.9 *Idealist.org.*

HigherEdJobs.com

HigherEdJobs is a good website to check out regularly for development jobs at colleges and universities (see Figure 1.10). As in the case of The Chronicle, nonprofit employers pay HigherEdJobs to advertise positions, which means that the site has a degree of quality control. HigherEdJobs has a View Our Job Listings page that provides a category listing of administrative positions with a click on the category Administrative. The category Development and Fundraising normally returns a list of hundreds of positions that can be filtered by date posted, institution, location, job title, or category. You can do an advanced search by Job Category (Admin – Development and Fund Raising) and location (by single state). HigherEdJobs also offers free services to save your searches and have your searches automatically e-mailed to you as you run them.

Personal Contacts

Don't hesitate to ask professionals you know either socially or from a previous job for advice about possible fundraising positions. Because so many professional fundraisers enter the profession through their commitment to a cause or organization rather than to fundraising in an abstract sense, it can also be vital to get

Figure 1.10 *HigherEdJobs.com.*

the advice and support of staff in nonprofits you have supported as a volunteer. For example, if you have demonstrated your passion for environmental protection through volunteer river cleanup work over a period of years, ask nonprofit staff who can speak to your commitment to do so. If you have put forth heroic efforts in a campaign to raise funds to eradicate a disease, call upon those familiar with your efforts to support your application to work for that particular cause.

Making a Good Impression on Paper or Online

Securing a fundraising position requires that you demonstrate your passion for the cause and your ability to communicate that passion effectively. Your response to an advertisement that interests you is your chance to display both your commitment and your ability to communicate. Your resume and cover letter will display your skills to people who may not have met you.

There is a wealth of advice on resume writing in books and on job search websites. Take advantage of all of that seems relevant to craft your resume. To hone in on how to make your resume resonate for a nonprofit audience, ask any contacts you may have in the nonprofit world to critique your resume.

Commitment to the cause matters to people making hiring decisions for a nonprofit organization. You may be prompted to apply for a position because of a personal connection to the cause. You may be an alumna or alumnus of the institution. You may have had a close family member who grappled with the disease for which the nonprofit is raising research funds. You may have grown up in the area the nonprofit is dedicated to preserving for posterity. You may have valuable insights gained over many years spent in a social service career related to the nonprofit's model for change. Never forget that when it comes to hiring decisions, a genuine personal connection and commitment can override any generic professional qualification in nonprofit management.

Each time you submit your resume for a nonprofit fundraising position, review it to see whether there is any way you might highlight your personal connection to the organization. Think in terms of your volunteer work. Any manner of volunteer experiences or life experiences that would not necessarily be considered relevant to other job applications might not only be relevant but crucial for an application for a fundraising position. This is not to suggest that your resume should be rewritten for each job application. It is a matter of looking at your background in terms of what you can bring to the mission of the nonprofit. The connection you make must be genuine.

Your response to a position announcement is the stage of the process when you can showcase your communication and marketing skills sight unseen.

Interviewing for a Position

The purpose of an application is to get an interview. If you are able to pique the interest of a prospective employer, you may get a phone call to set up a phone interview before you are actually brought in for a face-to-face interview. Should you receive a call, voicemail message, or e-mail message requesting a phone interview, you should be careful to set it at a time when you will be alone, relaxed, and not interrupted.

Most development offices will interview three or more persons for any open position. Assume that the situation is competitive and prepare accordingly. Learn as much as you possibly can about the organization before your interview. When you get to the interview, you don't want to ask any questions to which you could have found answers on your own.

Interview Formats

In general, there are three ways an interview may be set up. You may be called in by the decision maker and be interviewed by him or her alone. This sole interviewer could be the chief development officer or another development officer, depending on the place of the position in the organizational structure. If you happen to get on well with the interviewer, this is probably the easiest type of interview. If you don't, it is probably the hardest.

A more common interview format is the round-robin interview. Here you will be called in to meet with a primary interviewer and then sent around to meet at appointed times with other professionals at the nonprofit organization. It's important to keep your energy level up as you proceed through these meetings and to maintain your enthusiasm for the position throughout the day. You may circle back to your primary interviewer or you may not, but you can be sure that your primary interviewer will consult with all the people you have met with before contacting you again.

Another format you may encounter is the group interview. This may begin with a one-on-one interview with the decision maker, followed by a face-to-face meeting with a half-dozen people gathered in one room to ask questions and discuss your interest in the position. This group could include peers of your primary interviewer, support staff, persons who hold positions parallel to the one you are applying for, board members or other volunteers, or a consultant. These people are doing their interviewing work at the request of your primary interviewer, who is looking for second opinions about you. If you find yourself in this situation, you should resist focusing on one person in the group, even if someone emerges as a leader. Take care to look into the eyes of everyone at the meeting, and turn as you speak so that you connect with all persons present. Spread your enthusiasm equally, and make sure that everyone in the room senses your competence and passion for the position.

The aim of your interview is to get a job offer. You can expect to hear relatively soon after your interview about your status. Development positions normally need to be filled quickly. The time a position remains unfulfilled translates as time funds have not been raised.

You should not raise salary requirements in an interview situation. If they are brought up by your primary interviewer, you should be prepared to respond to her or him, but generally you should not discuss salary until you have an offer. If there is no salary range in the application notice, you can do some research early in the job search process. Salary averages and ranges for almost any development position can be found in the online resources of *The Chronicle of Higher Education*, the Association of Fundraising Professionals, and the various commercial online job search options covered earlier in this chapter.

DIALOGUE WITH A PROFESSIONAL: IRENE LUKOFF

Irene Lukoff has more than 28 years of experience in nonprofit administration and fundraising. Presently, she is a Director of Development in the Centers and Institutes unit of Penn Medicine Development and Alumni Relations at the University of Pennsylvania, with primary responsibility for the Institute on Aging, the Center for Neurodegenerative Disease Research, the Alzheimer's Disease Core Center/Penn Memory Center, and the Parkinson's Disease and Movement Disorders Center. In her 21 years at the University of Pennsylvania, she has also worked at the Center for Bioethics and the Wharton School, where she helped advance Wharton's $425 million Campaign for Sustained Leadership.

Among Lukoff's other notable accomplishments is the successful management of financial and development operations of the Chemical Heritage Foundation (CHF), from its days as a fledgling interdisciplinary Center at the University of Pennsylvania to what has matured into the premier resource for the study of the chemical and life sciences and related industries. Lukoff served as a key member of the development team that engineered the Foundation's transformation and move to self-sufficiency, including securing a $100 million bequest from the estate of Donald F. Othmer, raising $6 million to match the Othmer Challenge, and the purchase and renovation of the CHF's home at Independence National Historical Park.

Lukoff holds a B.A. from Brown University, an M.A. in museum studies from The George Washington University, and an M.S. in higher education from the University of Pennsylvania's Graduate School of Education.

After you got your M.A. in museum studies, you embarked on a long and successful fundraising career. What was your first development job, and what drew you to it?

What attracted me to and fueled my interest in fundraising was my long-term association with the Center for the History of Chemistry, which originated at the University of Pennsylvania and evolved into the Chemical Heritage Foundation (CHF). I started as Assistant Director of the Center and eventually became Director of Development for the Foundation.

I learned the craft of fundraising from one of the field's consummate masters, the renowned historian of science who founded the Department of History and Sociology of Science at Penn—Arnold Thackray, Ph.D. He later became President and is now Chancellor of CHF. Arnold's passion for the subject matter and his skill in connecting prospects to the mission of the organization and turning them into donors were awe-inspiring. It was a unique apprenticeship experience that I will never forget and will always be grateful for, since it allowed me to be part of one of history of philanthropy's amazing success stories—securing the "Othmer benevolency" (endowment)—that has transformed the Chemical Heritage Foundation into the international cultural and educational resource it is today.

What would you say are important skills for someone finishing an undergraduate or graduate degree and thinking about applying for a development position?

A basic understanding of how nonprofits operate—their governance and advisory board structure, fund and functional accounting, etc.—is quite helpful. It goes without saying that being organized, knowing how to interact with a variety of individuals, and having a customer service orientation are also desirable. However, most fundraising skills can be learned and perfected on the job. There are a number of certificate programs and even master's degree programs in nonprofit administration and development, but again, these are not critical in pursuing a career in development.

In large academic development shops like the one I am currently in—Penn Medicine Development and Alumni Relations (PMDAR)—there are numerous internal training opportunities. For example, at PMDAR or elsewhere in Penn development, the administrative assistant position is typically (but not always) the first step on the mobility ladder for a career in development. Probably the most important thing is having a strong commitment to the cause (for example, curing Alzheimer's or reducing global warming) and/or the organization and learning what motivates its constituencies to give. If you have that commitment along with a strong work ethic and are willing to ride the ups and downs of not only the economy, but also changes in Board and organizational leadership—external factors that you have no control over—all else will follow.

What kind of an educational background prepares a person for a successful career in development?

Any of the liberal arts that are geared toward the advancement and betterment of our society can provide good grounding for a career in development. Less frequently there are candidates who come to development from a background in science. Graduate studies in anthropology, psychology, social work, museum administration, or any of the humanistic fields that further reinforce our society's advancement and expose someone to interacting with many diverse individuals, their needs and aspirations, can also be helpful. Such studies can enhance analytical and research skills. There is no one typical path to a career in development.

What would you consider personally rewarding about your career in development?

Unlocking a donor's passions and matching those passions with the mission and needs of the organization is indeed the most rewarding aspect of this craft. You know you have achieved that objective when at the end of a cultivation process—be it as short as one visit or as long as 10 years—you hardly have to ask; rather, the prospect tells you what they would like to do for or give to the organization. Of course, depending on the case, there may be negotiations in between.

In my current role as Director of Development for Healthy Brain Aging & Neurodegenerative Diseases, knowing that private philanthropy can accelerate researchers' ability to find the causes and cures for debilitating neurodegenerative diseases is indeed the most rewarding feeling.

Have there been any special challenges?

There have always been challenges, as in trying to manage the expectations of donors, faculty, and organizational leaders. The economy is, of course, our biggest concern at this time. However, I don't believe we have seen its full impact reflected yet in transformational or major gift giving. If I recall correctly and if history is any indicator, transformational gifts can be given even in tough economic times. When we first started cultivating Donald F. Othmer for what ultimately became a $100+ million endowment, the nation and the economy were in a major slump, and we were still able to eventually secure such a unique transformational gift.

That said, in the aftermath of the recent economic crises and various political and financial scandals in 2008, philanthropists will be increasingly reluctant to part with their money and will certainly want to hold nonprofits to higher standards of account-ability for how their dollars will be invested. It will behoove leaders of the institutions seeking philanthropic support to make a better, more airtight case for how private support will be spent for the betterment of society.

I am pleased to say that we at Penn Medicine have been on track, if not ahead of schedule, for meeting our $1 billion goal of a total University goal of $3.5 billion dur-ing a capital campaign that is set to conclude in 2012. Our society is fundamentally altruistic and philanthropic, and I am confident that we will successfully pass through this economic turbulence and come out better for it—even if at Penn or elsewhere in the nonprofit development world we might have to adjust our campaign timeframes.

How could someone get development experience in order to qualify for an entry-level position?

There are plenty of opportunities for college students to get entry-level experience and embark on a career in development, including volunteering or doing work-study for development and alumni offices at their respective institutions, pursuing intern-ships in social work or aid/relief organizations (Red Cross, Habitat for Humanity, United Way, etc.) or other nonprofit organizations after graduation, joining and run-ning for leadership positions of student groups, organizing events, etc. Volunteering at nonprofit organizations, including service on governance or advisory boards, may also become an increasingly popular route for seniors who want to continue working beyond retirement and are considering a career move into development.

What suggestions would you offer someone who is working in the nonprofit sector and is thinking about making a career change by applying for a development position?

If seeking a change within your own organization, having any knowledge of the organization, be it technical, marketing/public relations, or administrative, is your biggest weapon, so play it up. You have an automatic leg up on any external candidate, so use it to your advantage. Come to the interview prepared to tell the hiring officers how you would use that competitive advantage in acquiring, cultivating, and stewarding donors. Turn the interview into an opportunity to role play with a mock prospect or donor.

If you are looking at other organizations, use a similar strategy to try to convince the hiring officer of the value you are bringing to the organization and how you can build on it. In today's economy, when so many jobs are being lost and whole industries are disappearing, it is good to show how flexible you can be and that you are willing to be retrained for a new generation of jobs. All of us have "transferable" skills; it's a question of how well we can market ourselves.

Are there any development training programs that have been particularly helpful to you and your colleagues?

As someone who has made her career in academic fundraising, I have been quite fortunate to benefit from numerous internal midyear and annual conferences and workshops. The two major organizations that put on training programs throughout the year and also run major annual conferences that I would highly recommend are American Association for Medical Colleges (AAMC) Group on Institutional Advancement (GIA) as well the Council for Advancement and Support of Education (CASE).

If at all possible, I would also encourage fundraising professionals to attend conferences put on by the professional associations of the organizations that they are fundraising for (for example, American Chemical Society, American Society of Bioethics and Humanities, American Society on Aging/National Council on Aging, Alzheimer's Association, etc.).

You've managed annual funds and you've worked on capital campaigns. How would you say they differ from an applicant's perspective?

Capital campaigns can be viewed as the pinnacle of a series of annual giving cycles whose scope and momentum are being accelerated. There is nothing magic about them. You are simply expanding your reach and intensifying your efforts to build on years of sustained donor acquisition, cultivation, solicitation, and stewardship, with the ultimate goal of substantially adding to your reserves.

While annual fund appeals are limited to sustaining and increasing the flow of operating funds to an organization, capital campaigns are usually comprehensive in nature—they target all funding streams: annual, capital, endowment, term, and planned giving. While there are certain aspects of capital campaigns that are similar across all organizations—for example, the length, its comprehensive nature, how dollars are counted, types of communication vehicles used (e.g. case statements, annual reports, press releases, etc.)—the goal of such campaigns varies depending on the type, size, needs, and constituency of the organization.

Chapter 2

The Annual Fund

- What Is the Annual Fund?
- Where Do Annual Fund Directors Come From?
- Determining Your Annual Fund Needs
- Greater Benefits from an Annual Fund
- Planning Your Annual Fund
- Finding and Working with Volunteers
- Mechanics of Solicitations
- Writing Letter Appeals
- Phone-a-Thons and Telethons
- Phone-a-Thon Scripting
- Acknowledging and Substantiating Gifts
- Your Professional Action Plan
- 90-Day Annual Fund Checklist

What Is the Annual Fund?

The annual fund is a year-round fundraising campaign that provides the bedrock funding that your organization will need to support general operations throughout the year. Unlike the capital campaign, which is aimed at one-time capital expenditures, such as buildings, infrastructure, and perhaps endowment, the annual fund is usually devoted to the day-to-day operations of your organization as set down in the annual budget.

An annual fund begins on the first day of your fiscal year and ends on the last day of your fiscal year. The day after your fiscal year ends, another annual fund will begin. Unlike a capital campaign,

---

MYTHS AND MISCONCEPTIONS

Myth: The annual fund will bring in a lot of big-figure donations.

Reality: The annual fund targets a wide range of donors, and most of those donors generally give in small amounts.

Misconception: The annual fund is a direct-mail appeal that involves sending a letter once a year to everyone who might possibly want to support your organization.

Reality: The annual fund is a campaign. It should consist of multiple communications in various forms. These "touches" should be consistent and should happen throughout the year.

Misconception: If a startup nonprofit has a multiyear grant from a foundation, it would make sense to try to secure additional large foundation grants rather than putting time and effort into developing an annual fund.

Reality: You should do both. Keep in mind that if one foundation has helped in the creation of your organization, it will probably be difficult to attract sustaining funding from other foundations. Starting up an annual fund is the first step to take to diversify your gift and grant support. Broadening your sources of support with an annual fund will help to make your nonprofit more attractive to foundations, which rarely want to sustain a nonprofit by themselves. Also, a successful annual fund is essential for building other fundraising programs that will further your funding diversity. A nonprofit can rarely survive in the long term with just one source of support.

---

which extends over a period of several years, each annual fund campaign will be completed at the end of 12 months.

Most annual fund contributions will be unrestricted and therefore can be used for anything contained in the annual budget. Expenses such as staff salaries, computer equipment, office supplies and equipment, postage, and all of the regular business expenses your organization incurs throughout the year can be—at least in part—covered by proceeds from your annual fund campaign.

An effective annual fund campaign will always involve multiple methods of contact to prospective donors. You will carefully script out your plan for the 12 months in advance and roll it out month by month.

Where Do Annual Fund Directors Come From?

Annual fund directors come from all walks of life. Frequently, they come from within an organization itself. People who intern, teach, or perform other functions in a nonprofit organization are often attracted to annual fund work when a position opens up. Their institutional knowledge gives them a jumpstart. Professionals in fields such as sales, marketing, or public relations often find that their skill sets enable them to make a smooth transition into development work via an annual fund position. Sometimes people are attracted to the work simply due to their belief in the mission of the organization. Perhaps more so than any other area of fundraising, annual fund work attracts people with no prior development experience.

> Annual fund work is characterized by high turnover and tremendous potential for advancement.

Opportunities Abound

Nearly every nonprofit has or aspires to have at least one professional managing its annual fund. Large nonprofits, such as research universities or national associations, may have dozens of annual fund professionals on staff.

Annual fund work probably has the greatest turnover of any area in development. This is because the experience gained in an annual fund lends itself to advancement up the ladder. Successful annual fund professionals very frequently "move up" to become major gift officers or capital campaign staff.

> Whatever the state of the economy, annual fund positions will continue to be available because they are critical to the survival of nonprofits.

At any given time, you will find vacant annual fund positions across the nonprofit sector. Regardless of the state of the national economy, nonprofits cannot afford to let these positions go unfilled because the annual fund is essential for sustaining the organization.

Determining Your Annual Fund Needs

Understanding your organization's annual operating budget is an important step in understanding your organization's annual fund needs.

As a new annual fund professional, you may find your annual fund goals given to you on your first day. This is likely if you are taking over for someone who has moved on from an annual fund position. If you are hired to start up or revive an annual fund effort, you may begin with little but high hopes and expectations. In either case, your first step is to get a handle on your organization's annual needs.

It is essential that you understand the annual operating budget well enough to discuss your organization's needs with the general public. Seek out the advice of your chief development officer, who may be able to provide you with enough information to get going on your annual fund plan. If questions remain, you might request a meeting with the financial officer of your organization and any other executives (such as the chief development officer) who might need to be present.

Become fluent in discussing your needs in detail.

At the end of your meeting on the annual operating budget, you should feel comfortable that you have a start on what can and what should not be discussed about your organization's needs. There is often a balance to be maintained here, because privacy and confidentiality issues can make it unwise or impossible to reveal some details concerning financial information to the public. On the other hand, your nonprofit organization has to file a public record of expenditures. You will need to have a very clear understanding of this balance. Usually, the more specific you can be about needs, the more appealing and compelling your case will appear to a donor.

Unrestricted Funds

In an ideal world, all of your annual fund gifts would be unrestricted. Your organization would be able to use revenues from the annual fund for whatever budgetary priority needs your executives and board have approved. With an unrestricted gift, a donor does not specify the target department, item, or purpose for the expenditure of the gift.

A generation ago, most annual fund gifts were unrestricted. In recent years, more and more donors want even relatively small annual gifts to be designated for a specific purpose. You will want to emphasize that your organization's greatest need is for unrestricted gifts. However, you will need to structure your annual fund plan to accept restricted gifts so long as they match your organization's needs and do not impose an administrative burden.

Although unrestricted contributions to the annual fund are highly prized, you will probably find it necessary to offer donors opportunities to make restricted gifts in order to motivate them to contribute.

Restricted Funds

Donors may have a variety of reasons for wanting to specify how their money will be utilized. A graduate of your engineering program may have a particular affinity for the engineering school and want her gift to support it. A grateful patient may want his gift restricted for a specific hospital program he has found to be of benefit. At educational institutions, the need for scholarship funding usually far exceeds the amount available in the budget, so this is a relatively easy restricted gift to accept. Most other nonprofits have areas that are logical for designated annual giving because the need greatly exceeds available funding.

If a donor contributes to your annual fund with a restricted gift, the restriction must be honored.

Once a donation with a spending restriction has been made, you must always honor that restriction. If you fail to honor the donor's intent, the donor is unlikely to sue to get his or her money back in the case of a modest annual gift. However, it would set a dreadful precedent. Rerouting restricted funds without consent is likely to end your relationship the moment the donor becomes aware of the situation. And the news is likely to spread, hurting your chances of raising money from other prospective donors who hear about your misstep.

Be careful about accepting restricted gifts. They must always align with the mission of your organization.

Your organization should have a gift acceptance policy that outlines what kind of restricted gifts are acceptable. Restricted gifts that do not align with your organization's mission should not be accepted. Restricted gifts that would give rise to a bureaucratic nightmare might cost more than they are worth. Your financial officer will help you to draw up a gift acceptance policy if you don't already have one. Every gift acceptance policy is written specifically for the individual nonprofit, so no two are identical. If you do an Internet search for the key phrases "gift acceptance policy" and "sample nonprofit gift policy," you will find examples.

In-Kind Contributions

In-kind contributions can be a part of your annual fund. These can include services or tangible property.

Examples of in-kind contributions solicited in an annual fund include:

- Trucks
- Boats
- Computers
- Construction equipment
- Telephones
- Buses

Many nonprofits include truck, boat, and car donation programs as part of their annual fund. When people in a donor pool buy new vehicles, they may choose to donate their old vehicles to your worthy cause. The nonprofit organization then sells the vehicles at auction. The nonprofit receives the money from the auction, and the donor may be eligible to claim a tax deduction for the fair market value of the vehicle.

Be very careful with these kinds of gifts to your annual fund. Tax laws and IRS rules are constantly changing, and what might be an acceptable practice today may be unlawful next year. Know the law. Consult your organization's attorney for advice on vehicle donations. You might also want to consult with an attorney who specializes in gift tax law and practice.

When a donor makes an in-kind contribution to your annual fund, you should issue a gift receipt that accurately describes what your organization has received. See the sample in-kind contribution acknowledgment letter in Figure 2.1. Do not write the value of the donation on the receipt unless the gift has recently been appraised by a professional appraiser and you have documentation of the appraisal in writing. In such an instance, an attorney should be involved to ensure that you are following the law.

Services are generally not tax deductible unless the donor can prove that he or she has paid for the services to be performed, so services will probably not be offered as an annual fund in-kind gift.

SAMPLE IN-KIND CONTRIBUTION ACKNOWLEDGEMENT LETTER

Include name(s) of donor(s) and address
in all acknowledgment letters.

FR. MEGER
CENTER
FOR SOCIAL JUSTICE

January 1, 2022

Mr. John Doe and Mrs. Jane Doe
125 Park Avenue
New York, NY 10011

Dear Mr. and Mrs. Doe:

Note and describe an in-kind gift, but
do not assign a dollar value to the gift.

I write to thank you for your gift of computer equipment, which was delivered today.
Please know that this equipment is much appreciated, and will be used to benefit the
lives of homeless people.

For your records, I provide you with a list of the equipment received today:

> 1 HP Color Scanner (Model XC243)
> 4 Dell 22" LCD Monitors (Model D223)
> 4 Dell Quad-Core Pentium Computers (Model WW222)

The Fr. Meger Center for Social Justice thrives because of gifts like yours. In this
time of giving, we are truly grateful to count you as a supporter of the Fr. Meger
Center and our mission to lead through innovation so that homeless people live with
freedom, dignity, and distinction.

Sincerely,

This letter functions as a gift receipt
and should contain a footer noting
that no goods or services were given
to the donor in return for the gift.
You should regularly review your
wording for tax law compliance.

Timothy Kachinske
Vice President for Development

*Please note for your tax records that no goods or services were provided to you in
consideration of this gift.*

Figure 2.1

Greater Benefits from an Annual Fund

An annual fund can provide benefits to your nonprofit organization far beyond the gift dollars you receive. Ideally, your annual fund will build relationships with donors. Each consecutive annual fund will help to maintain and nurture those relationships. The relationship-building that results from a successful annual fund often yields huge rewards. Million-dollar bequests and successful capital campaigns usually have their roots in annual fund relationships.

Making Your Donors More Than a Source of Income

The annual fund can serve to increase volunteer involvement and pave the way for major and planned gifts.

Because it is about relationships as well as dollars, your annual fund must involve more than a request for money. Long-term goals include increasing volunteer involvement and laying the groundwork for major and planned gifts. The relationships built up as a result of annual fund involvement will sustain your organization in a variety of ways.

Increasing Volunteer Opportunities and Involvement

An important side benefit of your annual fund is the opportunity for increased volunteer involvement. Correspondence appeals to prospective donors should ideally come from a volunteer. A donor who regularly receives a letter from a volunteer may consider becoming a volunteer. The more a prospective donor thinks about you, the more likely it is that he or she will become active within your community.

The more active your volunteers are, the deeper their commitment to your organization will become.

It is important to involve volunteers in soliciting gifts, whether by phone, by correspondence, or in person. The volunteers you select to assist you will be donors to the annual fund who are able to explain their own reasons for support. Volunteer gift solicitors for the annual fund become important ambassadors for your nonprofit organization.

Ideally, annual fund involvement fosters a deepened commitment to further the mission of your organization. Your volunteers may go on to serve on committees or even to lead committees. They may help to develop or manage correspondence and paperwork. They may get involved in delivering services or serving as spokespersons for your organization.

You will want to train, nurture, and support them because effective volunteer solicitors can build public confidence and trust in your organization. Because no one is paying them to say good things about your organization, people will value what they say. In many cases, the volunteer is a peer of the prospective donor. Research shows that peer solicitation of gifts is generally more successful than development staff solicitation.

Whatever they do, you should ensure that your volunteers have a positive experience and are thanked for their efforts.

Volunteers bring credibility to your fundraising efforts because they are not employed by the organization.

Laying the Groundwork for Major Gifts, Capital Campaign, and Planned Giving

Managing an annual fund involves laying the groundwork for great gifts ahead. When you read about a successful capital campaign resulting in many millions of dollars raised, you can be certain that many (if not most) of the donors first contributed to that organization's annual fund. Similarly, when you hear about a nonprofit receiving a multimillion-dollar bequest, you can usually assume that it was the culmination of a relationship that grew over a period of years and included contributions to the annual fund.

Huge donations nearly always have their roots in an annual fund.

Planning Your Annual Fund

Your annual fund plan will lay out a 12-month strategy for meeting your organization's immediate needs and accomplishing your long-term objectives. Structuring it requires a vision for the whole project as well as the organizational skills and discipline needed to break down the project month by month.

Annual fund planning involves developing a timeline and matching your efforts with donor interests, concerns, and need for recognition.

Creating a Timeline for Seeking Gifts

Your annual fund will be a year-long campaign that is comprised of multiple contacts with prospective donors. Ideally, you will send letters and e-mail messages throughout the year. You might contact donors through social networking sites. You might coordinate a telethon to ensure that all prospective donors receive a personal solicitation. Exactly what you do over the course of the annual fund year will depend on your objectives and the resources available to you. Figure 2.2 provides an at-a-glance look at how your annual fund year might roll out.

Sample Annual Fund Timeline

JUL
Publish list of previous year's annual fund donors.

AUG
Begin lining up leadership gifts.   Secure board commitment.

SEP
Prepare fall mail appeal.

OCT

NOV
Prepare and mail end-of-year tax appeal.

DEC
Send holiday greetings.

JAN
Send gift receipt letter noting value of all gifts from donor in the tax year.

FEB
Send spring appeal to non-responders of fall appeal.

MAR
Begin spring phone-a-thons.

APR
Use board and other volunteers to contact previous year's donors who have not yet contributed this year.

MAY
Prepare "draft donors list" and send to all non-donors with a response envelope.

JUN
Wind up annual fund year with special event for volunteers.

Figure 2.2

Moving on from Figure 2.2, let's assume your fiscal year starts in June this time. If that's the case, your timeline for the annual fund might look something like this:

June: Annual fund donor list. At the beginning of your fiscal year, you should send your donors a publication listing donations made in the previous fiscal year. This publication will list all donors by level and should include stories about projects that your organization has been able to undertake because of the generous support of everyone on the list. If your organization publishes a magazine, your annual fund donor list could be a special issue of that magazine. If you publish a quarterly newsletter, your donor list could be a special issue or section of that newsletter.

July: Summer appeal letter and leadership gifts. Send a letter to all prospective donors outlining the new projects and initiatives that your organization is implementing throughout the summer and fall. This letter should contain some kind of call to action for the donor. Educational institutions often delay their first letter appeal until the fall.

Begin soliciting leadership gifts or commitments from board members and an identified group of potentially larger donors.

September: Fall phone-a-thon. Organize volunteers to call every prospective donor on your annual fund list with a personal appeal. The volunteer callers will be donors who have a high level of commitment to your organization. If you work for an educational institution, they might be parents or students.

November: November year-end appeal letters. Send another letter of appeal. By November, many of your prospective donors will be poised financially to make a year-end donation. Some will be looking for an additional tax deduction before the end of the tax year. Right at the time they are looking around for that tax deduction, your donation envelope should appear in their mailbox.

January: Thank-you letters. At the beginning of the tax year, send your donors a thank-you letter from your students or staff. This communication should also contain a gift receipt. It will actually serve three purposes: to thank them, to provide the required receipt for taxes, and to ask for additional funds.

How you lay out the 12-month timeline for your annual fund will depend on your objectives and the resources available.

The annual fund year will coincide with your organization's fiscal year.

March: Spring appeal letters. Send an appeal letter to prospective donors in the form of an update on your organization's activities and needs. This communication should not repeat anything your letters have said earlier in the annual fund year. Use this letter as an opportunity to highlight new programs. Invite your prospective donors to events. Be creative. This letter will serve a dual purpose: to keep donors informed about what's happening at your organization and to seek a gift.

May: Year-end appeal. Send out a final appeal near the end of your fiscal year. Consider sending out a draft proof sheet of the annual donors list asking for corrections before publication. Tell your donors that this is their last chance to be included in the year's list of donors. You may well receive checks from the ones who are motivated by public recognition but whose names are missing from the draft list. In organizations where the donors know each other, this works very well.

Avoid Overwhelming Your Donors

When a donor responds to your first appeal by sending a contribution, subsequent communications should take that contribution into account.

Your annual fund is a campaign, and donors may contribute to this campaign at any point throughout the year. If you send six mailings per year, what do you do when someone donates money on the first appeal? Generally speaking, that donation should trigger a less aggressive campaign for the donor. You may cut out further appeals, with the exception of appeals directed at all prospective donors, such as those sent at end of the tax year and the end of your fiscal year.

Structuring Donor Levels

Donor levels provide a way to publicly acknowledge donors based on the size of their contribution.

It is good psychology to structure donor levels. Doing so gives donors the sense that they are joining a club. The higher the donor level, the more exclusive the club.

Within each donor level, donors can expect to receive specific benefits and/or recognition for gifts that fall within a range of dollar amounts. For example, donors might be given a lapel pin at the Silver Level, a special reception at the Gold Level, and a plaque in the lobby at the Platinum Level.

At the end of your fiscal year, when the annual fund results are published, donors should be listed by level. This way, those who have given more will be acknowledged accordingly.

Always remember that annual fund gifts are normally outright gifts, which is another way of saying that the gift is from a donor's disposable income. You will want to study your annual fund donor base when creating donor levels of giving. Donor levels involve suggestions of amounts to give, and those amounts should look reasonable to your audience. Also keep in mind that you are setting a precedent. You will need to stick with whatever structure you set up so that your donor base becomes accustomed to the donor levels in succeeding years.

Take some care in creating donor levels and avoid changing them from year to year.

Tables 2.1 through 2.3 outline a few examples of donor levels. Be creative when you are creating your own levels. The top levels might be named after the founder of your organization or the year it was organized. The dollar amounts might have significance—a reference to a year or a street address that everyone knows, for example.

Table 2.1 Sample Generic Donor Levels

Friend/Individual	$35–99
Benefactor	$100–$249
Patron	$250–$499
President's Circle	$500–$999
Founder's Society	$1,000–$9,999

Table 2.2 Sample College Annual Fund Levels

Donors	$50–$99
Friends of the College	$100–$249
Old Main Club	$250–$499
Bulldogs Club	$500–$999
Heritage Society	$1,000–$2,499
Legacy Society	$2,500–$4,999
Dean's Society	$5,000–$9,999
President's Society	$10,000–$24,999
Chairman's Society	$25,000+

Table 2.3 Sample Nonprofit Association Annual Fund Levels	
Donor	Up to $100
Friend	$100–$499
Benefactor	$50–$999
Sponsor	$1,000–$1,999
Patron	$2,000–$2,999
Leadership Circle	$3,000+

Finding and Working with Volunteers

Where you find your volunteers will depend on the kind of non-profit organization you serve. As you get to know your organization, you will become acquainted with the possibilities.

Board Members

Your board is a logical source for annual fund volunteers because board members share a fiduciary responsibility for your organization.

Board members are the ideal volunteers for soliciting leadership gifts.

Whatever type of organization you work for, look for volunteers for your annual fund amongst your governing board. All of them share a fiduciary responsibility for your not-for-profit organization. All of them should make some contribution to your annual fund. If the board doesn't have a development or advancement committee, they will need to form one. Try to get some board members directly involved in recruiting leadership gifts—those in the highest category of your gift levels. Other board members can help in other ways, such as hosting a telethon or signing a fundraising appeal letter.

Colleges and Universities

Colleges and universities have a built-in volunteer force in their current student body and their alumni association. Alumni are your most important source of gifts for a college annual fund, so you want to instill a sense of the significance of giving even before a student graduates. Senior class gift campaigns are important, even if the amount is small, because these prospective donors are only a year away from being alumni.

Colleges and universities often rank themselves by alumni participation. This ranking is based on the percentage of living or known alumni who have made a gift to the most recent annual fund. Traditionally, private institutions have been much higher in participation than their counterparts in the public sector. However, support for public colleges and universities is growing rapidly because of an understanding that private support is essential in order for public institutions to remain competitive. Alumni have a vested interest in maintaining an institution's reputation, because the perceived value of their degree depends upon it. No institution of higher education can afford to ignore the potential of its alumni when it comes to the annual fund.

Alumni will be your best source of volunteers. They know the college, its needs—and often each other. They can call their old classmates and ask for funds in the context of an enjoyable conversation. Old friendships may provide access you wouldn't otherwise have to wealthy alumni.

Alumni participation in the annual fund is an important measure of the vitality of a college or university.

Current students also make excellent volunteers. Most alumni will be receptive to a call from a student currently enrolled at their alma mater. Current students can update former students about campus news. Scholarship recipients are particularly effective at soliciting contributions for scholarship support because of the credibility they bring to the appeal.

Current parents can also help. You might divide your efforts by class and organize parents to solicit other parents in their child's class year. Most private schools will have a parent organization that actively works with the annual fund and in some cases even engages in mini-campaigns that complement the annual fund's revenues.

Alumni and parents of current students bring credibility to your annual fund solicitations.

If you work at a college or university, it is vital to make friends with the director of the alumni association and do everything possible to make sure you maintain a good working relationship. Cooperation between these two functions is so necessary that often an alumni director's job description will include assistance and support of the annual fund.

Schools

Normally you can't look to students as volunteers for your annual fund efforts at a private school. However, you can expect an even greater commitment from the ranks of your parents and alumni. Various studies have shown that if a person has attended a private school, the affinity to the school grows stronger with age.

Private-school communities are characterized by gratitude and a strong shared commitment to the values of the school.

Recent graduates of a college, university, graduate school, or professional school can be expected to have a keener affinity to the institution they most recently attended during their first years after graduation. After all, if you are an engineer or a lawyer, you have your professional school to thank for that great job you presently enjoy.

For individuals whose old school ties go back before college, sentiments about college days and experiences tend to be overshadowed eventually by those school memories that extend back to the formative years. Unless for some reason they had terrible experiences (in which case you probably won't even meet them), alumni of private schools tend to be fiercely loyal. They tend to care very much about the future of the school and to take a personal interest in maintaining its standards and traditions.

The oldest alumni of a private school tend to have the strongest feelings when it comes to securing the future of the school.

If you take an annual fund position at a private school, start looking to your oldest alumni classes first, both for annual fund contributions and as a source of volunteers. You will quickly realize that classes beyond the 15-year mark have a closeness and passion for the school that are stronger than anything you might experience in higher education. You may find volunteers willing to do almost anything to ensure the success of your annual fund.

Social Service Organizations

Business and community leaders are often ideal volunteers for social service organizations. Fraternal organizations of religious denominations are an excellent source of volunteers.

Finding volunteers in social service organizations can sometimes be challenging. If the majority of your clients are living at the poverty level, you may need to look elsewhere for your annual fund volunteers. Seek out community leaders who have a known interest in your particular client groups. Often a business executive or a public office holder with a family member in need of client services is an excellent person to give you advice in recruiting volunteers, and perhaps even to assist you directly.

If your organization is faith-based, seek the help of church guilds. Members of service and fraternal organizations, such as the Episcopal Knights of St. John or the Catholic Knights of Columbus, can be enlisted to help in a social service agency's annual fund.

Healthcare

Large research hospitals as well as community hospitals draw their annual fund volunteers from hospital volunteer committees. Hospitals have special projects for specific groups, such as children or the elderly, that attract civic-minded people. Hospital and healthcare delivery organizations typically have leadership committees that attract local citizens who want to contribute to their community or who have seen the organization do something special for a friend or family member.

> Hospital annual fund volunteers often come from the ranks of civic-minded community leaders and grateful patients.

Mechanics of Solicitations

Planning out the schedule for the annual fund is only half the battle. Next, you must actually implement the campaign. Before you begin, you will need to know some practical information about the mechanics of running your e-mails, letters, phone calls, and other interactions.

Business Reply Mail

Assuming you have the budget, every letter sent to donors should include a business reply mail envelope. These allow the return to be sent back to your address without a stamp. When a donor sends you a check in the business reply envelope, you will be charged for the first-class postage. If you wish, you can put a note on the left-hand side of the envelope saying something like, "You can help us to save on our postal expenses by affixing a stamp to this envelope."

> If you can afford it, include a Business Reply Mail envelope with your annual fund solicitation.

When printing your business reply envelopes, make sure you follow the strict US Postal Service guidelines for creating Business Reply Mailers (BRM). Obtain the latest copy of Quick Service Guide 507a from your local US Postal Service business office or from the US Postal Service website to make sure you have the latest specifications for business reply mail. See Figure 2.3 for an example of such an envelope.

> Always follow the United States Postal Service guidelines for Business Reply Mail.

If you opt for budget or other reasons to use preprinted envelopes without the USPS prepaid reply service, you are free to design the envelope in any manner that conforms to size requirements. Generally speaking, a plain envelope with conservative printing of your address is best.

Nonprofit Bulk Mail Permits

The US Postal Service offers special discounts for some nonprofit organizations. Anything sent at a nonprofit bulk rate must have NONPROFIT ORGANIZATION imprinted in the upper-right corner of the mailer. The bulk mail permit number must also

> To qualify for a nonprofit bulk mail discount, you must apply for a permit.

Figure 2.3

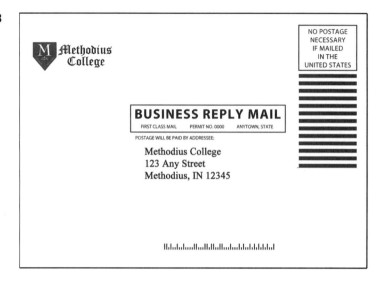

Only mailings that support your non-profit mission will qualify for a non-profit bulk mail discount.

appear. You will need to apply for a bulk mail permit at your local postal service business office. Depending on the class of mail you are sending, you may need between 200 and 500 pieces to qualify for the bulk rate.

It's important to note that nonprofit discounts are offered on a per-mailing basis and not on a per-organization basis. The Postal Service reserves the right to reject your mailing discounts if your mail pieces are not aligned with your nonprofit mission. In other words, if you are a social service organization, but your mailer is an advertisement for a sponsoring organization, your mailer is likely to get rejected. Even putting "Sponsored by XYZ Company" on your postcard can invalidate it for purposes of a nonprofit mailer.

Alliance of Nonprofit Mailers

The Alliance of Nonprofit Mailers is a good source of information about mailing regulations.

If you are sending mass letters through the Postal Service, you should consider joining the Alliance of Nonprofit Mailers. The Alliance is a group dedicated to advocating on behalf of nonprofit mailers, and it has a wealth of information about updated mail regulations. For more information, go to www.nonprofitmailers.org.

Credit Card Capability

Before your organization can accept credit card payments, you will need a merchant account. These are obtainable through your bank or through a third-party vendor. Some accounting programs, such as QuickBooks and Peachtree, also offer merchant accounts.

Getting a merchant account usually requires that your organization have sufficient credit to obtain a similar account, such as a credit card. If your organization is not in a position to be approved for a credit card on its own, it is unlikely that it will be approved for a merchant account.

A merchant account is needed to accept credit card payments.

Merchant accounts usually charge extra for a payment gateway, which is a required add-on if you are going to take credit cards online. There are many options for payment gateways, but one of the most popular is authorize.net.

Once you have a merchant account with an online payment gateway, you can integrate your online store with the payment gateway. Your web designer should be able to add a shopping cart to your website. Your Internet service provider may also offer a shopping cart option that can be integrated into your payment gateway.

You will also need a payment gateway. Some development software systems enable you to automate gift collecting with credit cards.

Purchasing a system such as Convio Internet software may make it a lot easier to accept online donations. Some fundraising-specific software, such as DonorPerfect, also has online components for collecting funds by credit card.

If you are a small nonprofit, you can get a free merchant account through PayPal, which offers an account with no setup fee, $0.30 per transaction, plus a 2.9% transaction fee.

The United Way and the Combined Federal Campaign (CFC)

You should consider joining the CFC and/or United Way as part of your annual fund if you are not already a member. The United Way is a national fundraising cooperative that pools fundraising resources for thousands of nonprofits nationwide. Many employers make it easy for their employees to donate to the United Way through payroll deductions.

Contact your local United Way to determine whether your organization qualifies to participate in the United Way campaign. Upon joining, you will receive a United Way number. Anyone giving through the United Way can designate your number as the recipient charity.

The CFC is the government-sponsored employee-giving campaign for government and military employees. In fact, the CFC is the largest annual employee-sponsored giving campaign in the world. Particularly if you are a national organization, joining the CFC can contribute significantly to your annual fund bottom line. Like the United Way, the CFC will assign your organization a number. You can find more information about the CFC at www.opm.gov/cfc.

Joining the CFC and the United Way can greatly increase your annual fund revenues. Ensure that your donors know your organization's unique number.

Just joining the United Way or CFC can potentially bring in masses of new donations. It is necessary, of course, to make sure that your prospective donors know you are a member. When they make their commitment to support you at their workplace, they will be asked to fill out a form. They will be given a list of all member organizations with their numbers, and they will need to be able to pick yours out. If your organization's name is at all similar to that of another organization, make sure your prospective donors know which one is yours.

Corporate Matching Funds

Many companies, especially large companies, have corporate matching programs in place. These matching programs will match any donations made by employees to 501(c)(3) charitable organizations. Some corporate matching programs even double or triple contributions.

Doing the work required to secure matching funds can reap generous rewards.

If you have an annual fund donor who works for a company that matches employees' gifts, you may have to do some work to secure those matching funds. Generally speaking, it is well worth the trouble. In fact, some universities are able to garner $500,000 to $1 million per year in matching funds from a single company if they have a large number of alumni, parents, and friends who work there.

Certain basic information is necessary to obtain matching funds. In each instance you will need to know where your donor works, whether the employer has a matching program, and if so, whether your organization qualifies for participation. (Most programs match tax-exempt charities in general, but some companies rule out certain kinds of nonprofits.) Then you will need to obtain a form from the company that you can give to your donor. You may be fortunate and have a savvy donor who knows that all this needs to be done and will do it for you. But you need to be prepared to do all the work yourself.

In years past, consolidated information about corporate matching gift programs could be found in annual publications, such as the one published by the Council for Advancement and Support of Education (CASE). Now there are online services that enable you to search companies for current matching gift information or to search your own donor files for matching gift eligibility. Depending on your budget and the quality of your own donor data, you can automate a lot of your searching for matching gift opportunities.

Online services can assist you in your efforts to identify which of your annual fund donors is eligible for corporate matching programs.

The CASE website (www.case.org) is an excellent resource for current information and vendors who offer these services.

Web Fundraising

Web fundraising is in its early stages in comparison to other methodologies, such as mail appeals and phone-a-thon solicitations. You probably will want to begin your annual fund career with these tried-and-true methodologies before branching out into the web. However, every day various new services, networking sites, and technological improvements make it clear that the web will eventually be just as important in annual fund work as conventional communication. See Chapter 9, "Fundraising with Social Media and Web 2.0 Technologies" for information and a discussion of web fundraising techniques, services, and advances.

Although you will probably want to begin with traditional fundraising methods, it is important to check out the possibilities presented by web fundraising.

E-Mail Solicitations

E-mail is a good way to interact with prospective donors, but it should not be your primary method of communication. The reason for this is simple: Most e-mail sent in bulk will never be read. On average, a mass e-mail sent to your donor base will have around a 20- to 30-percent read rate.

Mass e-mails should always be sent with a service that tracks read rates. This way, you'll know who read the e-mail, how many times they read it, whether they forwarded it to someone, and so on. If someone opens your e-mail 20 times, then maybe you should give that prospective donor a personal call. E-mail services generally embed a one-pixel graphic file that, when downloaded from the service's website, tracks the fact that the e-mail has been read. Swiftpage (www.swiftpage.com), ExactTarget (www.exacttarget.com), and Constant Contact (www.constantcontact.com) all offer statistical information about mass e-mail campaigns. Many nonprofit fundraising software applications, such as Convio, also include mass e-mail services.

If you decide to send a mass e-mail, always utilize a service that tracks read rates.

Be careful about sending mass e-mails through your internal e-mail servers. If you send a lot of e-mails from your internal servers, it is likely that you (or your entire organization) will get blacklisted. Do a Google search for "blacklist servers" for resources about how to avoid getting blacklisted. If a blacklist server identifies you as a spammer, anyone who subscribes (or whose ISP subscribes) to the blacklist will never get any e-mails sent from you or anyone at your organization.

To avoid getting blacklisted, don't send mass e-mails from your internal servers.

Here's a sample scenario: You send 5,000 solicitation e-mails. XYZ blacklist service identifies you as a spammer. You get added to their blacklist. Verizon, Comcast, and AOL all subscribe to that blacklist. From this point forward, you can't send any e-mail of any kind to anyone who uses these ISPs to host their e-mail servers. Nonprofit groups have had to go so far as to change their domain names because it is so hard to get off the blacklists. Using a service such as Swiftpage, ExactTarget, or Constant Contact can help you avoid the blacklist issue because these services send e-mails from whitelisted servers.

Any mass e-mails sent from your organization should be CAN-SPAM compliant. The CAN-SPAM law governs any mass unsolicited e-mail sent within the United States. It requires, among other things, that each mass e-mail sent includes your mailing address with an option to unsubscribe from your mailing list. If anyone unsubscribes, you are required to honor that request for all non-transactional e-mails.

Social Networking

The annual fund is primarily focused on sending correspondence to prospective donors in a consistent campaign over the course of a year, and social networking can be a great tool to easily (and inexpensively) send out annual fund solicitations.

Social networking sites can be used for annual fund solicitations if you can accept donations made by credit card.

If you have a group of 5,000 friends on MySpace or Facebook, these social networking sites will let you send mass messages with just a few clicks. If you use social networking for sending annual fund solicitations, it's imperative that you have a credit card merchant account with the ability to take donations online by credit card.

Writing Letter Appeals

Drafting letter appeals is probably the most important writing task you will have as an annual fund professional. Study a variety of models to get the hang of how it's done, but always create your own letters from scratch. Never, ever copy anything verbatim. It won't work. Your organization needs to be unique in a donor's mind in order for your communication to prompt a gift.

Drafting letter appeals is an important part of any annual fund professional's duties.

Develop a Library of Appeal Samples

As you begin your work as an annual fund professional, you should develop your own personal reference library of fundraising appeals. Save every fundraising appeal you receive in the mail, regardless of the cause or type of institution. Ask your family and friends to save theirs for you as well. This will be helpful in understanding how mailing lists are segmented because it's likely that your family members and friends are receiving different and possibly more appeals than you.

Develop your own personal library of appeal letters as a resource for techniques and strategies.

Collecting letter appeal samples will give you many ideas that can help you as you draft your own appeals. It will also show you what your competition is doing.

In a matter of a few months, you will have garnered dozens of sample pieces. You will supplement these with letters, postcards, and brochures that you have picked up in your continuing professional education. The point of collecting samples is to get a look at appeals that are currently being sent. Eventually, you should develop a vertical filing system for these pieces.

Books on direct marketing and letter writing are well worth checking out.

There are many books available on direct marketing and fundraising letter writing. These are well worth reading and include lots of samples, many of them from years past, but you will also want to see current examples for ideas, the look of layout and printing, and the enclosures that are inserted, which change in style frequently.

Crafting Your Appeals

Writing fundraising letters is a craft. There are direct-mail companies that will do everything for you, from conceiving and drafting letters to producing and mailing them. Do a web search for links, sites, and books on the subject, and you will find more than you can possibly read. Direct mail is a big industry.

If you have a donor or membership list in the thousands, you may well be using some or all of the direct-mail services available from private companies that specialize in this work. Small nonprofits and colleges often do all the work in-house, including everything from writing and printing letters and enclosures to stuffing envelopes and hauling the mail to the post office. Larger organizations may outsource most of this work.

Annual fund managers with thousands of donors often outsource to direct-mail services for assistance in managing the annual fund process.

The one thing you do not want to outsource is the wording of a letter appeal. You should always have control of this, as you would of any other correspondence you write. Even if a consultant has given you a draft to work with, always consider it a pre-draft. Your first work on the draft is the real first draft.

Whatever you do, don't outsource the writing of your appeal letter.

Author's Voice

There are many things to consider in writing a fundraising appeal, but two things stand out: the author's voice and the audience. Ideally, letter appeals will be signed by a volunteer, such as a board member or an annual giving chairperson. In some cases, annual appeal letters may go out under the signature of your chief executive officer. You will always be writing as someone else, not as yourself.

When you draft an annual fund appeal letter, you will be writing in someone else's voice.

Knowing the person signing the letter is important because hers is the voice you must capture on paper. Don't start drafting anything before meeting or talking to this person. Listen carefully until you are confident you know her well enough to write in her voice. It will also be helpful to discuss her with colleagues who know her and to read anything she has written, including informal correspondence with colleagues. What you see, hear, and read should give you a sense of how and what to write.

Don't take it personally when you are asked to revise an annual fund appeal letter. Revision almost always improves the final product.

Be careful not to invest personal feelings in anything you write for another person's voice. Be prepared for your author to change, revise, and delete your wording. In fact, that is a good thing when it happens. What you want is a finished product that your author feels is in her voice. Yours is the role of a craftsperson who enables your author to communicate your organization's needs effectively.

Audience

The audience is simply the reader of the letter. To a certain extent your sense of audience is inevitably going to be abstract. You can't actually get to know all the recipients of your letter, sit with them as they read, and gauge their responses. What you can do is talk to previous donors, or members or alumni, or anyone who might be on your annual fund list.

Knowing a few constituents will give you a broad sense of the audience you are addressing. If you are working at a private school, talk with alumni and parents. If you are working for a national policy or advocacy organization, talk with members. If you are working at a college or university, talk to alumni, many of whom will be volunteers and easy to meet. These conversations will give you an idea about such issues as tone (familiar or formal) and the level of detail required to be thoroughly understood. For example, an appeal for medical research funds sent to a lay audience might require details an audience of scientists would find insulting.

> For your annual fund appeal letter to be effective, you must know the audience you are writing for. Getting to know your donors is the best way to improve your sense of audience.

Drafting the Letter

An appeal for funds needs to be written in paragraphs, so once you have a sense of author's voice and audience, you should draft an outline of the letter showing what each paragraph will contain. Start with the opening and closing paragraphs, because you know what they will be about. If you are sending an appeal to past donors, your opening should begin with a statement of thanks for past contributions. Then lead into your current year. Likewise, the closing should remind the reader that you are grateful for past gifts and hopeful for a contribution again this year.

> An effective annual fund appeal letter begins with an outline setting down what each paragraph will contain.

Whatever goes between the opening and closing paragraph will depend on your creative instincts. If you are writing for a college or private school annual fund, you might say something about the current freshman class in terms of demographics, academic qualifications, and the sheer number of new people on campus. Then you will likely go into detail about the need for scholarships, offering some facts and figures to substantiate the need.

> Needs that are known to exceed the funds available can provide you with a compelling and believable appeal.

If you are not working for an educational institution, you should include needs that are analogous to scholarships in that they typically far exceed the funds available. For example, if you are a food pantry, it is obvious that the need automatically expands as joblessness and poverty increase. If you are involved in finding a cure for a disease, there is never enough money until the cure is found. Figure 2.4 provides a sample annual fund appeal letter with a compelling case for support in a volunteer's own voice.

SAMPLE ONE-PAGE ANNUAL FUND APPEAL

FR. MEGER
CENTER
FOR SOCIAL JUSTICE

January 1, 2022

Mr. John Doe and Mrs. Jane Doe
125 Park Avenue
New York, NY 10011

> A personal story, especially a testament, in an appeal can be more compelling to donors than a summary catalogue of your needs.

Dear Mr. and Mrs. Doe:

I write to ask for your support of the Father Meger Center's annual fund. You may know of the Institute's good work. I want to share with you my own personal story, and how I came to know the good people at the Father Meger Center.

Some years ago I was homeless. This is not an uncommon experience for Vietnam War veterans. And just when I thought my life bottomed-out, I found shelter in the Father Meger Center. They gave me a place to live, and got me taking computer courses paid for by the GI Bill. Soon I got an entry-level technology support job and moved into my own apartment. To make a long story short, Father Meger and his good people saved my life.

Today I have my own business, and I volunteer in my spare time at the Father Meger Center. I miss Father Meger, just as countless other people do. He touched so many lives. When I got my first job, he made me promise not to forget the people I was leaving behind.

So today, in this time of giving, we would be truly grateful to count you as a supporter of the Father Meger Center. Your gift will help homeless people live with dignity.

Sincerely,

> Try to have your letter appeals signed by volunteers rather than staff.

Timothy Kachinske
Chairman, Fr. Meger Volunteers

Figure 2.4

Segmenting Your Appeal

Annual fund appeals are most effective when letters are tailored specifically to individual recipients. Mail merge software makes this relatively simple to accomplish. A letter intended for first-time donors will not be identical to the letters you send to past donors. The letters you send to your biggest contributors will be highly individualized.

The more specific your appeal is, the more effective it will be.

For previous donors, the solicitation itself should request a specific dollar commitment or gift to the annual fund. You will base this on gifts given in the past year or previous years. If your organization has giving levels, you will want to judge whether it would be reasonable to ask the donor to "jump up" to the next donor level—for example, from the $125 Benefactor Level to the $250+ Patron Level.

Whenever you can, it is a good idea to differentiate your appeal letters based on donor characteristics.

If your annual fund donors fall into subgroups, such as class years or residents of a specific city, you may wish to vary the appeals so that you can describe needs that are of specific interest to that particular segment of your donor base. Older alumni may be interested in renovating the chapel, whereas younger alumni might be more inclined to support renovating the fitness center.

Phone-a-Thons and Telethons

Another important way to solicit annual fund gifts is via telephone. You will want volunteers to make these calls, not only to increase the labor force but primarily because volunteers over time have proven to be the most effective gift solicitors.

Phone-a-thons and telethons enable you to extend your letter appeals with a personal contact. Phone-a-thon calls are made by volunteers but directed and managed by annual fund professional staff.

Annual fund telephone solicitations are done with events called *phone-a-thons* or *telethons*. If you listen to public radio, you are certain to have heard phone-a-thon progress reports. If you are a viewer of public television, you have probably seen a telethon in progress—a host soliciting viewer contributions as rows of volunteers take calls in the background. If you have attended a college or university, you are almost certain to have been on the other end of a phone-a-thon solicitation call from a volunteer.

Phone-a-thon methodologies were first used by colleges, which remain the leaders in terms of actual annual fund dollars raised by this method of solicitation. However, many nonprofits outside higher education now use phone-a-thons effectively to reach people who will welcome a friendly phone call from a volunteer but might shred your letter without reading it.

Volunteer versus Professional

Get competent legal advice before entering into a relationship with a telemarketing company.

Some nonprofit organizations use telemarketing firms to make solicitation calls for their annual funds. At first glance, this may seem like an easier route than putting in the effort required to organize, support, and coordinate volunteers. However, commercial telemarketing firms are not satisfactory if you want to build a volunteer base. Nor are they effective in sustaining annual fund donor relationships over the long term.

If you use a telemarketer, the potential presented by volunteer involvement in the annual fund is lost.

If you are considering entering into a business relationship with a telemarketing firm, you should know exactly what you are getting into. Research the company thoroughly and talk to other development professionals who have worked with the firm. It can be complicated to ensure that a telemarketing firm meets state legal requirements and adheres to national and state standards. You should get competent legal advice before engaging a private firm.

Volunteer solicitation programs help not only to build your base of annual support from year to year, but also to pave the way for greater gifts when you are ready to undertake a volunteer-led capital campaign.

Where to Hold Your Phone-a-Thon

A phone-a-thon can be held wherever you have access to enough phone lines to accommodate your volunteers. Volunteers with businesses are a prime source of phone-a-thon sites.

All you need to hold a phone-a-thon is an office where there are a number of desks or workstations available for your volunteer solicitors. You can hold a phone-a-thon at your organization's offices if you have enough phone lines to make that a practical choice, but it may be better to ask your volunteers to find offices where you might hold your phone-a-thon. If you bring together volunteers in cities where your nonprofit does not have an office, the alternative of renting office space and phone lines will probably be cost prohibitive.

Holding a phone-a-thon offsite showcases your organization in the community.

Phone-a-Thon Scripting

If you give a script to your volunteer callers, you will be able to direct them in a way that will be most effective for your annual fund. Writing a script is probably the most important part of organizing a phone-a-thon. A script enables your volunteers to feel secure and comfortable talking with people they have never met. It provides structure and allows them to jump right into the task with a minimum of preparation beforehand.

Volunteer callers should receive lists comprised of names, phone numbers, and (if available) an amount that can be requested reasonably of the prospective donor based on past giving.

Part I: Introduction and Initial Solicitation

The typical annual fund phone-a-thon script has two parts. The first is a simple introduction script that tells the caller how to introduce him/herself quickly and effectively, explains the reason for the call, and asks for a gift in a specific amount.

If your callers are undergraduate students, the introduction script will go something like this:

> Good evening, _____. I am [volunteer caller's name]. I am majoring in [volunteer caller's major] at Methodius College. How are you doing this evening? I'm here with a group of students on campus tonight making calls to alumni and friends of Methodius. We are grateful for your past support of the Methodius annual fund, and I'm wondering whether you would consider a gift of $_____ this year?
>
> PAUSE for response.

Provide your volunteers with language to structure their conversations with potential donors. Have your volunteers rehearse phone-a-thon scripts aloud prior to making their phone-a-thon calls.

Part II: Scenarios

The second part of your annual fund script will be more complicated than the introduction and initial solicitation. The PAUSE that you insert in the script will be followed by a set of suggested reactions to what the prospective donor might say when asked to make a contribution.

Provide your phone-a-thon volunteers with scripts that guide them through typical scenarios.

Some phone-a-thon scripts have a complex set of potential donor reactions and suggestions for further engagement of the caller. For example, if a prospect says, "No," the script will suggest wording such as, "I understand. Would you feel comfortable making a gift of $___?" If the answer is still no, the caller might then be prompted to say, "Well, thank you for your time. I hope that you will come to an event soon at Methodius."

You will have one or more scenarios for people who say, "Yes." The caller might then be scripted to say, "Would you like to make your gift with a credit card, or would you like us to send you a pledge reminder in the mail?" At this point in your script, instruct the caller to record information.

Give your phone-a-thon volunteers cards on which to document each call.

Scenarios will also be needed for other situations. Consider having a "maybe" script scenario if a prospective donor hedges, says he needs time to think about it, or has a question about your organization. In such cases, you would want to have a scripted response, such as, "We have someone here from the development office who would be pleased to talk to you about your concerns." The point of the "maybe" script would be to keep your volunteers working at "yes" and "no" reactions, while taking prospective donors with more complicated attention needs offline so you can handle them yourself, perhaps at a later date.

If a prospective donor does not answer the phone, this situation will also require a script if you want your callers to leave a message. It should be written by you, not improvised by the volunteer caller. The message should be simple, for example:

This is Methodius College calling. Sorry to miss you tonight. We'll try back later. Thank you.

If you want to leave a recorded message that lets the recipient know that a pledge or reminder will be sent in the mail, it might look like this:

This is _____ from Methodius College calling on behalf of the annual fund. Sorry to miss you tonight. We will be sending you a pledge card. Thanks so much for your past support of Methodius College.

Figure 2.5 shows the flow of a basic phone-a-thon script.

Preparing Your Volunteer Callers

Have your volunteers read a phone-a-thon script aloud prior to beginning their calls. Listen and encourage volunteers as they practice their calls.

Once your volunteer callers are assembled, give them all a chance to read the script aloud to themselves. When they are comfortable and have no more questions or comments, give them their call lists.

It is helpful to develop a system of cards, one for each prospective donor. That way you can provide essential information for the caller together with a place on which to note the donor's reaction to a gift amount request, as well as credit card information if the donor wants to pay at the time of the call. The card can also

Basic Phonathon Script

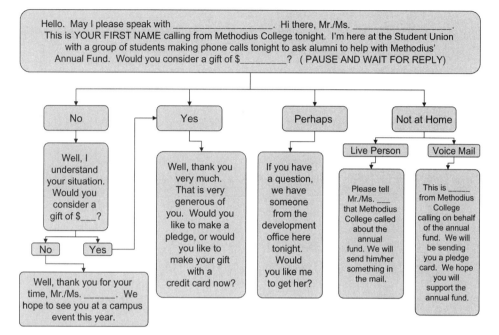

Hello. May I please speak with _____. Hi there, Mr./Ms. _____.
This is YOUR FIRST NAME calling from Methodius College tonight. I'm here at the Student Union with a group of students making phone calls tonight to ask alumni to help with Methodius' Annual Fund. Would you consider a gift of $_____?   (PAUSE AND WAIT FOR REPLY)

No

Well, I understand your situation. Would you consider a gift of $___ ?

No   Yes

Well, thank you for your time, Mr./Ms. _____. We hope to see you at a campus event this year.

Yes

Well, thank you very much. That is very generous of you. Would you like to make a pledge, or would you like to make your gift with a credit card now?

Perhaps

If you have a question, we have someone from the development office here tonight. Would you like me to get her?

Not at Home

Live Person

Please tell Mr./Ms. ___ that Methodius College called about the annual fund. We will send him/her something in the mail.

Voice Mail

This is _____ from Methodius College calling on behalf of the annual fund. We will be sending you a pledge card. We hope you will support the annual fund.

Figure 2.5

record pledge information if the donor prefers to get a reminder in the mail and pay by check. Cards are useful for recording any interesting points of conversation between caller and donor. Specific positive or negative comments are important to collect, and the card is the easiest place for a caller to note them.

Make certain that each caller's list contains at least one prospective donor that you have reason to believe will make a gift. This is important. A volunteer will find repeated refusals disheartening and may not wish to volunteer again. You can ensure that your volunteers feel successful by giving all of them lists that include known loyal contributors.

Monitor volunteers as they complete call cards and ensure that they are completing them correctly.

Volunteers who have been around for some time may want to redistribute the call list based on their personal knowledge of prospective donors. Accommodating volunteers' wishes in this case will increase the likelihood of success. If you can match volunteer callers with people they know ahead of time, so much the better.

Coordinating Written Communication with Your Phone-a-Thon

Review your current donors list and gift records for the annual fund before beginning starting up a phone-a-thon session. Remove any current donors on the list of prospective donors to call.

Begin your annual fund with letter appeals, and then hold your phone-a-thon. You will need to have up-to-date reports on responses to your letter appeals. Calling donors to request an annual gift is a serious faux pas if they have already pledged. So before each phone-a-thon, it is important to review donors against the list and call cards so that you can remove current donors.

Acknowledging and Substantiating Gifts

Whether annual fund gifts come as checks in a response to a letter appeal or as credit card payments at a phone-a-thon, all gifts should be acknowledged promptly. By the time you are sending out your first letter appeal, you should have your gift acknowledgement procedures set up and ready to go.

Acknowledgement Timing

Gift acknowledgment letters are important tax documentation for your donors. Ensure that the gift date and amount are correct on each letter.

A gift acknowledgement letter is not a piece of junk mail. It is an important record for your donor's tax files. Annual fund gift acknowledgements should be processed the day you receive them in the mail or the morning following an evening phone-a-thon. Acknowledgement letters should be sent first-class mail on the day they are produced.

Some organizations that receive large numbers of incoming annual fund gifts will generate their gift receipts with software. They utilize computer programs that automate the production of small printed receipts based on the previous day's batch of recorded gifts. The printed receipt will contain the name and address of a donor, the amount and date of the gift, and also verbiage to document that no goods or services were given in return for the gift. If you have such software in place, it is worthwhile to send the receipt with a hand-signed cover letter to give it a personal touch.

Information You Should Include in the Acknowledgement

Using a word processor to merge gift acknowledgement letters saves time and increases your productivity.

Most annual fund gift acknowledgement letters are generated with a word-processed letter. This letter has several important elements: an expression of gratitude, the dollar amount of the gift, the date of the gift, and a footer noting that no goods or services were given in return for the gift. See the sample annual fund acknowledgement letters in Figures 2.6 and 2.7 for examples of word-processed letters.

SAMPLE ANNUAL FUND ACKNOWLEDGEMENT LETTER

Civil Policy
Association

January 1, 2022

Ms. Jane Doe
125 Park Avenue
New York, NY 10011

Revise your acknowledgement letter openings as you begin a new annual fund campaign. This example takes advantage of your new CEO's recent appointment.

Dear Ms. Doe:

One of my first pleasures upon becoming Executive Director of the Civil Policy Association is having the opportunity to express thanks to you for your gift of $150 to the annual fund of the CPA.

Note dollar amount of gift.

Each new day brings more appreciation for the unique work of the CPA.

I know that as a Sponsor you too appreciate the work of the CPA, and I am grateful that you have contributed so generously. Unless you object, we plan to note your name on the CPA annual fund Honor Roll of Donors.

On behalf of everyone at the Civil Policy Association, I extend thanks and best wishes to you for the coming year.

Sincerely,

This letter functions as a gift receipt and should contain a footer noting that no goods or services were given to the donor in return for the gift. You should regularly review your wording for tax law compliance.

Timothy Kachinske
Executive Director

Please note for your tax records that no goods or services were provided to you in consideration of this gift.

Figure 2.6

SAMPLE LEADERSHIP ACKNOWLEDGEMENT LETTER

January 1, 2022

> Note amount of gift in first line of acknowledgment letter. Make sure your letter has a footer that notes no goods or services were received in return for the gift.

Mr. John Doe and Mrs. Jane Doe
125 Park Avenue
New York, NY 10011

Dear Mr. and Mrs. Doe:

May I thank you on behalf of the entire Meger Academy family for your leadership gift of $2500.00 to the Meger Academy annual fund.

The Meger Academy thrives because of gifts like yours. We believe in excellence. We want to instill values in our students, we want to challenge them intellectually and physically, and we want them to learn of the spiritual grounding that makes for a meaningful life. We cannot accomplish our goals as educators without the support of donors like you, those people that recognize that education needs "the extra mile" of giving.

Quite simply, your help is invaluable.

> Leave plenty of space for a hand-written note of thanks.

Sincerely,

Timothy Kachinske
Head of School

Many, many thanks for this generous gift, but more importantly, for the gift of Johnny and Sue. I very much enjoyed our September talk and hope to see you again soon.

Please note for your tax records that no goods or services were provided to you in consideration of this gift.

Figure 2.7

Anonymous Gifts

From time to time, donors will ask to be anonymous. You should always respect this wish and assume that there is a good reason for the request, even if you don't know or understand that reason. You annual fund will need a set of procedures to keep anonymous donors out of any public donor lists, stories, or other public recognition. Obviously, someone at your institution besides you may need to know about this donor's gift, as you will be processing a check with the donor's name and you will be generating correspondence to provide a gift receipt in some form. If you are the annual fund director, it will be your job to ensure that any colleagues who must know about the donor of such an annual fund gift be informed that the donor requests anonymity.

> Respect any donor's wish to be anonymous. Have procedures in place that ensure that you and other staff at your organization can carry out this wish.

Your Professional Action Plan

As a new person at your organization in charge of the annual fund, you will want to develop a plan that enables you to improve and keep current your knowledge of annual fund methodologies. Your plan should help you to be successful in your current position as it prepares you for career advancement.

Develop Your Continuing Education Program

Each year, the Council for Advancement and Support of Education holds a series of conferences on the annual fund. Most institutional members of CASE are colleges and universities. If your new annual fund job is in higher education, it will be obvious once you arrive that CASE is the place to go for knowledge and contacts because you will be seeing colleagues in other areas of development heading off to CASE conferences. CASE will soon become the most important part of your continuing education plan in your new job as an annual fund professional. It is very likely that you and a colleague in alumni relations at your organization will attend the same conferences.

> Broaden your knowledge of annual fund methodologies by attending national and district conferences sponsored by the Council for Advancement and Support of Education (CASE).

Colleges and universities have led the way in developing methods and technology for the successful annual fund as we know it today. You will want to profit from what CASE has to offer even if you are not working in higher education. CASE is important to all annual fundraisers because CASE conferences on the annual fund bring together the largest concentration of annual fund professionals and vendors in the country.

Each year CASE offers a general conference called *Successful Annual Giving*. Other conferences are devoted to specific areas of annual giving, such as phone-a-thons, matching gifts, or direct marketing. CASE conferences offer information and structure for your learning, and you will not be disappointed with the conference materials, speakers, and discussions. Just as important will be the informal sharing of information. There will be tables where annual fund and alumni directors place remainders of publications that you are free to pick up. You can count on leaving the conference with a substantial library of samples for your use later.

Visit the CASE website at www.case.org.

Be creative in searching out other workshops and institutes on annual giving, too. If you do a search on the web with key phrases such as "annual giving conference" and "alumni relations and annual giving," you will find many conferences and workshops offered by nonprofit and commercial enterprises. You may befriend people at CASE conferences who will in turn alert you to workshops of mutual interest. Such workshops are often informally organized by practitioners and are free or modest in cost. They are not always heavily advertised or easily found with a web search.

In your first year, you should aim to attend all annual fund-related workshops that are within a day's travel and at least one that takes you outside your region. Very likely you can connect your conference travel with annual fund business, such as meeting with a regional volunteer group, personal solicitation of leadership gifts for your annual fund, and meeting with vendors. If you have budgetary limitations for conferences and training, attendance at CASE conferences should be your priority.

Develop a Mentoring Plan

From day one on your new job in annual giving, you will want to think about people as a source for answers to questions or solutions to problems. This is especially true if this is the first annual fund you have ever managed, or if you are taking over an annual fund from another person. You may not be able to consult with your predecessor, but even if you can, you will still need the counsel of someone you can trust who knows your field. You will need mentors who have considerable experience in managing an annual fund.

Develop a network of mentors among your peers. CASE conferences are the best place to find a concentration of people with significant experience in operating an annual fund. You will find that annual fund managers tend to be extroverted and easy to talk to—especially about their work.

Each annual fund in education has a highly specific donor constituency comprised primarily of alumni and parents. There is little donor crossover among institutions. As a result, you will find the annual fund managers at educational institutions very willing to share techniques, experiences, and publications. Take advantage of this.

> Seek annual fund mentors outside your organization. Most annual funds have distinct donor constituencies and are therefore not competing among the same set of prospective donors.

During seminars and workshops, your peers in turn will reach out to you. Informal dinner groups form easily, as meals tend to be on your own at these conferences. Start conversations before and after every session, get calling cards or contact information from the people you chat with, and make notes on each one. These are people you can call later when you want to try out a new idea or resolve a problem. It would be a reasonable goal to leave a CASE annual fund conference with a list of 10 potential mentors.

90-Day Annual Fund Checklist

✓ You understand your employer's expectations for annual fund support.

✓ You have a good grasp of your organization's annual budget and needs, and you feel comfortable discussing those needs with people outside your organization.

✓ You have created an annual fund timeline that you are comfortable with.

✓ You have met with board members and other volunteers who have assisted with the annual fund in the past.

✓ You have a list of potential signers of appeal letters.

✓ You have looked for new annual fund volunteers and have a list of more than five volunteers whom you want to bring on board.

✓ You have drafted correspondence for letter appeals and gift acknowledgments, and you have shared these drafts with staff and volunteers.

✓ You have secured a volunteer to host your first phone-a-thon, and you have a list of three potential hosts whom you'd like to host future phone-a-thons.

✓ You have signed up for the CASE Successful Annual Giving conference, and you have attended a local workshop on annual giving.

✓ You have met at least one person outside your organization whom you have identified as a potential mentor, and you have called or written that person.

Chapter 3

Special Events

- What Are Special Events?
- The Role of Special Events in Fundraising Efforts
- Reporting Structure in Special Events
- Costing Out a Special Event
- Strategies for Negotiating a Hotel Contract
- Types of Special Events
- Volunteers
- Cause-Related Marketing
- Special Events with Tax Implications
- Develop Your Continuing Education Program
- Develop a Mentoring Plan
- 90-Day Special Events Checklist

What Are Special Events?

Special events are fundraising activities that bring prospective donors into your organization's environment. Gala events, parties, open houses, art exhibits, grand openings, and celebrity events all fall under the header of special events. In general, special events serve two main purposes:

1. **Publicity.** Special events are a great way to energize your base of supporters. They can inspire major gifts, and if properly executed, they can leave attendees with a favorable attitude toward your organization.

2. **Fundraising.** Special events can make money for your organization. Note the use of the word "can" in the previous sentence. Later on in this chapter, we'll talk about budgeting your special event. Unless your special events inspire major donors to make large contributions, your special events probably won't serve as a major source of fundraising dollars.

The Role of Special Events in Fundraising Efforts

All large nonprofit organizations employ professional managers of special events. Unlike the other development positions or areas of competence discussed in this book, special events may not appear in the title of a position or the heading of an advertisement for an opening. So you will need to look for the phrase "special events" in the finer detail of a position description or advertisement. However, since nearly every nonprofit, large or small, needs special events management in order to be successful, you will find many opportunities to do this engaging and rewarding work.

Special Events in Large Organizations

The size of an organization will determine whether it has a dedicated professional for special events management, or whether special events duties are combined with other fundraising responsibilities. A large research hospital or comprehensive university will most likely have at least one development professional dedicated to special events. These nonprofits tend to have broad, national constituencies of supporters, and special events often take place far from the organization's home city.

MYTHS AND MISCONCEPTIONS

Myth: Because you have celebrity involvement, your gala event is guaranteed to be well attended, hugely successful, and financially rewarding for your organization.

Reality: Most gala events barely break even. It's pretty common for a hotel or conference center to charge upwards of $150 per person for the meal alone. An expertly-managed gala event can make money, but the vast majority are break-even publicity events.

Misconception: Special events run themselves.

Reality: Holding a special event is one of the most time-consuming types of fundraising. There are countless details that need to be addressed, most of which you haven't even thought of. For example, let's say you are hosting a dinner. What is your plan for guests who have a peanut allergy? You may need to have one.

Misconception: People will be motivated to come to your special event because the tickets are tax deductible.

Reality: If someone receives goods or services in exchange for money that they provide your organization—even if your organization is a recognized charity—they won't be able to deduct the fair market value of the goods or services. For example, if someone comes to your gala event and pays $150 for the ticket, and it costs you $150 per person to buy the food served to them, they received full value for the ticket in goods and are not eligible for a tax deduction.

Large national advocacy groups that have broad membership and influence will have a fundraising professional dedicated to managing special events, but a local organization will probably include these responsibilities as one line on a job description that incorporates a variety of other duties. An organization that operates one or more national fundraising events a year, such as races, cook-offs, or galas, may have a chief special events manager who has a staff of fundraising professionals to assist her.

Special Events in Smaller Organizations

Smaller hospitals and educational organizations, such as liberal arts colleges and private schools, may often fold management responsibilities for special events into Director of Development or Director of Annual Fund positions. Some small colleges may have a special events manager reporting to the Director of Annual Fund or the Director of Special Gifts.

Small nonprofits with only one or two fundraising professionals typically fold special events into the existing positions that will also likely include annual fund and major gift responsibilities. There are many part-time opportunities in special events in smaller organizations.

Special Qualities Needed for Special Events

A fundraising professional in special events needs to have a special set of qualities. Perhaps the most important is attention to detail. While it is true that every position and area of competence in fundraising management requires attention to detail, no other area has quite so many details to manage as special events. These details will start with complicated financial spreadsheets and membership lists, leading to a potentially exhausting number of considerations and actions discussed later in this chapter.

A special events development professional also needs to have first-rate people skills. With the possible exception of prospect research, all fundraising jobs require good people skills. But most development positions will require meeting and dealing with individuals frequently and only occasionally with very small groups.

Special events professionals deal with large groups on a regular basis, so the special events fundraiser must be a person who likes people, enjoys meeting new people, and can make the people he or she meets feel comfortable and valued. Special events can be a very rewarding role for the right person, but it is not the job for someone who tends to be introverted.

Reporting Structure in Special Events

Typically, the fundraising positions and areas of competence discussed in this book report directly to the chief development officer, who holds an executive position usually at the vice-presidential level of a nonprofit organization. This executive is generically known as the chief development officer, and titles can range from Vice President of Advancement or Vice President of Development to Director of Development.

Special events fundraising can often be an exception to the norm of reporting to the chief development officer. Unless your events are responsible for $1 million in gifts per year, you likely will be reporting to another development officer, who in turn will report to the chief development officer.

Special Events and Capital Campaigns

Many special events fundraising positions are created for an organization's capital campaign. These positions will always report to whoever is doing the day-to-day managing of a capital campaign. You could report to the Vice President for Development, or you could report to a Director of Major Gifts who has been put in charge of a campaign.

In a sense, these are "temporary" positions created for the duration of a multi-year campaign. Often these temporary positions become permanent if post-campaign events continue to be successful in growing capital gifts. If you are looking at a special events position that was created for a capital campaign, you will want to know the material in Chapter 7, where capital campaigns are covered in some detail.

The sample development office organization charts in Figures 3.1 through 3.5 are offered to give you an idea of where you might be in the reporting structure, depending on the size of your non-profit organization or depending on the amount of gifts your events might generate.

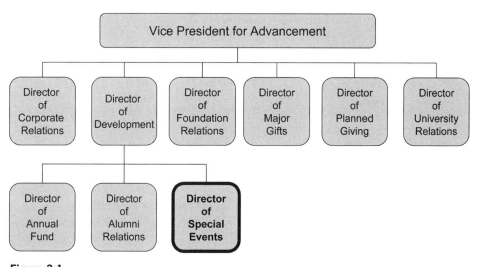

Comprehensive University
Sample Reporting Structure for Special Events Professionals

Figure 3.1

Research Hospital
Sample Reporting Structure for Special Events Professionals

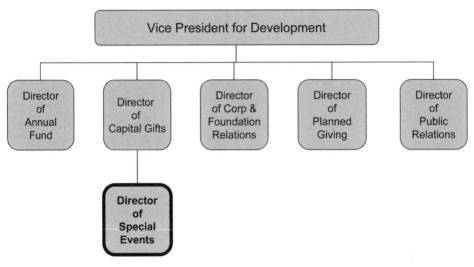

Figure 3.2

Liberal Arts College
Sample Reporting Structure for Special Events Professionals

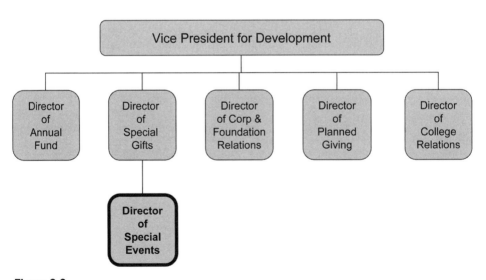

Figure 3.3

National Policy or Advocacy Organization
Sample Reporting Structure for Special Events Professionals

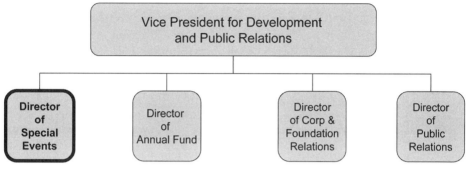

Figure 3.4

Independent (Private) School
Sample Reporting Structure for Special Events Professionals

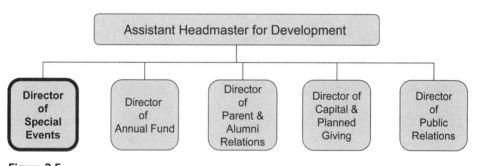

Figure 3.5

Costing Out a Special Event

Now that you have decided to take a position in special events fundraising, your first concern will be costs. You will want to tread carefully from the beginning with your costs.

Galas can be enjoyable events that drive participation in your organization, but they are rarely huge moneymakers.

Your annual gala event is coming up, and everyone is very excited about it. The whole staff has devoted significant time to preparing for this event, and you have more than 1,000 people committed to attending. The ticket price was high this year—$125. You raised the price because the gala lost money last year, so everyone is sure that this year's event will be a huge success.

With this scenario, let's take a look at your budget for the event:

Food and beverage for attendees	$85,000 ($85/person)
Food and beverage for staff	$1,000
Security guards for event	$1,000
Insurance	$3,000
Hotel rooms for staff	$1,000
Plaques for donors	$1,000
Two hours cash bar	$2,000
Pyrotechnics fee from hotel	$3,000
Signage	$1,000
Hidden hotel costs	$3,000
Staff salaries	$65,000
Total cost for event	$166,000

When creating your cost/benefit analysis for an event, be sure to include staff time in the analysis.

You charged $125 per person for tickets to the gala event. This means that your total income for the gala will be $125,000 for your 1,000 attendees. You just spent $166,000 to make $125,000 in revenue. Even though the price of this year's gala went up, you still lost money.

A staff salaries line item is included in the budget, and you should always consider this when planning an event. If running a gala requires that you devote two staff positions to the prep work for the event for six months, you should include that cost in your budgeting. Staff salaries are, after all, an actual cost to your organization. Many nonprofit organizations fail to consider the value of their internal time, but the salary position is often the item on the budget that tips an event into the red. Without considering the staff positions, you would have come close to breaking even.

The point of this chapter isn't to discourage you from hosting galas or other events. However, if you are going to host a special event, you must be very mindful of your budget. If the event loses money, that may be an acceptable outcome if your organization feels that the publicity and goodwill generated by the event outweigh the loss.

In the case of the aforementioned gala scenario, you might consider asking guests to donate money at the event to make up for your shortfall. You might do a video presentation to showcase the good work your organization does throughout the year. On the tables at the gala, you could leave envelopes for guests who wish to write a check. You might run a silent auction. There are lots of ways to capitalize on this captive audience in order to supplement your income.

Hotel Contracts and Hidden Costs

If you are renting a facility from a hotel or banquet hall, negotiating a good hotel contract can mean the difference between success and failure for your special event. In general, hotel contracts are written by hotel lawyers for the purpose of protecting hotel interests. You will most likely have to sign a version of the hotel's standard contract, but it is important to remember that you can *always* negotiate a specific line item in the contract. Hotels will expect that savvy organizations will ask for changes in the hotel contract.

Since margins are generally slim on special events held at a hotel, make sure you understand all of the hidden costs in your hotel contract before committing to either the event or the hotel.

If your organization has an attorney, you should have that attorney approve any hotel contract before it is signed. Many attorneys specialize in dealing with hotels, so if you do not have one on staff, you should hire an attorney who can safeguard your organization's interests.

In this section, you will find issues you should be aware of when negotiating a hotel contract.

Insurance and Liability Issues

You undoubtedly have car insurance. You also have homeowner's insurance or renter's insurance. You are a responsible person. You will want to carry the same responsibility over to your professional work in special events and secure the appropriate insurance for your event.

Event insurance is a must for any organization of any size. If you are bringing people together for any purpose, make sure you have liability insurance in case anyone gets hurt.

Many nonprofits can purchase an insurance plan that covers all of their events for the year.

What if someone dies at your event? What if someone gets drunk and is hit by a car on the way home? What if someone slips and falls on water accidentally spilled on the dance floor? What if your CEO puts out a cigar in the trashcan and causes the hotel to burn down? What if someone has a medical incident and ends up severely injured because nobody on your staff provided first aid? You should have insurance to cover your event so that, in the event of a lawsuit, you don't end up losing a lot of money due to unforeseen, accidental circumstances.

Keep in mind that all insurance policies for special events have payout limits. You will probably have an aggregate limit, a per-occurrence limit, a personal injury limit, a social host liability limit, and a limit to physical damage to the property. When negotiating an insurance policy for your event, it's a good idea to make the event coordinators, premises owner, co-promoters, sponsors, and other key individuals listed as named-insured on the policy. Make sure your policy covers setup and takedown—the days before and after your event. Make sure there is a liquor clause in your policy if you are going to serve alcohol at the event.

Don't skimp on the insurance. The cheapest policy is not always the best policy, and not all insurance policies are equal.

LEGAL DISCLAIMER
The information contained in this publication is not intended to convey or constitute legal advice on any subject matter. Readers should not rely on the information presented in this publication for any purpose without seeking the legal advice on the specific facts and circumstances at issue from a licensed attorney. Readers should not consider the information presented in this publication to be an invitation for an attorney-client relationship, and providing the information in this publication is not intended to create an attorney-client relationship between you and any author or contributor to this publication. The information in this publication contains general information that is intended, but cannot be guaranteed, to be always up to date, complete, and accurate. Any representation or warranty that might be otherwise implied is expressly disclaimed. The authors and contributors expressly disclaim all liability or responsibility in respect to actions taken or not taken based on any or all of the information contained in this publication.

ADA Compliance

If you are renting a conference room, and the hotel has storage boxes blocking the handicapped access ramp to the front door, both you and the hotel can be separately sued for noncompliance with the Americans with Disabilities Act. According to the ADA, places of public accommodation must make reasonable efforts to be accessible to people with disabilities. In your hotel contract, there should be a very specific clause that shifts responsibility for ADA noncompliance to the hotel or banquet hall.

If you put the storage boxes on the ramp, and if the hotel could not have avoided the blockage with reasonable effort, then the responsibility may still remain with you, so even if you have a clause that shifts responsibility back to the hotel, make sure your staff are aware that they have to accommodate handicapped persons throughout the event.

> Make sure there is a clause in your hotel contract that indemnifies you in case the hotel fails to provide an ADA-accessible space for your event. Make sure your staff is aware of any people with disabilities.

Banquet-Room Fees and Setup Charges

Most hotel contracts will offer free basic room setup. You should know what "basic" specifically means. For some hotels, a basic room setup involves a certain number of tables and chairs. If you need anything specific, be sure it's laid out in your hotel contract upfront.

> Anticipate hidden charges and make sure they are laid out in the contract specifically.

Here are a couple examples of situations that might not be covered in a basic room setup charge:

- **Power.** If your event requires that each attendee plug in a laptop, you'll need power strips set throughout the banquet hall. This is very rarely included in a basic room setup and sometimes requires additional hardware to tap into the main hotel power grid. If you show up at the event and say—at the last minute—that you need power for everyone, you may not be able to get it at any price.

- **Internet.** If you need Internet access for the presenter, make sure this charge is laid out in advance. Some hotels charge as much as $1,000 (or more) per computer for Internet access in a ballroom.

- **Trash removal.** Let's say your group leaves trash on the tables. Some hotels will charge you to take it away.

- **Storage.** If you ship materials to the hotel the week before an event, the hotel might charge you for the storage of these materials.

> Don't sign any hotel contract that refers to a fee without an explanation of how much that fee will be. Scrutinize Internet access charges for every meeting room or ballroom.

- **Extra chairs/tables.** If you have specific chair/table requirements, make sure they're laid out in advance.
- **Union labor.** Check your contract for union clauses. They may require that you hire local union labor to move chairs, set up the room, and so on.

Most of these items aren't laid out in a hotel contract. This is done on purpose. Let's say you ship a number of boxes to the hotel in advance of your gala. Since the price of storage isn't laid out in advance, you are at the mercy of the hotel when those boxes arrive. They can charge whatever their "standard" fee is— and it may be a lot!

Audio-Visual Fees

Expect that most high-end hotels will charge you to use your own AV equipment, unless you pre-negotiate otherwise.

There are speakers in the ceiling of the hotel, and when you did the run-through, you figured that you could just patch into them with your own microphone. There is, after all, a mic plug in the wall.

Wrong. Most hotels will levy a charge to use in-house AV systems. Sometimes they will also require that you pay for one of their staff members to be available throughout your event to tend to the AV equipment. Overhead projects, LCD projectors, sound, mixers, microphones, laser pointers, and just about any other type of AV equipment will cost extra.

The rental fees for audio-visual equipment can sometimes be as much—per day— as it would cost to purchase the equipment outright.

Most hotels—even big convention centers—outsource their AV departments to third-party companies. Most of these companies store their equipment off premises, so make sure you are upfront about your AV needs. If you need an extra projector at the last minute, you may be out of luck.

If you have your own overhead projector, you may still have to pay the hotel to use it. If you are planning on using your own AV equipment, be sure that is allowed in your contract. Some hotels charge an AV equivalent of a corkage fee. Use their projector, and it costs $500 per day. Use your own projector, and it will cost you $450.

Hotel Taxes and Recovery Fees

If you are tax exempt, make sure the hotel knows about this before signing the final contract.

Your hotel may charge you tax, but you may be able to avoid some of these taxes by providing a tax-exempt certificate. Do this upfront, and make sure it's clear to the billing office at the hotel that you won't have to pay some or all of the taxes on the account.

Known Expenses

You may be surprised how many fees can actually be hidden within known expenses. For example, your group might have to pay a deposit toward the master account with the hotel. The hotel, in turn, may charge you a service fee for accepting the deposit. If you want to transfer that deposit to a specific fund within your master account, you may incur a funds transfer fee.

Be sure to talk to the hotel about these types of fees. If you ask specifically about these fees, the hotel meetings staff will usually be upfront about them. If you don't ask, however, they are not likely to point out the hidden charges.

It is worth noting that luxury hotels usually have more fees than budget hotels. If you are having a small meeting at a two-star hotel, that hotel is almost never going to impose a food and beverage surcharge for the meeting. In fact, many of them offer free breakfast.

Even though you may think you've found all of the hidden fees in your hotel contract, get the hotel to agree in writing that you don't agree to pay any fees not specially laid out in the contract.

Hotel fees are higher and more numerous in luxury hotels.

Cancellation and Rebooking Fees

You are fairly certain that your special event will go as planned, but what if your CEO has a heart attack? What if you don't meet your required attendance number? What if another unforeseen circumstance causes you to cancel the event?

You have probably been to a wedding for a marriage that ended in divorce. Think about that when booking your venue. You never know what is going to end up making you cancel the event. Make sure you have an exit/rebooking strategy.

You probably won't be able to get rid of a cancellation clause in the contract, but make sure it is set on a realistic timeline and a sliding scale to minimize your liability.

Force Majeure

Make sure your hotel contract has a *force majeure* clause. This will limit both your liability and the hotel's liability for acts of God. Floods, earthquakes, volcanoes, wars, riots, and other emergencies that are beyond the control of the parties are all covered under a *force majeure* clause.

In case you were wondering, *force majeure* is French for "superior force."

Let's say you are organizing a conference in San Francisco. An earthquake hits two weeks before your event, and half of your attendees cancel because the airport was destroyed in the disaster. The hotel remains standing, and because you don't have a *force majeure* clause in your contract, you have to pay for all of the hotel rooms and conference facilities, even though you had to cancel your event.

Force majeure clauses in your contracts protect you from natural disasters and wartime disruptions.

Don't ignore the *force majeure* clause, no matter how remote the possibilities may seem.

Many people glaze over when they look at the sorts of situations covered by a *force majeure* clause. It's very real, though, and you should take it seriously. What if there is a terrorist attack that results in people being afraid to travel to your event? That's a very real possibility, especially if your event is held in a major city.

Force majeure clauses usually specifically cover:
- Wars
- Hurricanes
- Rebellions
- Insurrections or invasions
- Hostilities where war is not declared
- Floods
- Fires
- Earthquakes
- Storms
- Natural disasters
- Revolutions
- Military conflicts
- Interruption of utilities, such as electricity or telephone
- Blockages
- Embargoes
- Labor disputes or strikes

Housekeeping and Resort Fees

Resort fees usually include bottled water, newspapers, pool access, and Internet access.

If you are staying in a luxury property, your organization may be nickel-and-dimed with a resort and/or housekeeping fee. Resort fees typically cover bottled water, newspapers, use of the pool/hot tub, and other amenities that you would probably expect to be freebies in most hotels.

Make sure your staff is aware of resort or house-keeping fees.

Some resorts include high-speed Internet access in their resort fees, and you can sometimes leverage this fee to negotiate Internet access in the ballrooms. Especially in larger hotels with separate banquet facilities, the wireless Internet access available in hotel rooms sometimes won't extend into the ballroom areas, so you'll need to negotiate for ballroom access if this is something important for your event.

Food and Beverage Requirements and Minimums

Most hotels with catering service available will have a food and beverage requirement for any of their meeting spaces. If you're planning on having an event announcing a new initiative, and you don't really *need* food to be served at the event, you may not have a choice.

Make sure you have—in writing—all of the food and beverage requirements for your meeting space. Find out if breakout sessions are required. Find out if the serving of coffee is required if you are holding the meeting in the morning. Above all, make sure you know what the food and beverage fees are before signing the contract. Coffee for meetings, for example, is usually sold by the gallon. A gallon of coffee may cost upwards of $100, which makes the local coffee shop look like a bargain basement.

Expect your hotel contract to have a food and beverage minimum charge in four- and five-star hotels.

It's normal for a hotel to have per-person or per-event minimum charges for food and beverage service. For your 100-person meeting, this could add up to thousands of dollars in hidden extras. What's worse is that sometimes these minimum charges will be enforced even if you don't use them. So, if you have a meeting and you don't provide your guests with appetizers, you could end up having to pay for them anyway.

Make sure all food and beverage requirements are clearly laid out before signing the contract. After signing, you will have very little room for negotiation.

If you need to plan an event without food at a hotel, try looking at two- and three-star hotels. Some have nice, though usually small, meeting facilities. And because most two- or three-star hotels won't have onsite catering services, they are unlikely to have mandatory food and beverage minimums.

Cash Bars Aren't Free

If your event is going to have a cash bar, be advised that you will probably have to pay for the privilege of having the cash bar available during your event. Find out what these fees are and be advised that you'll probably have a per-bartender charge for each cash bar station.

Get drink prices from the hotel upfront. A bottle of water that costs $9 could be off-putting to your potential donors. You may want to subsidize a cash bar by charging a portion of each drink ordered to the master account, or you may consider using a drink coupon system, where every attendee gets a drink coupon. After that first drink, they have to pay for each drink ordered.

If you run a cash bar to save money at your event, make sure you have budgeted for bartender fees. These fees can be upwards of $100 per hour per bartender and do not include any drinks for your guests. Know the costs of everything, including a bottle of water.

You may also consider using a wristband system. Donors who have given more than $X to your cause get a wristband, and they drink for free. Or, if you want to be more subtle, you could give out a handful of drink coupons in advance.

Attrition Clauses

If you commit to a room block, be prepared for hefty fines if you don't meet the number of anticipated room nights.

If your special event involves a room block in a hotel, be careful about the attrition clause. If you commit to 150 room nights and only end up booking 100, you will probably have to pay for the extra 50 room nights.

If the hotel is agreeable, consider adding a clause that specifically states that both parties agree to waive any fees for room block slippage.

Mitigation Clauses

Having a mitigation clause in your hotel contract can limit your liability in the event that you don't make your room block. Mitigation clauses require the hotel to attempt to sell unsold rooms to other hotel guests, and if successful, these non-related guest rooms can count toward your room block.

If you have a room block booked as part of your special event, you may not meet this room block. You should always make sure that any hotel contract that includes a room block also includes a clause that requires the hotel to resell vacant rooms if you haven't met your room requirements by a certain date. These are usually called *mitigation clauses*.

Most standard hotel contracts do not include this clause. Let's say you have a room block of 100 rooms for an event that lasts three nights. You only sell 50 rooms each night, leaving 150 total room nights unsold in your room block. Without a vacant room clause, the hotel doesn't even have to try to resell those rooms to other guests. They can let the rooms sit empty because you've already purchased them.

With a vacant room clause, though, the hotel will be forced to open your room block to other visitors. If the hotel sells out for the nights of your conference, you'll end up getting out of the room block.

Cancellation Charges

Expect a cancellation charge in your hotel contract.

Make sure you have the financial support to pay a cancellation charge before booking a venue.

Most hotel contracts will have some kind of cancellation clause. Make sure this cancellation amount is something your organization can afford. If the meeting doesn't pan out, can your small nonprofit afford to fork over $150,000 in unnecessary expenses? If not, you might consider choosing another venue, or you might want to decide against holding the event.

Cancellation charges should be on a sliding scale, and they should be written out clearly in the contract. If you cancel one year before the event, the charge is $100. If you cancel a month before the event, the charge is $200. If you cancel the day before, the charge is $500. Get wording like this in your contract.

Resolving Disputes

Look over the sections of your hotel contract that discuss dispute resolution. Who is going to pay attorney fees in the event of a dispute? Is arbitration required before any issue goes to court?

In the event that a lawsuit is the end result of your contract, what will the governing state be? If your attorney practices in New Jersey but the contract stipulates that all conflicts will be resolved in Florida, you could find yourself having to hire a Florida attorney if you get sued.

When signing a hotel contract, try to name the venue for disputes as your local jurisdiction. Otherwise, if a dispute arises, you may end up having to fly to that jurisdiction for each hearing.

Strategies for Negotiating a Hotel Contract

By using these simple strategies for negotiating a hotel contract, you can save your organization a lot of headache, liability, and money.

Rule #1: Get Everything in Writing

This may seem cynical, but it can save you a lot of money in the long run:

Do not believe anything that is told to you. Only believe that which is written in an official contract.

If a hotel employee tells you not to worry about a specific fee, get it in writing. If the banquet manager says there isn't a fee for doing something, make a note of it and make sure you get it in writing. If you're worried about a specific resource being available during the conference, get it in writing.

Don't believe anything told to you in person. Get everything in your hotel contract in writing. Any promises made orally are virtually unenforceable.

The hotel is only contractually obligated to provide what is offered in writing, and if you didn't get it in writing, you'll be out of luck if they decide not to fulfill the terms of the oral promise.

Some hotel salespeople will be a bit more aggressive in offering products or services than they can actually deliver on. Just be careful that you don't fall into that trap.

Request regular reports in writing.

You should also ask for regular reports from the hotel in writing. Room block status updates, food and beverage charge summaries, and cancellation reports should be sent to you in writing on a regular basis. Once your event starts, you'll probably want to have these reports delivered daily.

Always Look for Hidden Fees and Read Your Contract Thoroughly

Never sign a contract without reading it first. You, or whoever at your organization signs the contract, should understand every fee. Before signing, make sure your attorney approves the wording.

Scour your hotel contract for hidden fees. If the contract mentions any fees, it should specifically lay out what the fees will be. For example, you would never want to sign a contract that alluded to a non-specific resort fee. You would want to say what the resort fee includes, what the final cost would be, and what situations would call for an overage of that fee, if any.

One of the simplest things you can do to save your organization money is to read the contract thoroughly. If you don't provide your own hotel contract, then make sure you know everything that is in the contract provided to you. Read the contract with a skeptical viewpoint, and remember that the contract was written by lawyers with the hotel's best interests in mind. The contract is in place to protect and serve the hotel, not you.

Consider Using Your Own Contract

If you start negotiations with your own hotel contract, you'll be less likely to end up forgetting a clause that could save you liability and/or money if a dispute arises. Your organization should have an attorney who can help you with developing your own contract.

The hotel will send you a contract, but most hotels will also accept a contract written by your attorney. It would probably be worth the investment to have a boilerplate contract written specifically for your organization. This way, every time you need a hotel for a special event, you can start the negotiations with a contract that serves your organization's specific needs and interests.

Asking your organization for a boilerplate hotel contract can also protect you in the event that they deny the request and a bad hotel experience costs your organization money. If you asked for a hotel contract during your first 90 days on the job, and if your superiors did not feel that this would be a good use of resources, you can always point to your original suggestion if a bad hotel contract sours one of your galas, book signings, conferences, or other special events.

Before signing, go through the contract and identify fees that look negotiable. Go back to the hotel with a list of fees you'd like to see lowered or eliminated. Often, they'll agree.

Don't Forget to Ask for a Handout

As a development officer, your whole job revolves around asking people for money. You ask donors for money. You ask strangers for money. You ask companies for money. Why not, then, ask for a freebie as part of your hotel contract?

When negotiating with a hotel, keep in mind that there are a lot of things that the hotel can throw in for free. Internet access, lowering of excessive fees, extra banquet space, and additional staff are all things that can be negotiated.

If your event includes a room block, you can generally expect to get one free room night for every 40 or 50 guest nights purchased. You can use these free rooms to offset the hotel costs for internal staff.

Make your requests for freebies reasonable, such as an extra room for staff meetings. Ask for something you think won't cost the hotel money.

Remember that meeting space is often a very negotiable part of hotel contracts. Plan out all of your meeting room needs in advance. If you need a meeting room for staff preparation the day before the event, ask for it. You'll likely get it for free, especially if you are spending a lot of money in other parts of the hotel.

Don't Be a Pain

Most of this chapter is devoted to helping you identify places in a hotel contract where your organization can lose money. However, don't lose sight of the fact that the hotel has to make money, too. You don't want to nickel-and-dime your hotel to the point that they become resentful of you.

Treat the hotel staff as you'd like to be treated. Try not to get into a situation where you are the customer that all of the hotel's sales reps talk about around the water cooler. Special events are high-stress situations for all staff—yours and the hotel's.

Chances are good that you've worked with someone in your professional life who is a pain. You are less likely to give this person freebies. You're less likely to go out of your way to help this person, and you're probably less likely to help this person to avoid costly situations. You don't want to annoy your hotel salesperson to the point where you are viewed as a pain.

Keep the relationship with the hotel salespeople friendly. Only complain to supervisors in extreme situations, and whenever you negotiate something, make sure that you have someone within your organization other than you who can be the bad guy. This way, you can stay on the good side of the hotel staff. You may need their help at some point during the event.

When you are negotiating with the hotel, put a mirror on your desk or cubicle. When you're talking on the phone, look into the mirror and smile. Try this. If you're looking at yourself smiling while talking on the phone, you come across as a more pleasant person. Everyone prefers to deal with pleasant people, including hotel salespeople.

Types of Special Events

Galas are probably the most common special events for nonprofit fundraising. There are, however, lots of other opportunities for nonprofit organizations to gather supportive prospective donors for an event.

All of the events described in this section are time consuming. They'll drain your internal staff resources, they probably won't yield high-dollar donors, and they might not actually break even. Some special events are successful, however, so I've highlighted a few events in each section to use as an example of a successful event.

Keep in mind that success doesn't necessarily translate to high revenues. A successful special event might be one that raises awareness for a cause or organization, even at a monetary loss.

Galas and Other Meal/Entertainment Events

Gala events are often not profitable. Careful planning is required to make money on these types of special events because of the high cost of production.

Galas are usually large dinner banquets. Usually held in the evening, they sometimes require formal attire and often involve speakers, awards, and remarks from the leadership of your organization.

When putting together a gala event, consider joining forces with other like-minded non- profit groups. While it may initially seem as though you would make more money hosting the event yourself, don't underestimate the amount of time required to coordinate a gala.

If you can spread this out across multiple staff at many organizations, you can probably save a lot of upfront headache. A large gala might also be able to negotiate a better hotel contract. Your per-person fees for a 1,000-person dinner will probably be less than you'd pay for a 100-person event.

Your first inclination for a gala might be a fancy hotel. Consider alternate events that might be cheaper. If you are a nonprofit that works with schools, consider hosting your event in a school auditorium. You won't be bound to the excessive hotel fees covered earlier in this chapter, and you might be able to better highlight some of the great successes of your organization—right in the location where you do work.

Colleges and universities often have topnotch banquet space available for rental by nonprofit groups. You may need a staff or faculty sponsor to rent the space, so this would be a good reason to develop relationships with faculty at a local university.

Volunteers are essential for a successful gala. You'll need registration staff, helpers to stuff bags, a band or other entertainment, and general workers to do tasks that come up throughout the course of the evening. Make sure you have a volunteer committee. As a nonprofit, you can usually pull from groups of people friendly to the organization. There's no sense in paying hotel staff to do a job that your volunteers could do better.

You would be smart to create a gala committee. Add members of your staff, your board, and volunteers to this committee. Having a solid committee in place is a good way to get people to commit to helping out with the event. Make sure this committee is staffed with people who will actually help out. You might have an honorary chairman or two, but not more than that.

> Volunteers are an essential element of most gala events. Where else are you going to get hundreds of temporary workers for a one-day event?

Consider having a corporate sponsor for your gala event. Events are a great way for companies to show civic responsibility, and it usually won't cost you much to post banners throughout the event that advertise the organization. Also, if your organization hasn't yet ventured into online registration for your gala event, take a look at how other organizations are using the web for this purpose. See Figure 3.6 for an example of how a prominent hospital uses the web to register donors for its gala.

After your gala is over, don't forget to publicize the event. Try to get an article published in a newspaper, accompanied by pictures taken during the event. Circle back to the gala attendees with this information, and use it as an opportunity to encourage them to donate extra money to your cause.

Competitions and Races

Every year for more than 20 years, the Whitman-Walker clinic in Washington, D.C. has sponsored an event called the AIDS Walk. The AIDS Walk is a 5K fundraising event that takes place each October.

> Walkathons, 5K races, and other contests can all be turned into multi-level marketing-type fundraising events.

Individuals or groups can register for the AIDS Walk (see Figure 3.7). In the process, they set a personal fundraising goal. Leading up to the event date, each participant asks friends and colleagues to sponsor them in the walkathon. Once the personal fundraising goal is completed, the person can participate in the AIDS Walk.

Figure 3.6

Online gala signup form for St. Jude's Children's Research Hospital.

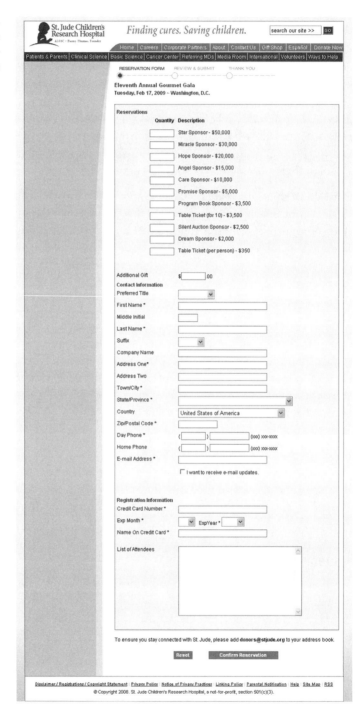

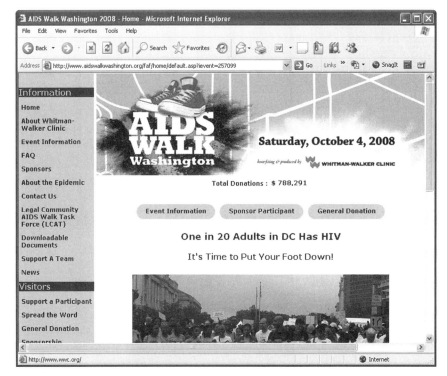

Figure 3.7 *AIDS Walk Washington online event registration.*

Competitions and races like the AIDS Walk can be great fundraisers because they gather a large group of people for donations—more than you could gather without the structure of the event. You may be able to get 100 people to donate money this month, but if those 100 people ask 10 friends each, you've now got 10,000 donors for the same event. This can really boost overall donation revenue.

Competition events can broaden your fundraising base to include friends and relatives of people within your circle.

Grand Openings

You just moved to a new facility. The building your organization has been working to secure for many years just opened its doors. Last year, you were able to secure enough funding to open a new school for disabled children.

If you are opening a new facility, consider turning that grand opening into a fundraising event.

Any time you have a new building or group to show off, you can use this event as an excuse to get potential donors to come to your facility and learn about the great things happening in your organization (see Figure 3.8).

Figure 3.8
Sample grand opening announcement.

SAMPLE EVENT INVITATION

DENHAM
MEMORIAL HOSPITAL

John Doe Cancer Wing
Grand Opening

Please join us as we celebrate the opening of the John Doe Cancer Wing. This latest addition to Denham Memorial Hospital is the most state-of-the-art cancer unit in the tri-state area, and it shows our continued commitment to providing the highest level of care to our patients. Major funding for the new wing was provided by the John and Jane Doe Foundation.

Tuesday, February 21, 2021
3:00pm – 5:00pm

Denham Memorial Hospital
21 South Jones Street
Denham, MN 55454

Please RSVP to:

Timothy Kachinske
Director of Special Events
rsvp@denmemhosp.com
218-555-1212

Refreshments provided by
Denham Catering Services, Inc.

Make sure your visitors have a good impression. Pay attention to catering refreshments and setting up a special display that gives people something to look at and talk about.

Grand openings can be great fundraising events because they generally happen at your facility. You won't have any of the excessive charges that might come up if you had to rent a space to hold the event.

You should definitely cater any grand opening event and consider having booths set up throughout the facility where donors can interact with staff, learn about your organization, or get updates on the progress of specific fundraising activities.

Antique Shows

Every year, the St. Barnabas Health Care System in northern New Jersey is the beneficiary of the Annual Two Rivers Art/Antiques Show and Garden Tour (see Figure 3.9). This antique show is the primary fundraiser for the Wilentz Breast Center and annually draws more than 1,000 attendees. The

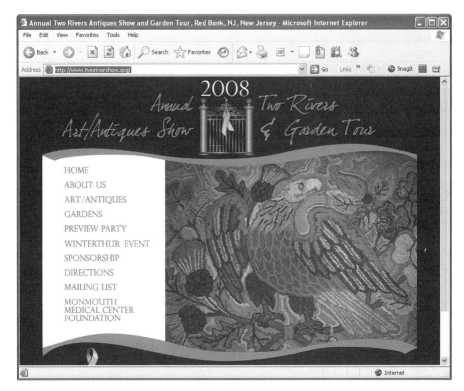

Figure 3.9 *Sample home page for an antique show.*

group has raised $2 million over the last 14 years, and this money has been put to good use helping women with breast cancer overcome the disease.

The event gathers local antiques dealers and artists, who sell items at the antique show. To get into the show, the general public pays $30 to $35 for an entry ticket, and a portion of the proceeds goes toward the Wilentz Breast Center. For more information on the Two Rivers Art/Antiques Show and Garden Tour, go to www.tworivershow.org.

A show like this really needs a champion within your organization. It's a lot of work to coordinate and execute an event like an antiques show, and if you are going to run one within your organization, you'll probably want to find this champion before committing to the event. The champion might be a retired donor with an interest in antiques, a wealthy patron with extra time to devote, or someone with special expertise in art or antiques. Expect an antiques show on the level of the Two Rivers event to require a full-time staff position year round.

Bingo Nights

Bingo nights can be a lot of fun, and they're fairly easy to coordinate. You'll need basic bingo equipment, but many party supply stores will rent you a bingo machine. Even if you have to purchase one, they are relatively inexpensive and can sometimes be found secondhand. Party supply stores often sell bingo cards, blotters, and other necessary equipment for running a successful bingo night.

If you are on a budget, you can download and print bingo cards on your printer (see Figure 3.10). You can also create your own bingo cards from ping pong balls. Write numbers on the balls with a permanent market and put them in a bucket. Your total expense with this low-budget route could be as little as $30.

Ideally, your bingo night will offer a donated prize. This way, you can keep all of the cash raised from the event. Consider offering

Figure 3.10
Sample bingo card.

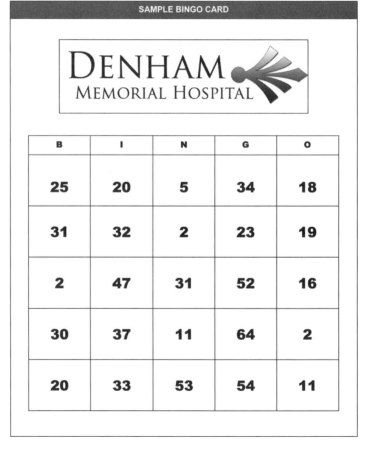

B	I	N	G	O
25	20	5	34	18
31	32	2	23	19
2	47	31	52	16
30	37	11	64	2
20	33	53	54	11

vacation packages, airfare vouchers, trips to spas, and other valuable prizes.

Whatever you do, make sure you are licensed by the state to hold a bingo event. In Massachusetts, for example, the state agency with domain over charity bingo nights is the Massachusetts State Lottery Commission Charitable Gaming Division. In 1973, when charitable bingo was legalized in Massachusetts, the State Lottery began licensing charities to hold bingo nights.

It's a big business. One year, there were more than 64,000 weekly players at charity bingo events, and there are more than 400 organizations in Massachusetts licensed to conduct bingo events. The State of Massachusetts collects a 5-percent tax on bingo events, but considering that more than $37 million is spent each year in bingo environments, you should be able to budget 5 percent of revenues.

Some states do not allow bingo or related gambling events. Know the law.

Beyond the tax, you'll need to get a permit to conduct bingo. That may require a significant amount of paperwork and planning on your part. This planning process may make bingo less desirable.

Bingo regulations vary from state to state, so be sure to contact your local regulatory board to make sure that you are in compliance before running a bingo event. If you don't, you could end up in a lot of trouble.

It's worth noting that any money "donated" to your organization through a bingo night is not considered a charitable contribution and will not be tax deductible for the patron.

Raffles

Raffles are probably the easiest to administer of all of the special events covered in this section (see Figure 3.11). Organizing a raffle can be as easy as taking a trip to an office supply store to buy a roll of tickets. You can run a 50/50 cash raffle, or you could raffle off prizes. You can hold a raffle online, at a specific event, or you could hold a long-term raffle for which participants are able to buy raffle tickets at multiple venues or events over a long period of time.

Raffles tickets purchased at your events are generally not tax deductible.

St. Jude Medical Center runs a very successful raffle in which they raffle off a house. Tickets cost $100 per chance to win, and the dream house for the winner is valued between $300,000 and $700,000. Although this is a nationwide raffle, St. Jude has set up

Figure 3.11
Sample raffle ticket.

a website where prospective participants enter their Zip code of residence to see whether local laws prohibit them from participating.

Raffles can be a quick way to increase revenue at an event, especially if you can solicit free prizes to raffle off.

One sticking point with a raffle like this is that the IRS generally requires taxes to be paid on winnings greater than $5,000. Let's say you won the $700,000 house. You may—immediately—end up owing the IRS as much as $350,000 in taxes on that income. A lot of the people who win major prizes like this aren't aware of the tax implications and end up with tax bills (accruing interest) that they aren't prepared or able to pay. Winners could quite possibly end up having to take out a mortgage on their free dream home.

The $100 fee per ticket is possibly not tax deductible, since it involves purchasing a chance to win something. Any receipt provided for a raffle should specify that the money received by your organization was exchanged for a raffle ticket chance to win a prize. A winner of a raffle would definitely not be able to write off any portion of the fee paid. You should refer to your tax attorney for updated information and an opinion on this subject.

Most state or local governments regulate the sale of raffle tickets. You should be sure to contact your local authorities before holding a raffle to avoid severe penalties and/or prosecution.

Currently, for example, Tennessee has no legalized gambling. If you're in Tennessee, you can't hold a raffle. Period.

Concerts

Concerts can attract donors on a large scale, especially if you can get the talent (the singer or band) to run the concert for free.

Concerts can be a great way to attract potential donors. They can be economical events from an administrative perspective, especially if you can get the entertainers to perform for free or for a reduced fee.

There are many examples of high-profile concerts run as fundraisers for organizations or causes. One of the most notable is Farm Aid (see Figure 3.12). Organized more than 20 years ago by Willie Nelson, Neil Young, and John Mellencamp, Farm Aid has held a concert every year to support local family farmers.

Cultivate performers such as singers or musicians who might perform for free or at a reduced rate.

Figure 3.12 *The Farm Aid website has information about the annual concert and much more.*

Celebrity Events

You might be able to harness the allure of meeting a celebrity to promote an event for your organization. A well-known speaker might bring a crowd of supporters that would not otherwise come together for an event.

Celebrities usually require payment to participate in your events.

Celebrities might include pop stars, politicians, speakers, sports figures, newsmakers, television personalities, actors, or just about anyone with star power.

One of the biggest misconceptions about celebrity events is that most celebrities will not want to be paid for an engagement. Unless a celebrity has a very strong link to your organization, they probably won't show up at your event for free. It doesn't matter that you are a nonprofit, and it doesn't matter that you are supporting a great cause. There are lots of great causes out there, and celebri-

Money paid to attend a celebrity event is often not tax deductible because you might not be able to pinpoint, for example, the fair market value of a golf outing with Tiger Woods.

The cost to book a celebrity may outweigh the benefits.

ties are in the business of selling their time and branding. Whenever they give either time or branding to you, they lose the opportunity to sell that amount of time or branding elsewhere.

You might work through a talent agency, such as Celebrity Talent International, to book a celebrity for an event. However, the cost to book a celebrity may outweigh the benefits.

Book Signings

Book signings tend to be inexpensive, and they can be a great way to show off the accomplishments of people close to your organization.

Let's say you work for a liberal arts college. One of your alumni has just published a book, and it has hit the bestseller list. Chances are good that this alum has committed to doing a book tour for the publisher, and you might have a great opportunity to co-brand one of these events as a special event to highlight your college.

Hosting a book signing serves a number of purposes. It highlights the accomplishments of your alumnus, which in turn enhances your reputation. It brings people together for a common purpose related to your organization, which presents an opportunity for donor cultivation. It can also be a learning experience for your existing students, staff, or patrons.

Silent Auctions

Silent auctions can be highly profitable events, especially if the items auctioned off are donated to your organization.

A silent auction can be a great way to raise money because there is no cost for the items sold. Silent auctions are often conducted in conjunction with another special event. For example, you might have a banquet and hold a silent auction beforehand. Usually the goods or services auctioned off will have been donated by companies or individuals friendly to your cause. Some examples of things you might auction off are:

- Airline tickets or vacation packages
- Spa services
- Hotel stays at a resort (see Figure 3.13)
- Rental of vacation properties
- Restaurant packages
- Donated goods
- Cars, boats, or motorcycles
- Dinner with your CEO or a famous celebrity
- Artwork

If you are running a silent auction, make sure you have the ability to process credit cards. You can get a merchant account

SAMPLE SILENT AUCTION BID SHEET

DENHAM
MEMORIAL HOSPITAL

7 Night Caribbean Vacation
Cancun, Mexico

Package for Two

Stay in the beautiful Los Calamo resort, a five-star luxury five star resort in Cancun, Mexico. This vacation package includes:

- Airfare from any major US city
- Lodging
- Hotel transfers
- Meals
- Local alcoholic beverages

Generously donated by:
XYZ Travel
Denham, MN
218-555-1245

Name	Bid

Figure 3.13
Sample silent auction bid sheet.

through most banks, through your accounting software company (such as QuickBooks or Peachtree), or through wholesale clubs, such as Costco. PayPal also offers merchant accounts to nonprofit organizations. When it comes time to pay for items purchased in a silent auction, the worst thing that can happen is for money to be left on the table because the attendee was only able to pay for a big-ticket item by credit card.

You might also opt to run your silent auction online. eBay will run a traditional auction for a charity, but niche sites, such as cMarket.com, are more geared toward fundraising auctions.

Consider doing a silent auction online.

When issuing receipts for any items purchased at a silent auction, be sure to clearly describe the item purchased. Generally, the purchaser will not be able to deduct the fair market value of the goods received, but if the donor offered $5,000 for a toothbrush, they'd probably be able to deduct a large amount of the purchase price as a charitable contribution.

DIALOGUE WITH A PROFESSIONAL: FARRAND O'DONOGHUE

For several decades, Farrand McDonald O'Donoghue has served in development positions that have required special events expertise. Her impressive accomplishments offer a model for anyone looking at a fundraising position that involves special events.

Presently, she serves as Development Director at the Bishop John T. Walker School for Boys, founded in Washington, DC to honor the memory of the first African-American bishop of the Episcopal Diocese of Washington. This school serves boys and their families in a chronically underserved area of southeast Washington, DC.

Previously O'Donoghue served as Director of Leadership Gifts at the United States Navy Memorial in Washington, DC. At the Navy Memorial, O'Donoghue's fundraising responsibilities included specials events in Washington, DC and locations throughout the country, as well as a campaign to fund and erect Lone Sailor and Homecoming statues on the waterfronts of cities across the U.S.—some of these individual statue projects topped $3 million in costs.

O'Donoghue also has held fundraising positions at the Smithsonian Institution, Washington National Cathedral, and The Catholic University of America. At both the Smithsonian and Catholic University, O'Donoghue's special event responsibilities included planning and accompanying groups of Smithsonian supporters on travel excursions to Europe, South America, and sites across the U.S. As Director of Regent & Development Activities at The Catholic University of America, O'Donoghue was responsible for managing the American Cardinals Dinners, an annual gala held in a different U.S. city each year. O'Donoghue's fundraising goals for each Cardinals Dinner exceeded $1 million.

How did you get into fundraising?

I had owned my own small business and decided to close it and seek a new career path. Over many years, I had volunteered for a variety of nonprofits, including chairing numerous special events, so I had solid, hands-on experience.

At first, I worked with a presidential campaign that involved special events and, at the campaign's conclusion, I looked for a job in the nonprofit sector. I became the Director of Regent & Development Activities at The Catholic University of America, which put me in charge of the university's national fundraising board and the annual American Cardinals Dinner. It turned out to be an excellent launch pad for my career as a professional fundraiser and special events expert.

How could someone get special events experience if he or she is a recent college graduate?

Well, I would say take a hard look at internship opportunities. Many larger special events advertise for paid, part-time help. Be proactive and seek out a forthcoming event whose mission appeals to you and then telephone or write to the person managing it. Ask whether they are looking for an intern.

That often can prompt someone to think about adding an internship to help get the job done. If you're creative in development, it's usually respected. Don't be afraid to reach out and create your own opportunity by offering insightful suggestions that you can carry out on your own.

You can also volunteer. If I were looking at someone with significant volunteer special events experience, I would consider that as good work experience. Perhaps you had an important role in getting out invitations or solicitations, updating RSVP lists, leading a group of volunteers in manning a phone-a-thon, handling the registration desk at an event, working with VIP guests—all of that constitutes solid experience, so don't underestimate what you may have accomplished.

What do you recommend for persons who are looking for reentry into the job market, a career change, or part-time work?

Reentry: Look at what fundraising or special events work you might have done at your children's schools, a local hospital, your place of worship, and other charities. Have you ever chaired a fundraising committee, planned the charity's annual gala, planned an annual special day at a school, place of worship, etc.?

That will have provided you with broad experience that can be translated into work experience. Save copies of invitations, press releases, promotional materials, event booklets, photos of decorations, and solicitation letters that you designed for various events. Organize them into a portfolio that you can take to job interviews to show your creativity and capability.

Career change: The tips that I suggested for reentry also apply to making a career change to special events fundraising. Also, think about probably having to accept a lower salary than you might have anticipated, because nonprofits do not have the large budgets for salaries that would be comparable to private-sector companies. Likewise, benefits packages at nonprofits tend to be less attractive for the same budgetary reasons.

Part-time: Special events fundraising can be the perfect solution for people who prefer part-time employment. It's possible to link up with one, two, or several charities to work on their annual events for a limited timeframe, and at the same time each year. This provides a stable option for both the part-time employee and the nonprofit organization.

What are important skills?

Organizing skills are very important because without them you will be frustrated and unable to keep the many balls in the air that special event fundraising requires. You need to be a person who can work with a myriad of "to-do" lists and manage a calendar with hundreds of minute details. Imagine putting together a spectacular birthday party or dinner party, then multiply all the work and details by 100, 1,000, and even more. Be organized! That's the best way to avoid feeling overwhelmed.

But, it's also important to enjoy this kind of work. You need to like working with people—lots of people.

Learn how to read your paid assistants as well as your volunteers and try to match their strengths with appropriate jobs. If someone says they are not particularly good at a certain task, give that person something to do that they can accomplish with success and that will interest them as well.

Computer skills are a must. You'll need them for almost everything you do. You'll need to be expert at word processing for so many things—getting out invitations, solicitations, and other mailings. You'll also need to know how to use Excel spreadsheets for all kinds of tallies, including (but not limited to) responses to invitations, names of guests, table assignments for dinners, who has paid and who still owes for the event, and thank-you notes following the event.

You might have to learn the particular development software that an organization uses. Ease in working with e-mail is a must, as is familiarity with the web. You don't have to be a webmaster with technical knowledge, but you should know how events and fundraising can be done on the Internet and convey that to the organization's web administrator.

What was your most interesting or rewarding special event?

That's so hard to say. I've really enjoyed my work. When I managed the American Cardinals Dinner at The Catholic University of America, our fundraising supported scholarships for students in need of financial aid. Literally hundreds of students were helped each year.

My work at the Smithsonian Institution, the world-renowned, free-admission museum complex that showcases America's national treasures, was both rewarding and fascinating as our funds went toward educating millions of visitors from across the globe that came to the Smithsonian each year.

Right now I'm working to support a private school for boys in a very poor area of Washington, DC. I feel it's vitally important, probably the most important work I've done yet. This is a faith-based, tuition-free school, so the need is huge. But the impact is huge, too, on the lives of the boys and their families.

But I think everyone who works in fundraising and special events has similar feelings. Doing a good job that results in supporting a great cause is, undoubtedly, the best part of special events fundraising. After an event, there's always a feeling of exhilaration when the job is done and you get to see how your fundraising work helps people. That's where you can get a lot of personal satisfaction.

Do you have any advice for someone who is thinking about applying for a development job that has special events responsibilities?

You definitely want to understand your responsibilities upfront—"other duties as assigned" is a clause in job descriptions that often can take you away from what you will be expected to produce and what will be discussed in your annual review. If you get an interview, it's not always easy to ask a lot of probing questions. It's a good idea to do as much due diligence as you can before going to an interview.

Use the Internet to learn all you can about the organization—its track record in fundraising, its longevity, has there been constant staff turnover (a negative sign), and what is the ratio of funds raised to funds distributed to the charity's good works. Ask around to see if anyone you know has personal knowledge of the organization.

Were there any special challenges?

Definitely, always count on special and unplanned challenges. Being prepared and flexible to handle last-minute changes is important, and you should learn to take these issues in stride, although it will not seem easy to do at the moment. I'll never forget the black-tie fundraising dinner I planned for 1,000 people in Los Angeles when I was working at The Catholic University of America when, very unfortunately, a major earthquake struck, and the honorary chairman of the dinner decided it would be best to cancel the event and hold it the following year.

The university was depending on the $1 million for scholarships that the dinner traditionally raised, so we had to find another city that would host the dinner on short notice, find new co-chairmen, and put on a gala affair. We did it! This is an example of a big, last-minute change, but there will be many smaller changes that will need attention and immediate decisions—stay calm, keep a sense of humor, and you will survive!

Volunteers

Staffing is usually the second highest expense (behind venue costs) for special events. Having a corps of volunteers to help run your special events can drastically increase the profitability of these events. This section will include tips for where to find volunteer labor.

Colleges and Universities

College students make great volunteers. Let's say you're running a telethon. You could hire a staff of cheap labor to call alumni to ask for money, but if the people making the calls don't know anything about the university, their lack of knowledge is likely to negatively affect the outcome of the fundraising event. However, if students are making the calls, the alumni contacted will be inclined to engage in conversation.

If you are running a gala event to raise money for a university, it might actually help your cause to have students working the event. When an alum shows up at the gala looking for a name badge, he or she would probably prefer to see a student worker

Colleges and universities are great places to find volunteers because students will be friendly to your cause, and they often have time to devote to volunteer activities.

behind the registration desk rather than an outsourced worker from a staffing agency.

Don't forget about tapping into your alumni base for volunteer efforts.

When looking for volunteers at colleges and universities, you might turn to your fraternities, sororities, and service organizations for help coordinating. Many fraternities and sororities require that their members complete service projects, so that might be a great fit with your event.

If you are trying to recruit volunteers for a specific event, try coordinating with your on-campus housing department. You might hold a contest. The Resident Assistant who coordinates the most volunteers gets a $100 bonus. That might motivate your RAs to get people on their floors to pitch in. You might also post signs in common areas, dorms, cafeterias, and other places that will have high visibility for the student body.

Alumni are also a good source of volunteers within a college or university. Check out the alumni association leadership for help coordinating alumni support.

Primary and Secondary Schools

When looking for volunteers in a school environment, make sure you have parental consent if the activity requires it.

In schools, you generally have two main sources of volunteers: parents and students. Whether you tap into the parent pool or the student pool will often depend on the type of event and the level of responsibility required of volunteers.

For example, if you are running a charity auction for a secondary school, some of the volunteers may need to drive auction items from one location to another. In cases like this, you might need to tap more into the parent pool because parents are more likely to have cars and driver's licenses.

Don't be afraid to tap into your parent organization for assistance with events. Work with the leadership of your volunteer groups.

To coordinate student volunteers, consider reaching out to specific extracurricular clubs, homerooms, specific classes, sports teams, or other preexisting groups within the school. Getting the entire football team to volunteer for your gala dinner might be easier than finding 40 individual students, especially if you have buy-in from the football coach.

Most schools have a PTA, PSTA, Mother's Club, or Father's Club. Whatever your school calls the parent-teacher association, reach out to them. One phone call to the PTA president might be all it takes to get 20 volunteers to show up for a special event. Whenever possible, reach out to existing groups. Identify a figurehead who can coordinate your volunteer list, and then interface primarily with that figurehead. Dealing with the president of your parent organization is a lot less time consuming than dealing with 40 individual parents.

Social Service Organizations

Social service organizations should always maintain a database of potential volunteers. Anyone who has given you money should be in this database. Anyone who has signed up for your newsletter is a potential volunteer. Anyone who has attended one of your events might be willing to participate in a special event.

Your goal when creating a list of potential volunteers for a social service organization will be to always be on top of the list of people who are friendly to your cause.

Web 2.0 technologies can help greatly in organizing volunteers in social service organizations. If you are an animal rights group, you probably have a Facebook or MySpace page. On this page, you can communicate with friends, send updates, and solicit volunteers. Posting a message on your My Space page might be all it takes to bring in 20 volunteers to man booths at your special event.

Social service organizations should tap into Web 2.0 technologies to gather lists of potential volunteers for events.

Healthcare

If you are a hospital, hospice organization, nursing home, or other healthcare organization, you will want to maintain a list of people whose lives have been touched by your organization.

While maintaining this list, be sure to not violate any HIPAA privacy laws. For example, let's say you're a breast cancer research center. If you need volunteers to talk about their experiences with breast cancer, and if you sent out this invitation as an e-mail where all recipients are CC'd, you would have essentially revealed the medical history of everyone on the recipient list. Penalties for breaches like this can be stiff and definitely outweigh any benefit you would get from soliciting volunteers.

You might consider creating an opt-in list of former patients, family members of patients, and others who specifically would like to volunteer for your hospital or organization. If your state-of-the-art equipment saved someone's life, they're probably going to be inclined to attend the fundraiser geared toward acquiring more equipment.

Always be aware of privacy laws when contacting volunteers in a healthcare environment.

Actively gather a list of people who would be willing to volunteer for your activities. Don't wait until you need them to have this list of volunteers ready.

Make sure your staff is aware of privacy laws.

Churches and Religious Institutions

Use your church bulletin to advertise volunteer opportunities. Consider using automated phone calls for your clergy's messages.

If you are a church, it's probably easy to get volunteers for an event. Every weekend, most of your church members attend religious services. At the end of the service, the pastor can solicit volunteers for whatever is needed.

Churches may benefit from purchasing a subscription to a robo-call service, like those used by political campaigns. The concept is simple. Sign into the robo-call service, record a message, upload a list of phone numbers, and everyone on the list gets called and played the message. Having your pastor record a message calling for volunteers might be a good way to remind members of your church about an upcoming need.

Cause-Related Marketing

Consider cause-related marketing to highlight your cause and organization and bring in new income.

Cause-related marketing involves pairing corporations and non-profit groups to create a co-branded marketing campaign. The primary aim for these campaigns is usually to sell the service or product from the corporation, with a small portion of the profits donated to the designated charity.

Cause-related marketing campaigns have become more and more popular in recent years. It is likely that you have seen a breast cancer product. KitchenAid, for example, makes a line of pink products and donates a portion of the proceeds to cancer research.

Website retailers, such as TigerDirect, also team up with cancer research companies to offer shoppers a chance to direct their buying power toward a charitable organization.

American Express

In the first major cause marketing campaign, American Express increased new card-members by 45 percent and at the same time raised $1.7 million for restoration of the Statue of Liberty.

American Express actually first coined the phrase *cause-related marketing* in the early 1980s. Since then, they have been one of the most successful marketers of co-branded causes. In 1983, American Express launched a campaign to restore the Statue of Liberty. Every time someone charged a purchase on their American Express card, the company would donate a penny to the Statue of Liberty restoration project.

Very soon after commencement of the campaign, new card-members increased by 45 percent. Card purchases on existing cards increased by 28 percent. By donating a penny to a good cause, American Express made a lot of money. And cause-related marketing was born.

More than $1.7 million was raised for the Statue of Liberty project. A decade later, American Express launched another cause marketing scheme with Share Our Strength (SOS). The campaign was called Charge for Hunger, and American Express raised more than $21 million and springboarded SOS into a large national advocacy program. Suddenly, they were on the national scene with the kind of advertising campaign that few nonprofits could afford.

Susan G. Komen for the Cure

Susan G. Komen for the Cure was started in 1982 by Susan Komen's sister, Nancy Brinker. Since then, this organization has raised more than $1 billion for cancer research. Much of the income comes from a brilliantly executed cause-related marketing system.

Susan G. Komen for the Cure has been one of the most successful cause marketing organizations, raising more than $1 billion in its history. Many of the organization's donations come in the form of proceed shares with co-branded pink products.

You've probably seen the pink products that provide support to Susan G. Komen for the Cure. There are hundreds of pink products on the market today, including:

• Better Homes and Gardens pink cookbook

• Belkin pink iPod case

• Garth Brooks *Ultimate Hits* CD (the cover is pink)

• Pink watches

Every time you buy one of these (or other) Susan G. Komen products, a portion goes to the nonprofit breast cancer foundation.

Project Red

U2 singer Bono and Bobby Shriver teamed up to create Project Red to support The Global Fund to Fight AIDS, Tuberculosis, and Malaria. The group sells products that are—you guessed it—red. Red shirts, red iPods, red shoes, red laptops, red printers, and red watches are all available for purchase.

Project Red sells red-branded items, with a portion of sales donated to The Global Fund to Fight AIDS, Tuberculosis, and Malaria.

The idea is simple. People can buy products that they would buy anyway. If you're going to get an iPod, you can get the red model, and part of your purchase price will go to help fight AIDS in Africa.

Major partners of Project Red include American Express, Apple, Converse, Dell, Armani, Gap, Hallmark, and Microsoft. You can get an American Express card that is co-branded as a Red card. You can buy a red Gap T-shirt that says INSPI(RED) on the front. With a little help from Bono and other celebrities, such as Oprah, Project Red's products have actually become quite fashionable.

Livestrong

Yellow Livestrong bracelets worn by Lance Armstrong on the Tour de France became an overnight sensation and raised millions of dollars for his foundation.

Livestrong yellow bracelets became a fashion accessory. Consumers had to have them. The yellow rubber bracelets have a simple design and have the word LIVESTRONG engraved into them. They are sold at thousands of retail outlets, mostly at checkout counters. With a price tag of $1 per bracelet, they are within the budget of most people.

Lance Armstrong wore the bracelet while he competed in the Tour de France. Almost immediately after doing so, it seemed like everyone in America had to have a Livestrong bracelet. John Kerry wore a Livestrong bracelet to the Democratic National Convention. More than 10 million bracelets sold out almost overnight.

In fact, the Livestrong bracelets were so popular that, after they sold out, may people sold their bracelets on eBay for more than 10 times the original price. Of course, none of that profit margin made its way back to Lance Armstrong's foundation, but it does underscore the popularity of the product.

GoodShop.com

If you're looking for a low-risk way to enter into cause-related marketing, check out GoodShop.com. National cause-related campaigns take a lot of time, effort, and planning but an idea with GoodShop.com can become a reality quickly.

GoodShop is one of a number of websites that co-brand corporate purchases with donations to charities. Dell, Best Buy, Expedia, Apple, Gap, Hotels.com, L. L. Bean, Kohls, and hundreds of other major retailers are available on GoodShop.

The concept is simple: People buy things they were going to buy anyway, but because they start that online shopping trip at GoodShop, they can designate the donation to go to any of more than 70,000 nonprofit organizations.

Signing up with a company like GoodShop might be a good idea because, with very little upfront effort, you can create a cause marketing campaign for your organization. If you are a small nonprofit, chances are slim that you could create a co-branding contract directly with American Express; however, if you sign up through GoodShop, you can get much of the same benefit.

Some Issues with Cause-Related Marketing

You are probably thinking, "Great! If we align ourselves with a corporate sponsor, then we'll be able to put our names on billboards in every subway station for a small kickback on everything they sell."

Be careful, though. When you enter into a cause marketing scheme, you're also lending your name to the product, which could backfire. If you align yourself with an organization that ends up having a scandal, lawsuit, recall, or other unfortunate situation, the company's misfortunes could end up negatively impacting your organization.

In the mid 1990s, the Arthritis Foundation entered into a co-branding marketing contract with Johnson & Johnson, which owns multiple arthritis medication brands. More than half of the states in the U.S. have filed suit against McNeil Consumer Healthcare, a division of Johnson & Johnson. The result was a settlement close to $2 million.

A few years later, the American Medical Association announced a scheme of co-branding marketing with Sunbeam home health products. After the contract was signed, the trustees of the association voted to end the project. A lawsuit ensued, and AMA ended up paying Sunbeam close to $10 million.

If you enter into a cause marketing contract, make sure you have legal insurance. Many insurance companies provide legal insurance, and the concept behind it is similar to other types of insurance. If you have car insurance, and someone hits your car, you're protected. With legal insurance, if someone sues you, the insurance company covers the legal expenses.

Some organizations, such as the Arthritis Foundation and the American Medical Association, have seen cause marketing deals backfire and end in costly lawsuits. Always have an attorney and insurance when engaging in cause marketing.

Special Events with Tax Implications

Sometimes the biggest consideration with a gift to a charitable organization is the tax benefit for the gift. You have to be mindful of this when holding a special event because special events usually have some kind of tax implication—both for you and for the donor. Whenever there is a question, you should consult an attorney who is an expert in gift tax law.

Raffles, Lotteries, and Auctions

Raffle and lottery tickets are rarely tax deductible.

All states regulate raffles and lotteries. Some even regulate auctions. The first thing you will need to do if you are hosting a raffle, lottery, or auction is get the necessary permits to hold the event within your jurisdiction. If your event is held online, that may affect the permits you need.

In some states, your organization could be subject to a gambling tax if you hold a lottery or raffle. Check with your state authorities to see whether this would apply to you.

If someone buys a lottery ticket from your organization, they're essentially purchasing a chance to win a larger prize. When someone gives your nonprofit organization money in exchange for goods, they can only deduct any money paid beyond the fair market value of the item received. In the case of raffles and lottery tickets, the fair market value of the ticket is the face value of the ticket, so none of the money paid would be tax deductible.

In an auction, a purchaser can deduct anything paid beyond the fair market value of the product or service purchased.

In the case of an auction, your donor would be able to deduct anything beyond the fair market value. So, for example, if someone purchases a spa package at your auction for $500, and if that spa package is advertised on the spa's website for $300, they would be able to deduct $200 for the auction. Be careful about specifying the fair market value of goods sold at an auction. You are a nonprofit organization, not a professional appraisal firm. Make sure that any market value dollar figures given by your organization are backed up by documentation from a third party, such as a manufacturer. As a courtesy to your donor, you might want to provide a newspaper clipping, website printout, letter from the manufacturer, or other third-party proof of fair market value.

Galas, Dinners, and Other Food-Based Events

Galas and other events where food is provided for a donation are usually not tax deductible.

Earlier in the chapter, we discussed a scenario in which you sold tickets to a gala for $125, but your costs to produce the event were more than $125 per person. This is the big tax catch with galas and dinners.

Most galas are break-even (or worse) events. The fair market value of that dinner someone just ate might be $125. If so, the event is not tax deductible for any of the attendees.

Trinkets

Be careful about giving out trinkets to your donors. If the trinket is valued at more than a few dollars, it will probably reduce the total amount that your donor can deduct. For example, if someone gives you $100, and you send them a gift basket valued at $30 as a thank-you present to cultivate the donor to giving more money in the future, you've essentially given this person goods in exchange for the donation. At this point, you wouldn't be able to write that no goods/services were received in exchange for the gift on his receipt, and he would only be able to deduct $70 for the gift.

Any substantial trinket will decrease the amount (for your donor) that he or she can deduct. Always know the current tax laws as they relate to trinkets. Laws change, so keep current. Attorneys with gift tax expertise can help you.

Unrelated Business Income Tax (UBIT)

UBIT is assessed if your organization performs business activities that are not related to your tax-exempt purpose. For example, if you are a small organization devoted to helping people with a specific disease, your organization couldn't open a grocery store and then claim the entire enterprise as a tax-exempt organization. Unrelated business income is a burden that you want to avoid if at all possible.

According to the IRS, activities by tax exempt organizations will be subject to unrelated business income tax when:

Before running any event for which gifts or services are provided to donors, check with your attorney to make sure that you won't be liable for any unrelated business income taxes as a result of the event.

- **Requirement 1:** If the activity is a trade or business. Generally, the term *trade or business* covers any activity in which you sell goods or services for a monetary kickback.

- **Requirement 2:** If the activity is not a regular activity of the organization.

- **Requirement 3:** If the activity isn't substantially related to furthering the exempt purpose of the organization.

Your activity must meet all three requirements for it to be subject to UBIT.

There are some exceptions to these requirements, though. If your activity results in less than $1,000 in income, for example, you must report the unrelated business income, but that income is not subject to the tax. There are a lot of loopholes to this law, and you should familiarize yourself with IRS Publication 598, which details many circumstances in which business activities that seem unrelated are actually not subject to UBIT. For example, if volunteers make up your staffing on an event, it's probably not subject to UBIT. Charity auctions and bingo tournaments are also not usually classified as subject to UBIT.

You may hold a meeting, seminar, or conference in which training about your cause is provided to industry leaders. The conference probably wouldn't be subject to UBIT, but it's possible that tangible personal property provided alongside the event might be unrelated.

If you run into a situation in which your organization performs an activity that meets the requirements for UBIT, the IRS essentially taxes you at the same rate you'd be taxed if you were a corporation. IRS Form 990-T is used to calculate and report unrelated business income tax.

Develop Your Continuing Education Program

Regardless of whether you are new to special events, conferences and seminars will broaden your knowledge. Plan to attend the annual CASE Conference on Special Event Fundraising. Go to www.case.org for information.

Whether you are new to special events or you are looking for a refresher, you will want to devise a plan over the year to build and update your knowledge. Fortunately, you have a great deal of opportunities. You can set up your personal continuing education plan right at your desktop.

First, do an online search for "special events planning courses." You will find that there are many online courses, webinars, and classroom courses. Some opportunities are offered by commercial training companies. Community colleges also offer night and online courses in event planning. This is a great place to start your search for a preliminary list of training opportunities.

Your most important continuing education opportunity will be the annual CASE (*Council for the Advancement and Support of Education*) on Special Event Fundraising. Sign up for it right away. Even if you are not working for an educational institution, you will still want to attend this conference. The Special Event Fundraising conference is likely the largest concentration of actively learning professionals with special events fundraising responsibilities. Typically, this conference covers everything from building a case for support and connecting with your special events donors to state-of-the-art discussions and demonstrations on protocols, policies, media coverage, publications, leadership, and volunteer recruitment.

One of the remarkable "take-aways" of this conference will be the sample plans, publications, and other materials that practitioners and presenters will be sharing with participants. Very likely many participants will bring stacks of publications, such as "save the date" cards, menus, programs, and flyers that are left over from past special events. These materials will typically be placed somewhere on an unmanned table, and they are there for your benefit. Be sure to take advantage of this sharing and build your own personal library of samples. This conference is a must, whether you are new to special events fundraising or you are looking for refresher information.

You should also search the Foundation Center website (www.foundationcenter.org) and its affiliates for short seminars on special events. These courses are often half a day or a full day, and they tend to have a modest registration cost if they are not free. You may be looking at the nearest Foundation Center library or affiliate for your own convenience, but you should cast your net wider and look for seminars in other cities. You may be able to work a seminar into your own development or personal travel plans.

Search the Foundation Center website regularly for new seminars on special events.

Develop a Mentoring Plan

You will also want to devise a mentoring plan from day one on your new job. If you are fortunate enough to have a colleague at your new place of work who has previously managed the events you are now managing, you will want to befriend this person right away. If you show the proper respect to this person's previous work, you will likely find that you have someone nearby whom you can consult from time to time. Just be sure not to overuse this person as a resource.

Seek out mentors both inside and outside your organization. Aim to leave each special events seminar with one potential mentor in mind. Aim to leave larger conferences with several potential mentors in mind.

Potential mentors will be present at every special events conference or seminar that you attend. Always think of a presenter as a potential mentor and have a goal of striking a conversation with every presenter who you think could advise you. At a multi-day conference, such as the CASE Special Event Fundraising conference, it would be reasonable to have a goal of connecting with at least three potential mentors.

At a smaller conference with one presenter, you would have a smaller goal. Whenever you strike up a conversation with someone at a conference or seminar, think about whether you would like that person as one of your mentors. Always get contact information, because it will be your responsibility to develop and maintain the relationship. If you do these things, you will quickly develop a host of experienced contacts whom you can contact when you need some advice.

90-Day Special Events Checklist

✓ You understand your employer's expectations for special events support.

✓ You have a good understanding of your organization's annual budget.

✓ You feel comfortable with the budget allocated for your special events expenses.

✓ You have created a timeline for all special events of the year, and you feel comfortable with your timeline.

✓ You have met with board members or other volunteers who have participated in special events of the past.

✓ You have a list of potential new volunteers and have contacted at least five on your list.

✓ You have costed out your special events of the year and projected fundraising returns on these events.

✓ You understand the tax implications of all special events planned for the year.

✓ You have signed up for the annual CASE conference on Special Events Fundraising.

✓ You have met at least one person outside your organization who works in special events, and whom you have identified as a potential mentor.

✓ You have called or written your potential mentor several times.

Chapter 4

Foundation Relations

- What Is Meant by Foundation Relations?
- Identifying Your Organization's Needs
- Matching Foundations' Priorities and Interests with Your Needs
- Categorizing Potential Sources of Foundation Support
- Undertaking Foundation Research
- Involving Others in Your Efforts
- Cultivating Prospective Foundation Donors
- Using Query Letters
- Using Concept Papers
- Writing Grant Proposals
- Post-Award Tasks
- Your Professional Action Plan
- 90-Day Foundation Relations Checklist

What Is Meant by Foundation Relations?

As a fundraiser focused on foundation relations, you will manage relationships with foundations that are prospective sources of support for your organization.

Philanthropic foundations are the backbone of the not-for-profit sector. For more than a century, private charitable foundations have had a leadership role in shaping American society as we know it. They have not only supported existing social and educational needs but have also helped to define problems and their solutions.

In the early 20th century, great American family fortunes gave rise to philanthropic giants such as the Ford Foundation, the Rockefeller foundations, and the various Carnegie foundations. The financial power of these foundations enabled them at times to be a force equal to the public sector. The tradition of such organized philanthropy continues today as successful entrepreneurs, such as Bill Gates and Warren Buffett, turn their attention to serving the public good.

You will be the point person for your organization's contact with the foundation world, and you'll involve staff and volunteers in your contact.

As a fundraiser focused on foundation relations, you will be dedicating your efforts to matching the specific financial needs of your not-for-profit organization with foundations that are likely to be interested in funding those needs. You will be the point person in your organization charged with managing the relationships with foundations considered to be prospective sources of support.

Don't expect that foundations will want to support your cause simply because it is worthy.

Universities and large nonprofits often have one or more development officers dedicated to foundation relations. Sometimes foundation relations will be combined with corporate relations in one position. In smaller organizations, a director of development may be charged with foundation relations as one of several areas of responsibility. Regardless of how your organization assigns foundation relations, the elements of the role will be similar.

Identifying Your Organization's Needs

Before you look for foundation funding, you must have a clear understanding of your organization's needs. As a development officer, you will be given priorities. Your job is to pull together a profile of financial and descriptive information about those needs so that you can strategize potential matches for foundation funding. In pulling together this profile, you will talk with your organization's financial officer for budgetary input and with program staff about the substance of the needs.

MYTHS AND MISCONCEPTIONS

Myth: Foundations have billions of dollars available and are just waiting to share the wealth.

Reality: Foundations are required to spend just 5 percent of their assets per year on charitable giving and associated administrative costs. Therefore, less than 5 percent is actually available for grants. The competition for these resources is intense. You can expect your application to be one of many.

Misconception: You can convince a foundation to support you solely on the merit of your need or cause, regardless of their mission or culture.

Reality: When a foundation states its mission or purpose, you need to understand and accept it. Geographical and other restrictions must be taken at face value. If a foundation states that it supports higher education, for example, you cannot expect that it will fund your preschool project simply because it is such a worthy cause.

Restricted and Unrestricted Funds

Every nonprofit organization categorizes its annual budget in terms of restricted and unrestricted funds. Restricted funds can only be used for a specific purpose. When you look for a likely foundation prospect, you may find a match by narrowing down your organization's needs to a specific restricted purpose. For example, a food bank might seek support specifically for the purchase of canned food.

Unrestricted support is wonderful but hard to come by. Most foundation support is restricted.

Unrestricted support can be used to further the general objectives of your organization. A food bank might use unrestricted support to fund salaries, utility bills, or any other general operating expense. Unrestricted support may be the most desirable type of support from the point of view of your board and executives, but it is not easily obtained. The majority of foundation grant dollars given out each year are dispensed as restricted gifts.

New Program Development

The nature of foundation culture is such that a good share of your applications for support will involve new program development. While it is true that occasionally you will find a foundation that does make grants of unrestricted or general support, most foundations that you will be looking to for support will require that your organization propose something new or innovative.

Foundations want to make an investment that will result in significant, long-term, positive change.

As a development officer, you will not be designing and implementing new programs. However, you will be in a position to bring a fresh perspective to the executive and program staff in your organization, based on your knowledge of what foundations are looking for and what they will consider to be new and innovative. Foundations are unlikely to be interested in simply maintaining the status quo.

The foundation culture is aimed at making relatively small grant "investments" in order to leverage significant and long-term change. The nonprofit culture, on the other hand, is often preoccupied with survival. You may find yourself poised between opposing cultural values and norms, and it will be your job as a development officer to structure a win-win situation for both sides.

Most foundations do not make ongoing operating support grants.

As an important part of understanding and being able to quantify and articulate your organization's needs, you will want to interface with the executive decision makers and program staff of your organization about the potential for developing new and innovative project ideas.

You might be able to glean existing or potential new program development ideas from internal planning documents. If this is possible, this is where you should start. You should also, at the very beginning, make a point of getting to know your colleagues on a personal level and finding out what their passions are. It is their passions that will generate excitement and drive success. With luck and perseverance, you should be able to find new program possibilities that will fit with both the foundation culture and the culture of your organization.

Matching Foundations' Priorities and Interests with Your Needs

Research is key to understanding foundations' priorities. Without research, you're not likely to get anywhere with a request to a foundation.

The key to success in foundation relations is finding a match between your organization's needs and the interests and requirements of foundations. Finding a match requires that you be thinking along two tracks at all times to be able to see how things look from opposite points of view.

It will be easier for you to understand your colleagues' perspective since you will naturally absorb the culture of your organization to a certain extent. However, it is important that you be able to stand apart from that culture in order to see your organization as it looks to outsiders, especially those who might be considering making a foundation grant.

Build Your Knowledge Base

A logical and helpful way to begin building your foundation knowledge base is simply to do some reading. A lot has been written about America's great philanthropists, and reading their stories will give you invaluable insights into the history of American philanthropy and how its culture has developed over the last hundred years or so.

To give away money is an easy matter and in any man's power. But to decide to whom to give it and how large and when, and for what purpose and how, is neither in every man's power nor an easy matter.
—Aristotle

This culture has given us great museums, parks, hospitals, and research centers. Our National Gallery of Art was given to the nation by Pittsburgh banker Andrew W. Mellon. Chicago's great Field Museum owes its existence to its first major benefactor, department store magnate Marshall Field. We would not have the glories of Colonial Williamsburg were it not for the vision and generosity of John D. Rockefeller, Jr. and his wife, Abby Aldrich Rockefeller.

I resolved to stop accumulating and begin the infinitely more serious and difficult task of wise distribution.
—Andrew Carnegie

Andrew Carnegie, whose name graces the portals of libraries across the country, also was responsible for establishing the first secure and attractive pension system for college and university professors. You may find that your own nonprofit pension plan can be traced directly to Andrew Carnegie's fortune. It is probable that the more you learn about American philanthropy, the more fascinated you will become. As a foundation relations officer, you will be entering an interesting and exciting world.

Identify Foundations That Fit Your Organization in Terms of Eligibility and Interest

You will also need to read a considerable amount of current information related specifically to your position. First, identify all foundations that are currently supporting your organization or have supported it in the past. Learn everything you possibly can about these foundations and the history of their relationship with your organization.

The secret to success in foundation fundraising is finding the fit between your needs and their interests.

You may be able to start with files and other printed material, but you will also want to talk with colleagues who have firsthand or secondhand knowledge of this support. Conversation can steer you in the right direction in terms of working toward future support. It can also reveal any problems in the relationship that are not apparent in written records and might require that you do some damage control. As the new staffer, you are in an ideal position to help repair or nurture relationships, and it is very rewarding work.

Your previous supporters are always on your list of potential supporters.

Generally speaking, your previous donors are always on your list of potential future donors. You will need to qualify the situation with facts about each individual foundation to determine whether you are eligible for another grant or whether it is appropriate to be thinking about another proposal submission. These past and current donor foundations will form your first list to review, and you will return to it regularly to review it again.

As you research the foundation history of your organization, you may discover information about unsuccessful applications. This type of information will be useful as background knowledge and relevant to any future strategies you develop. A proposal that did not get funded by the foundation approached may still have merit.

There are nearly 80,000 foundations in the United States. You'll need a strategy for figuring out which foundations are a good fit with your organization.

You might be able to retool the concept and present it successfully to a different foundation that is a better fit. Similarly, the experience of a rejection can provide helpful information about a foundation that can enable you to be successful with subsequent proposals.

According to the National Center for Charitable Statistics, there are nearly 80,000 charitable foundations in the United States. This means you need a strategy in order to expand your foundation donor base. You will need to look for foundations that are appropriate in terms of potential support.

You will need both electronic and paper filing systems to organize your research.

You may find it helpful to develop lists of foundations that support the various types of work your organization does. You can save a lot of time and energy by looking at the most recent annual reports of competing organizations. Ask your colleagues who they are.

All schools, colleges, universities, and hospitals publish an annual list of donors. Many other not-for-profit organizations also publish annual donor lists. These publications are a goldmine of information for you as a new development officer, because they show you who is supporting whom and for what. Publications

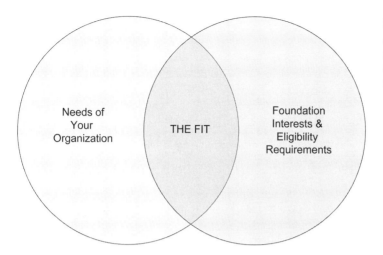

Figure 4.1
*Aim to match your
organization's needs
with a foundation's
interests.*

such as the *Chronicle of Philanthropy* and the *Chronicle of Higher Education* also give quick access to foundation grant information. Each issue lists the details of recently awarded grants.

Categorizing Potential Sources of Foundation Support

There are many types of foundations, which means you need a methodology and structure to guide your work. Foundations reflect the intentions, interests, and relative wealth of their donors, heirs, and trustees. Sometimes restrictions are based on activity.

Foundations can be categorized by interests and geographical restrictions.

One foundation may restrict its grants to healthcare in the developing world, for example. Another may restrict its support to higher education endowed chairs in a selected discipline.

Geography may also play an important role in foundation restrictions. Some foundations may give grants only in a particular state or region. To be efficient, you will need to be able to categorize your foundation prospects in terms of what they will and will not support. The Foundation Center (www.foundationcenter.org) is the place to begin.

National Foundations

National foundations are a good place to start because they are easily researched. National foundations are for the most part the largest foundations in the country, and they tend not to place geographical restrictions on their grant-making activities.

Identify national foundations that may be potential sources of support for your organization.

Since they are large, they often have broad interests with specific program areas for topics such as education, healthcare, social services, and policy. They are easy to find in a list in the *Foundation Directory* (published by the Foundation Center) or online.

You should be able to assemble a list of 50 to 100 national foundations that are worth reviewing, based on their assets and the scope of their grant-making activities.

Regional and Local Foundations

Identify regional and local foundations that focus on your geographical area.

You may find that a few of the largest foundations have some geographical restrictions. This will either eliminate you from the competition all together or give you a competitive advantage. You should know as much as possible about all foundations that operate solely in your state or locality.

Typically, every state or community has at one time or another published its own foundation directory. Even if these publications are out of print, they can be found in local libraries, and it will be worth your time to hunt them down. You can also do online searches using the Foundation Directory Online, narrowing your searches according to geographical restrictions. From this work, you will be able to pull together lists of all foundations that make grants restricted to your city, state, or region of the country.

You cannot assume that you are eligible for support simply based on location, but there is a good likelihood that you will be eligible for funding from some of the foundations on these lists.

Family Foundations

Relationships are often the key to securing support from family foundations.

The term *family foundation* does not refer to a specific type of legal entity. Instead, the term is used here to describe foundations that are driven by the interests of immediate family members.

There are many thousands of these foundations. Most of them are small and have a very low profile. Often, they do not publish an annual report or provide information on their grant-making interests beyond what is required by law. They may have very specific interests that may be impossible to determine from published sources.

This may sound discouraging. However, if you can discern a connection between your organization and the family (ideally, someone on the foundation's board), you should regard that foundation as a potential prospect even if it is across the country and most of the grant-making is random and local.

That personal connection can make all the difference when you are dealing with a family foundation. They have far more discretion than a large foundation that requires a more formal method for requesting and reviewing proposals. Your challenge as a development officer will be to orchestrate the relationship in such a way that will benefit both the foundation's interests and your organization's needs.

Foundation Challenge Grants

Foundation challenge grants are worth researching because of their potential to yield a significant return on your investment of effort. If, for example, your organization is planning to undertake building construction or a capital campaign, your vital contribution as a foundation relations officer might be your expertise on challenge grant opportunities.

Don't neglect to investigate the possibilities for foundation challenge grants.

Most challenge grants awarded by foundations are for partial funding of a project at a particular stage in its development, at which point the foundation's challenge is used strategically to complete the fundraising. Say you are halfway to completion of a new building, which has been funded thus far by trustees and other major gift donors.

A foundation challenge grant could be used effectively to fund the next 10 to 20 percent of the total need, as a matching challenge to all the donor constituencies in your organization. A successful foundation challenge grant can push you over the top by increasing the giving of current donors and bringing new donors on board.

Foundation challenge grants are complicated, but they can be very rewarding and can bring additional dollars to your organization.

You can search for challenge grants online or in the indexes of directories. Keep in mind that foundation challenge grants will probably involve going beyond your own areas of responsibility to involve annual fund staff or capital campaign staff.

Challenge grants can be a complicated undertaking that requires considerably more planning than the typical proposal project you will submit to foundations, but the rewards can be significant.

Non-Grant-Giving Foundations

Some foundations
are competitors,
not prospects.

Not every organization that has *foundation* in its name is a private charitable grant-making entity. Most public colleges and universities have a foundation. Many public school districts have a foundation. These are set up in order to take in gifts and grants in the same way that your own 501(c)(3) is set up to accept gifts and grants, and they do their own fundraising.

They are your competitors. However, there are some organizations called *foundations*, principally in the areas of causes and diseases, that do their own fundraising but also make grants for research and projects. These organizations are basically re-granting gifts that were given to them, and in some cases they have created endowments. This enables them to do new and innovative projects without actually having the research or program staff on their payroll.

Someone in your organization may have a research project or other program that could be funded by one of these foundations. If you are in the areas of cause advocacy, healthcare, or medical research, you will want to be aware of these foundations.

Undertaking Foundation Research

Today's foundation researcher has a vast array of tools, many of which are available online. Years ago, foundation research was confined for the most part to libraries and often involved travel. Records were often kept on microfiche or microfilm, which made the search process tedious. Now, most of what you need will be just a mouse-click away.

Finding and Analyzing IRS Form 990s

Foundation tax
returns are
public informa-
tion, and they
will tell you a lot.

The IRS Form 990-PF is officially entitled, "Return of Private Foundation." (See Figures 4.2 through 4.5.) It is the foundation counterpart to the IRS Form 1040 filed annually by individual U.S. taxpayers. However, it differs from the Form 1040 in one very important respect; the IRS Form 990 PF is freely available public information.

All private foundations must file the Form 990-PF every year. Perusal of a foundation's 990-PF will give you detailed financial information (for example, assets, grants paid, expenses, staff salaries) as well as information on its mission, significant activities, governance, management, and policies.

Form **990-PF**

Department of the Treasury
Internal Revenue Service

Return of Private Foundation
or Section 4947(a)(1) Nonexempt Charitable Trust
Treated as a Private Foundation

Note: *The foundation may be able to use a copy of this return to satisfy state reporting requirements.*

OMB No. 1545-0052

20**07**

For calendar year 2007, or tax year beginning , 2007, and ending , 20

G Check all that apply: ☐ Initial return ☐ Final return ☐ Amended return ☐ Address change ☐ Name change

Use the IRS label. Otherwise, print or type. See Specific Instructions.

Name of foundation — **NAME**

Number and street (or P.O. box number if mail is not delivered to street address)   Room/suite — **ADDRESS**

City or town, state, and ZIP code

A Employer identification number

B Telephone number (see page 10 of the instructions)
( )

C If exemption application is pending, check here ► ☐

D 1. Foreign organizations, check here . . ► ☐

H Check type of organization: ☐ Section 501(c)(3) exempt private foundation
☐ Section 4947(a)(1) nonexempt charitable trust ☐ Other taxable private foundation

2. Foreign organizations meeting the 85% test, check here and attach computation . ► ☐

I Fair market value of all assets at end of year *(from Part II, col. (c),* line 16) ► $ **ASSETS**

J Accounting method: ☐ Cash ☐ Accrual
☐ Other (specify) ....
(Part I, column (d) must be on cash basis.)

E If private foundation status was terminated under section 507(b)(1)(A), check here . ► ☐

F If the foundation is in a 60-month termination under section 507(b)(1)(B), check here . ► ☐

Part I Analysis of Revenue and Expenses *(The total of amounts in columns (b), (c), and (d) may not necessarily equal the amounts in column (a) (see page 11 of the instructions).)*

	(a) Revenue and expenses per books	(b) Net investment income	(c) Adjusted net income	(d) Disbursements for charitable purposes (cash basis only)
1 Contributions, gifts, grants, etc., received (attach schedule)				
2 Check ► ☐ if the foundation is **not** required to attach Sch. B				
3 Interest on savings and temporary cash investments				
4 Dividends and interest from securities . . .				
5a Gross rents				
b Net rental income or (loss)				
6a Net gain or (loss) from sale of assets not on line 10				
b Gross sales price for all assets on line 6a				
7 Capital gain net income (from Part IV, line 2) . .				
8 Net short-term capital gain				
9 Income modifications				
10a Gross sales less returns and allowances				
b Less: Cost of goods sold . .				
c Gross profit or (loss) (attach schedule)				
11 Other income (attach schedule)				
12 **Total.** Add lines 1 through 11				
13 Compensation of officers, directors, trustees, etc.				
14 Other employee salaries and wages				
15 Pension plans, employee benefits				
16a Legal fees (attach schedule)				
b Accounting fees (attach schedule)				
c Other professional fees (attach schedule) . . .				
17 Interest				
18 Taxes (attach schedule) (see page 14 of the instructions)				
19 Depreciation (attach schedule) and depletion . .				
20 Occupancy				
21 Travel, conferences, and meetings				
22 Printing and publications				
23 Other expenses (attach schedule)				
24 **Total operating and administrative expenses.** Add lines 13 through 23				
25 Contributions, gifts, grants paid — **GRANTS PAID**				
26 Total expenses and disbursements. Add lines 24 and 25				
27 Subtract line 26 from line 12:				
a Excess of revenue over expenses and disbursements				
b Net investment income (if negative, enter -0-)				
c Adjusted net income (if negative, enter -0-)				

For Privacy Act and Paperwork Reduction Act Notice, see page 30 of the instructions.   Cat. No. 11289X   Form **990-PF** (2007)

Figure 4.2 *Page 1 of IRS Form 990-PF has important information about a foundation's total assets and the total amount paid out in grants during the tax year.*

Part VII-B	Statements Regarding Activities for Which Form 4720 May Be Required *(continued)*

5a During the year did the foundation pay or incur any amount to:

    (1) Carry on propaganda, or otherwise attempt to influence legislation (section 4945(e))?   ☐ **Yes** ☐ **No**

    (2) Influence the outcome of any specific public election (see section 4955); or to carry on, directly or indirectly, any voter registration drive? . . . . ☐ **Yes** ☐ **No**

    (3) Provide a grant to an individual for travel, study, or other similar purposes? . . . . ☐ **Yes** ☐ **No**

    (4) Provide a grant to an organization other than a charitable, etc., organization described in section 509(a)(1), (2), or (3), or section 4940(d)(2)? (see page 22 of the instructions) . . . ☐ **Yes** ☐ **No**

    (5) Provide for any purpose other than religious, charitable, scientific, literary, or educational purposes, or for the prevention of cruelty to children or animals? . ☐ **Yes** ☐ **No**

  b If any answer is "Yes" to 5a(1)–(5), did **any** of the transactions fail to qualify under the exceptions described in Regulations section 53.4945 or in a current notice regarding disaster assistance (see page 22 of the instructions)?   **5b**

    Organizations relying on a current notice regarding disaster assistance check here . . . . . . ▶ ☐

  c If the answer is "Yes" to question 5a(4), does the foundation claim exemption from the tax because it maintained expenditure responsibility for the grant? . . . . ☐ **Yes** ☐ **No**

    If "Yes," attach the statement required by Regulations section 53.4945–5(d).

6a Did the foundation, during the year, receive any funds, directly or indirectly, to pay premiums on a personal benefit contract? . . . . ☐ **Yes** ☐ **No**

  b Did the foundation, during the year, pay premiums, directly or indirectly, on a personal benefit contract? . .   **6b**

    If you answered "Yes" to 6b, also file Form 8870.

7a At any time during the tax year, was the foundation a party to a prohibited tax shelter transaction? . ☐ **Yes** ☐ **No**

  b If yes, did the foundation receive any proceeds or have any net income attributable to the transaction? . . .   **7b**

Part VIII	Information About Officers, Directors, Trustees, Foundation Managers, Highly Paid Employees, and Contractors

1 List all officers, directors, trustees, foundation managers and their compensation (see page 23 of the instructions).

(a) Name and address	**(b)** Title, and average hours per week devoted to position	**(c)** Compensation **(If not paid, enter -0-)**	**(d)** Contributions to employee benefit plans and deferred compensation	**(e)** Expense account, other allowances
OFFICERS				

2 Compensation of five highest-paid employees (other than those included on line 1—see page 23 of the instructions). If none, enter "NONE."

(a) Name and address of each employee paid more than $50,000	**(b)** Title, and average hours per week devoted to position	**(c)** Compensation	**(d)** Contributions to employee benefit plans and deferred compensation	**(e)** Expense account, other allowances

Total number of other employees paid over $50,000 . . . . ▶

Form **990-PF** (2007)

Figure 4.3 *Page 6 of IRS Form 990-PF provides a list of board members.*

Form 990-PF (2007)   Page **10**

| **Part XIV** | **Private Operating Foundations** (see page 27 of the instructions and Part VII-A, question 9) |

1a If the foundation has received a ruling or determination letter that it is a private operating
foundation, and the ruling is effective for 2007, enter the date of the ruling . . . . ▶

b Check box to indicate whether the foundation is a private operating foundation described in section ☐ 4942(j)(3) or ☐ 4942(j)(5)

	Tax year	Prior 3 years			
	(a) 2007	**(b)** 2006	**(c)** 2005	**(d)** 2004	**(e)** Total
2a Enter the lesser of the adjusted net income from Part I or the minimum investment return from Part X for each year listed					
b 85% of line 2a					
c Qualifying distributions from Part XII, line 4 for each year listed . . .					
d Amounts included in line 2c not used directly for active conduct of exempt activities . .					
e Qualifying distributions made directly for active conduct of exempt activities. Subtract line 2d from line 2c . .					
3 Complete 3a, b, or c for the alternative test relied upon:					
a "Assets" alternative test—enter:					
(1) Value of all assets					
(2) Value of assets qualifying under section 4942(j)(3)(B)(i)					
b "Endowment" alternative test—enter ⅔ of minimum investment return shown in Part X, line 6 for each year listed . . .					
c "Support" alternative test—enter:					
(1) Total support other than gross investment income (interest, dividends, rents, payments on securities loans (section 512(a)(5)), or royalties) . . .					
(2) Support from general public and 5 or more exempt organizations as provided in section 4942(j)(3)(B)(iii) . . .					
(3) Largest amount of support from an exempt organization . . .					
(4) Gross investment income . .					

| **Part XV** | **Supplementary Information (Complete this part only if the foundation had $5,000 or more in assets at any time during the year—see page 28 of the instructions.)** |

1 **Information Regarding Foundation Managers:**

a List any managers of the foundation who have contributed more than 2% of the total contributions received by the foundation before the close of any tax year (but only if they have contributed more than $5,000). (See section 507(d)(2).)

b List any managers of the foundation who own 10% or more of the stock of a corporation (or an equally large portion of the ownership of a partnership or other entity) of which the foundation has a 10% or greater interest.

2 **Information Regarding Contribution, Grant, Gift, Loan, Scholarship, etc., Programs:**

Check here ▶ ☐ if the foundation only makes contributions to preselected charitable organizations and does not accept unsolicited requests for funds. If the foundation makes gifts, grants, etc. (see page 28 of the instructions) to individuals or organizations under other conditions, complete items 2a, b, c, and d.

a The name, address, and telephone number of the person to whom applications should be addressed:

b The form in which applications should be submitted and information and materials they should include:

APPLICATION INFORMATION

c Any submission deadlines:

d Any restrictions or limitations on awards, such as by geographical areas, charitable fields, kinds of institutions, or other factors:

Form **990-PF** (2007)

Figure 4.4 *Page 10 of IRS Form 990-PF provides details on application information.*

Form 990-PF (2007) Page **11**

Part XV Supplementary Information (continued)

3 Grants and Contributions Paid During the Year or Approved for Future Payment

Recipient Name and address (home or business)	If recipient is an individual, show any relationship to any foundation manager or substantial contributor	Foundation status of recipient	Purpose of grant or contribution	Amount
a *Paid during the year*				
GRANTS PAID				
Total . . . . ▶ **3a**				
b *Approved for future payment*				
FUTURE GRANTS				
Total . . . . ▶ **3b**				

Form **990-PF** (2007)

Figure 4.5 *Page 11 of IRS Form 990-PF lists all grants, including amount and purpose, and any grant awards approved for future funding.*

The 990 will give you the foundation's real name and mailing address, as well as the names and addresses of trustees. Particularly useful to you as a development officer is the itemized list of all grants paid during the year according to recipient, purpose, and amount. Also useful is the section on grants approved for future payment, which shows the foundation's financial commitments to organizations beyond the tax year you are looking at.

A foundation's Form 990-PF can be obtained in any of three ways—from the foundation itself, from the IRS, or from a centralized information source, such as the Foundation Center. There is almost never a good reason to go to the foundation itself, because you would do so only if a recent 990 wasn't available from one of these other sources, and if that is the case there is probably a good reason why.

You will want to learn how to obtain 990s and how to analyze them. In many cases, they will be your sole source of information about a foundation.

Getting information directly from the IRS can take more time than you have on your schedule, unless you do so through the IRS website. The Foundation Center provides an online search engine that makes the process of finding 990s simple and easy.

Internal Foundation Publications

All large foundations and many smaller ones publish guidelines, statements of interest, and annual reports. These are printed materials that you can request from the foundation. Most of these foundations also maintain a website from which you can garner information about guidelines and grant-making interests (see Figure 4.6).

Gather all the printed information you can find on foundations you have identified as potential sources of support.

Often you can download copies of their most recent annual reports. This is valuable information that you want to seek and study as you build your lists. You will want to maintain files containing these publications, and you will need to make sure you update them on a regular basis to ensure that you always have the most current information available. Simply requesting an annual report often places you on a foundation's mailing list and ensures that your files can be kept up to date automatically.

Bookmark foundation websites for quick access.

Reference Resources on Foundations

There are a number of indispensable reference resources that you will turn to on a daily basis in the course of your work in foundation relations. The Foundation Center in New York has historically led the way in developing tools and resources for foundation relations professionals.

Figure 4.6

Sample grant guidelines page from a major foundation's website.

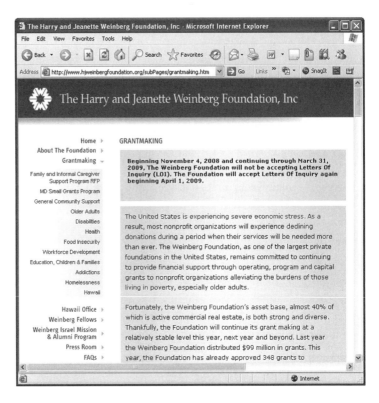

The Harry and Jeanette Weinberg Foundation, Inc - Microsoft Internet Explorer

File   Edit   View   Favorites   Tools   Help

Back   Search   Favorites

Address   http://www.hjweinbergfoundation.org/subPages/grantmaking.htm

The Harry and Jeanette Weinberg Foundation, Inc

Home
About The Foundation
Grantmaking
Family and Informal Caregiver Support Program RFP
MD Small Grants Program
General Community Support
Older Adults
Disabilities
Health
Food Insecurity
Workforce Development
Education, Children & Families
Addictions
Homelessness
Hawaii

Hawaii Office
Weinberg Fellows
Weinberg Israel Mission & Alumni Program
Press Room
FAQs

GRANTMAKING

Beginning November 4, 2008 and continuing through March 31, 2009, The Weinberg Foundation will not be accepting Letters Of Inquiry (LOI). The Foundation will accept Letters Of Inquiry again beginning April 1, 2009.

The United States is experiencing severe economic stress. As a result, most nonprofit organizations will experience declining donations during a period when their services will be needed more than ever. The Weinberg Foundation, as one of the largest private foundations in the United States, remains committed to continuing to provide financial support through operating, program and capital grants to nonprofit organizations alleviating the burdens of those living in poverty, especially older adults.

Fortunately, the Weinberg Foundation's asset base, almost 40% of which is active commercial real estate, is both strong and diverse. Thankfully, the Foundation will continue its grant making at a relatively stable level this year, next year and beyond. Last year the Weinberg Foundation distributed $99 million in grants. This year, the Foundation has already approved 348 grants to

Internet

You will be able to find a wealth of information through the Foundation Center. GuideStar has information about nonprofits.

Today, there are regional Foundation Centers in a number of other cities that offer a reference library and database access to all visitors. These centers also offer free or inexpensive training seminars. If you are new to foundation relations, you should look up your closest Foundation Center office, get on their mailing list (both snail mail and email), and visit them at your earliest opportunity. Visit the Foundation Center online at foundationcenter.org.

The New York and Washington, DC Foundation Centers have substantial research libraries. Keep them in mind when you travel to these cities for other reasons, and work in a visit if at all possible.

GuideStar (guidestar.org) is another huge online repository of information about not-for-profit entities. It casts a wider net than the Foundation Center, as it contains information about many types of organizations other than grant-making foundations. You will find it helpful.

Manage the Results of Your Foundation Research

As you do your research on foundations, you will be collecting materials, information, and notes. You will need a way to store all of this in a manner that will allow you to retrieve something specific at a moment's notice or look at the big picture. You will also want to be able to update your research results regularly.

The obvious place to start is with an electronic and paper filing system for every foundation prospect. You need both. Beyond that, it will be necessary to have some kind of spreadsheet or database that will allow you to track your efforts. This tracking system will include vital information, such as foundation interests, eligibility, deadlines for submission of queries and proposals, and a detailed history of contacts.

It is unlikely that whatever development software program your organization is using will work for this purpose. Your first option if you have no other resources is to create an Excel spreadsheet (see Figure 4.7). This will at least allow you to have at your fingertips all of your updated information in a format that will let you sort and filter it. However, it will eventually be difficult to track multiple activities on such a spreadsheet, and you will want to invest in a database.

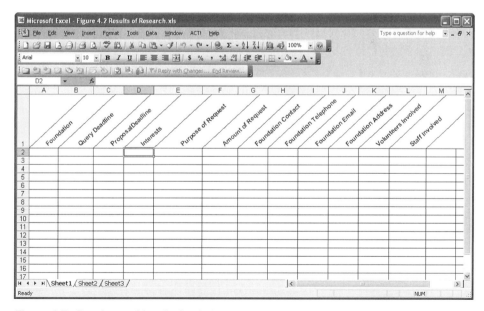

Figure 4.7 *Sample spreadsheet for foundation research.*

Involving Others in Your Efforts

Your work in foundation relations will involve others in your organization, as well as volunteers.

You may view yourself as the focal point for foundation relations efforts in your organization, but you should not be the only person involved. Other staff and volunteers add credibility to your efforts, and sometimes they can accomplish things that you could not do alone. Although at the outset it may seem as though it is a burden to involve others in your work, you will find that it pays off in the end.

Staff Involvement

Much foundation relations work takes place behind the scenes. Often you will find yourself coordinating contacts actually made by other staff members.

Staff involvement can come from the executive level of your organization or from program people engaged in its day-to-day work. As you develop strategies to approach specific foundations, you will begin communicating with them. In many cases, the ideal person for communicating will be your CEO, whether it is a college president, a hospital administrator, or a nonprofit executive director.

You will orchestrate the relationship and provide any assistance needed, such as providing background information, drafting correspondence, and arranging visits. Ultimately, any proposals you submit will come from the CEO, so it is wise to involve that individual early on.

You will be the primary source of expertise, and you'll assist with any details that the staff needs to promote your efforts at support.

Others at your organization can also be instrumental in developing a relationship with a foundation. Star research or program people can sell your message effectively because they are directly involved in the work.

There may be a case for making the dean of a college or university your ideal point person for developing this relationship instead of the president. You may not wish to call on the president's limited time due to other priorities, or you may wish to capitalize on the expertise of that particular person.

Volunteer Involvement

Volunteers can sometimes make your case more effectively than staff can.

Volunteer involvement can come from board members, students, parents, grateful patients, citizens, or anyone who is for one reason or another considered a friend of your organization. Board members can often be your best advocates. They are usually prominent individuals, and they often have connections that you or other staff members do not. It follows that they may be taken seriously when you or other staff members are not.

You need to tread carefully when involving board members, because goofing up may well get you fired. However, if you keep your wits about you, the involvement of board members can make the critical difference between success and failure.

Other volunteers bring credibility of a different sort. Alumni of educational institutions tend to have very strong feelings, and if you can harness those feelings for your efforts, you may have an advocate willing to work very hard on your behalf. Your volunteers are particularly valuable if they have some connection to the foundation you are planning to approach.

Often, volunteers have connections to foundations that will be a unique resource to add to your efforts.

Cultivating Prospective Foundation Donors

As you begin to marshal your research, you will want to develop a cultivation plan for each prospective foundation. The ultimate goal of each plan will be the submission of a proposal. You will want to avoid what are sometimes called *blind submissions*. In other words, you won't want to just look up a foundation's address and send off a generic proposal.

You need to develop a unique plan and strategy for each foundation, and the actions that result are your foundation cultivation efforts.

Your aim should be to ensure that any proposal you ultimately submit to a foundation will be welcomed. At the very least, this requires that your proposal be well-tailored to a foundation's interests and guidelines. In many cases you will want to have some direct communication between you or others from your organization prior to submitting a proposal.

Unless the foundation expressly discourages communication, your first cultivation efforts to follow up on research should be some type of direct communication.

Communicating by Letter and Phone

Letters or phone calls to a foundation should be carefully thought out. Foundation staff are very busy people. Often they are fielding communications and dealing with proposals from literally hundreds of organizations.

Plan your communications with foundations carefully. Make sure that everything you might need is in front of you before you pick up the phone.

You should never call a foundation officer for information that is available in the foundation's publications. Choose your calls carefully and be well prepared before you pick up the phone. When you do pick it up, be sure that you have everything at your fingertips that you might conceivably need to refer to.

For an initial contact, a formal letter requesting information is usually better than a phone call. In an initial contact you can be both the author and the signer of the letter if your purpose is simply to seek general information. If you are writing to request published information about guidelines or opportunities, it is fine to use a generic letter (see Figure 4.8). In subsequent correspondence you will probably find yourself drafting more complicated letters for others in the organization, either executives or program staff.

Visiting Foundation Prospects

As you move forward, you may from time to time request to visit a foundation. In general, this should not be a generic visit, but a meeting requested for a strategic purpose. In the case of new foundation prospects, you will need some time to develop a research-based strategy before you make your approach for a visit. However, you may well start out visiting foundations soon after you take your position as you strategize past and current foundation donors. Providing a personal report on a previous and successful foundation grant project is often enough to open the door, but you should have something in mind about the future as well.

Aside from the research you are pulling together to support your approach, you also will want to prepare materials to bring along on a foundation visit. If the person you are visiting is an alumnus or has some other personal interest in your organization, you might bring a tchotchke—a token gift branded with your logo or name. It should be something modest. If you are visiting an alumnus, it could be a mug, a pennant, or recent issues of a college newspaper.

If there is no personal connection between the person you are visiting and your organization, anything you bring should be relevant to the professional purpose of your visit. If you have not already sent a copy of your organization's annual report or college viewbook, bring one along. It would also be good to have copies of anything relevant to proposal project ideas you might want to discuss, such as newspaper clippings, magazine articles, special reports, or news releases. If you are planning a foundation visit for your CEO, you will want to prepare a planning document similar to the sample shown in Figure 4.9, and you will also want to assist in preparing follow-up correspondence, as shown in Figure 4.10.

SAMPLE GUIDELINES REQUEST LETTER

January 1, 2022

Mr. John Doe
The Doe Foundation
125 Park Avenue
New York, NY 10011

Dear Mr. Doe:

I write to ask for a copy of the current guidelines and grant application procedures of The Doe Foundation. I would also appreciate receiving the current annual report, if available, and any other current publications of the Foundation.

Thank you very much for your consideration.

Sincerely,

Timothy Kachinske
Director of Development

> Always ask for additional publications with your request for guidelines. This ensures that if they have a mailing list, they'll put you on it.

Figure 4.8

SAMPLE FOUNDATION PLANNING DOCUMENT

University
of the United States

University of the United States Advancement Office
Planning Document: The General Foundation

Time and Date of Visit: 10:00am   March 12, 2022

Place of Visit: The General Foundation
                                                      30 Rockefeller Plaza   (212) 555-4000

Foundation Official: John Doe, Executive Director

University Visitor: President John Johnson

Purpose of Visit: To continue dialogue established during President
                                                      Johnson's first visit to the Foundation on March
                                                      15, 2015.

According to Jane Doe, re-evaluation of the Foundation's grants program is still
continuing. It may be beneficial to cover the following items in a discussion with Jane.

University of the United States Achievements Over Past 3 Years

Major Foundation Grants:
          John and Jane Doe Foundation   Jim Smith Foundation
          XYZ Foundation   Great Foundation

Faculty Recipients of Fulbright Awards:
          Dr. Evelyn Smith   Dr. Jane Smith
          Dr. John Jones   Dr. Jim Davis

Endowment Growth
          2020: $105.5 million   2021: $188.5 million

Strengthened Liberal Arts Curriculum
          Endowed Chair in Religion   Endowed Chair in Classics

Figure 4.9

SAMPLE FOUNDATION CULTIVATION LETTER

University
of the United States

January 1, 2022

Mr. John Doe
The John Doe Foundation
125 Park Avenue
New York, NY 10011

> The opening of your cultivation letter should refer to your most recent contact with the foundation, if possible.

Dear Mr. Doe:

I want to thank you again for the very stimulating discussion last month. You have given me much to think about concerning my vision for a major initiative on the roles of law and religion in civil life and public policy. I intend to write you soon with some of my thoughts.

In the meantime, I would like to remind you about our forthcoming symposium on US-Poland relations. In conjunction with the Embassy of Poland, the University of the United States will convene the first ever international conference to assess the US-Poland Fundamental Accord. Please know that you are most welcome.

This symposium will prove to be a landmark event. Many of the senior US and Polish officials involved in negotiating the Accord have committed to speak, including former President Bill Clinton.

I should note that this symposium is funded by a grant from the Jim and Jane Smith Foundation, and several other private donors. Please do not hesitate to contact me if you want further information about the symposium.

Thanks again for your interest in the University of the United States.

Sincerely,

> This letter should be signed by your chief executive officer.

Timothy Kachinske
President

Figure 4.10

Hosting Foundation Prospects

Hosting a foundation visit can strengthen a relationship and position your organization for success.

From time to time you may have an opportunity to invite a foundation representative to visit your organization, or a foundation representative may ask to visit your organization. This will only happen after you have developed a relationship on the basis of some program or activity that is of special interest to the foundation.

This might be a simple visit, in which you coordinate the schedule and accompany the visitor yourself, or it could be a fairly complicated visit in which you will set up a series of meetings with executives and program staff at your organization. You will need to coach your staff intensively to ensure that such a visit is successful.

You will probably be responsible for all of the details, and it can be a lot of work. However, hosting a successful foundation visit can make a critical difference, particularly if a foundation is considering making a major investment in your organization.

Using Query Letters

Query letters have the advantage of getting a sense of whether you're on target without risking a formal rejection of the foundation.

Many foundations explicitly require that any initial request for support be done with a query letter rather than a proposal. Unless the foundation has special requirements for its query letters, you should aim to make this a one-page letter. Basically, you are writing to inquire about the foundation's interest in supporting whatever your research and strategy show you to be the right purpose and amount for a request.

Therefore, whatever you write must be done concisely. If your organization has elaborate letterhead, you may need to do some redesigning so that your query letters can fit on one page.

When a foundation does not explicitly require a query letter prior to proposal submission, it can sometimes nevertheless be to your advantage to send a query. Typically, when you submit a fully developed proposal to a foundation, your request goes into a hopper with many other organizations' proposals to await a decision that will be made at a designated time.

Foundations make decisions based on their funding, so normally they make their proposal funding decisions at a specific date on their working calendar. This may be once or twice a year. In most instances, a foundation will entertain only one proposal at a time from an organization and will expect that your single proposal reflects your organization's priority need. You should never submit multiple proposals during a grant cycle unless there is clear exception to this rule.

Query letters are advantageous because they can get you timely feedback that will tell you whether you are moving in the right direction. Unlike proposal submissions, query letters are usually answered as they are received, rather than at a fixed time on the foundation's calendar.

> Query letters also save time that would be lost waiting for a lengthy proposal decision.

Getting a reaction to a query letter can give you additional time within a grant cycle to develop another funding request, should the query response reject your initial idea. A positive query response can provide helpful information that can make your final proposal more competitive. Writing a query letter can prevent you from wasting time and effort developing an elaborate but unsuccessful proposal.

Determining the Query Letter Author and Recipient

The query letter is similar to a proposal in that it is a request for support. Therefore, it should be signed by the CEO of your organization. It should be addressed to a person, not to a generic "to whom it may concern."

> Try to make sure your query letter is addressed to the appropriate individual at the foundation. The query letter should not come from you; your CEO should sign it.

In the unlikely case that you can't determine the precise person who should receive your query letter, you can address it to the executive director, who will forward it to the appropriate person for a response. In most cases, you will be writing either to the executive director or to a staff person who is responsible for a particular program area.

If you have a board member who has a significant connection to the foundation, you may want that person to cosign the letter or you may want to orchestrate a follow-up letter from that board person to be sent immediately after your query letter is sent. A query letter should always refer to recent previous support, as shown in Figure 4.11.

Elements of a Query Letter

The first sentence of your query letter should make your inquiry clear, as the sample letter in Figure 4.12 shows. It should read something like, "I am writing to inquire whether Foundation X would be interested in supporting a program for ……. at …….."

SAMPLE ACKNOWLEDGEMENT AND QUERY FOR FURTHER SUPPORT

Methodius College

January 1, 2022

Ms. Jane Doe
The Jim and Jane Johnson Foundation
125 Park Avenue
New York, NY 10011

Dear Ms. Doe:

I am writing to thank the trustees of The Jim and Jane Johnson Foundation for the recent grant in support of Methodius College's project on eight city-center schools in Methodius, Indiana.

As you may know, the College is in the midst of a major initiative concerning the future of inner-city schools. The plight of inner-city schools in our country is of great concern to the scholars, students, and practitioners involved in this initiative. I can assure you that the study supported by The Jim and Jane Johnson Foundation will be of immediate benefit to these eight schools. I look forward to conveying to you the results of our research.

We plan to establish a Center for the Study of Inner-City Schools here at Methodius College. It is my hope that this Center will be in a position to offer planning assistance and research support to all schools in need of such assistance, especially those here in the area.

Once again, please extend my gratitude to the trustees of The Jim and Jane Johnson Foundation for their support of this project.

Sincerely,

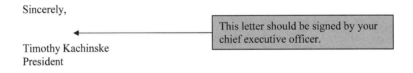

This letter should be signed by your chief executive officer.

Timothy Kachinske
President

Figure 4.11

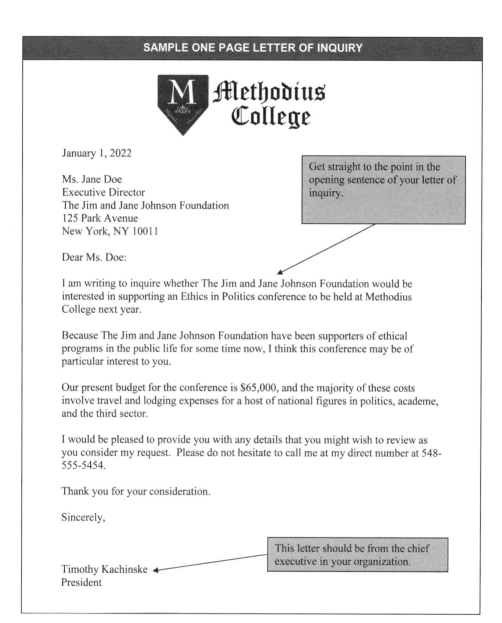

SAMPLE ONE PAGE LETTER OF INQUIRY

M Methodius College

January 1, 2022

Ms. Jane Doe
Executive Director
The Jim and Jane Johnson Foundation
125 Park Avenue
New York, NY 10011

> Get straight to the point in the opening sentence of your letter of inquiry.

Dear Ms. Doe:

I am writing to inquire whether The Jim and Jane Johnson Foundation would be interested in supporting an Ethics in Politics conference to be held at Methodius College next year.

Because The Jim and Jane Johnson Foundation have been supporters of ethical programs in the public life for some time now, I think this conference may be of particular interest to you.

Our present budget for the conference is $65,000, and the majority of these costs involve travel and lodging expenses for a host of national figures in politics, academe, and the third sector.

I would be pleased to provide you with any details that you might wish to review as you consider my request. Please do not hesitate to call me at my direct number at 548-555-5454.

Thank you for your consideration.

Sincerely,

> This letter should be from the chief executive in your organization.

Timothy Kachinske
President

Figure 4.12

Query letters must be concise.

It should not begin with a general statement about your organization or several paragraphs leading toward the point you are trying to make. If you do send a dense, multipage query letter that requires the reader to scour it simply to determine the purpose of your inquiry, the cost of the project, and the key personnel involved, you have defeated the purpose of a query letter.

It may be helpful to attach a page or two to the query letter in order to provide details, photographs, or graphics. However, the query letter must be able to stand alone. Some foundations are systematic in their requests for query letters and may ask for specific things in an attachment.

Potential Next Steps

Be prepared to go into action immediately if your query letter results in an encouraging response.

As soon as your query letter goes out, you must be prepared to react to it. Since the letter more than likely did not come directly from you, with your telephone number on it, you must make sure that whoever signed the query letter is aware that it is out there.

You want to make sure that the executive and his/her staff know that inquiries need to be dealt with immediately, and that you need to be informed about any phone calls or correspondence resulting from a foundation query letter.

Also, you want to be prepared to follow up by producing a detailed proposal. So while a query letter might contain relatively few budgetary details, a description, and other information, you will want to have most of the information needed for a detailed proposal already collected and surveyed before you send that query letter. If you do get a positive response to a query, you want to follow up immediately.

Using Concept Papers

Concept papers are rarely used, but when needed, they're invaluable in getting a sense of whether you are on target without risking a formal rejection.

Concept papers are rarely used, but in those situations where they can be used strategically, they can be very helpful to your case. A concept paper is more elaborate than a one-page query and may on the surface look like a short proposal. However, it will not state that you are requesting a specific amount of money for a specific purpose.

In other words, you won't be asking the foundation to make a decision on funding, as you would in a proposal. Your introductory wording for a concept paper would be something like, "[Your organization] requests a review of this proposed project idea by the X Foundation."

When and When Not to Use a Concept Paper

Concept papers are typically used after you and others at your organization have developed a relationship with foundation staff. You would never submit a concept paper without knowing that the recipient was interested in reviewing it. A foundation program officer might ask you for a concept paper in the course of discussions.

Used strategically, concept papers can strengthen the relationship between your organization and a foundation.

A concept paper can be useful to a foundation that is considering moving into a new funding area but has not yet publicized that interest, in which case your ideas can help them to develop their ideas. There again, you might propose the idea of a concept paper in the context of a discussion with a foundation staff person if, for example, your organization is developing a new program that you are not yet ready to flesh out into a full proposal.

A concept paper extends discussions between foundation staff and your organization and has the potential to strengthen your relationship. You are giving the foundation a chance to consider and circulate an idea without having to commit to a formal decision.

Writing Grant Proposals

As a foundation relations officer, you will become in effect your organization's chief proposal writer. Your experience and expertise may be called on by others in the organization for assistance with applications and proposals for individual support. Your responsibility will primarily be generating and coordinating all of your organization's proposals to foundations.

As the chief proposal writer of your organization, you will be called upon to generate many proposals.

Before you actually begin writing a proposal, you will have done your research and communication, and you will have worked out an outline. Even though after a while you may be able to borrow verbiage from one proposal to use in another, you will want to approach each proposal as a unique writing project (see Figure 4.13).

SAMPLE FOUNDATION LETTER PROPOSAL

FR. MEGER CENTER FOR SOCIAL JUSTICE

January 1, 2022

Ms. Jane Doe
Doe Charitable Fund
125 Park Avenue
New York, NY 10011

Dear Ms. Doe:

I write to thank you for your interest in the Fr. Meger Center for Social Justice, and to follow up on your recent phone conversation with Ms. Kim Johnson of the Fr. Meger Center. I would also like to answer your questions about our sources of support.

The Fr. Meger Center relies on contributions from a broad range of individuals, corporations, and foundations for support. Our educational and human services programs support people with autism and other disabilities in the King County area. I enclose a copy of our annual report, which contains a donors list on page 14.

I would also ask that the Doe Charitable Fund consider supporting the Kennedy Institute's annual fund this year in the amount of $25,000. Support in this amount would provide scholarships for children ages 6 months to 6 years in our Early Childhood Development center for autistic students.

Thank you once again for your interest in the Fr. Meger Center. Please contact me at your earliest convenience at 202-555-4554 x 321.

Sincerely,

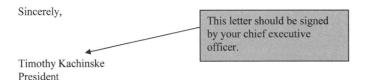

This letter should be signed by your chief executive officer.

Timothy Kachinske
President

Figure 4.13

Writing a One-Page Proposal Letter

In some respects, one page is the ideal length for a proposal. It is brief enough that you know it will be read in its entirety. Out of necessity, it must be clear and to the point, as the sample letter in Figure 4.14 is. It will take relatively less time to craft because it will not contain a lot of detailed information that needs to be organized and presented in a cogent way. Typically, small family foundations that have no particular guidelines will accept a one-page proposal.

> One-page proposals are ideal for foundations that will accept them.

Writing a Longer Proposal

Most of your proposals will not be one-page proposals. You will always want to outline your proposal to align with any guidelines the foundation has published regarding what should be included and in what order. The guidelines can ask for things that will comprise whole sections of your proposal, such as the purpose, budget summary, and key personnel involved. Sometimes guidelines require specific attachments, such as evidence of your tax-exempt status, letters of support, and resumes of principal investigators or key program people.

> Always follow a foundation's proposal guidelines exactly.

The hard-and-fast rule is that the organization of your proposal should follow the format of the foundation's guidelines. If it doesn't, it will appear to be an unsuccessful proposal written for a different foundation and recycled in the hope that it might meet with better luck the second time around. If there are no published guidelines, you must be creative and organize the proposal in a logical sequence.

Cover Letter

Proposals are always accompanied by a cover letter signed by the chief executive officer of the requesting organization. This is more than a formality. Cover letters are an essential element of routine practice because every foundation grant must be approved by your organization's board. You might find colleagues in your organization who tell you that they can sign the cover letter. Gently inform them that it's not usually done that way.

> Foundation proposal cover letters are nearly always signed by the CEO of the organization requesting support.

There may be exceptions to the CEO signing the cover letter. At a college or university, sometimes the chief academic officer can sign in the president's absence. Another rare exception would be a board member who has a particular interest in the project as a

SAMPLE FOUNDATION GRANT RENEWAL LETTER

January 1, 2022

Make your renewal request
specific in the first line of
your letter.

Mr. John Doe
Chairman
The Smith Trust for Charitable Purposes
125 Park Avenue
New York, NY 10011

Dear Mr. Doe:

I write to request that The Smith Trust for Charitable Purposes renew its support of the graduate nursing program at Methodius College with a grant of $25,000. The Smith Trust for Charitable Purposes has been a generous supporter of this important program, and it is my sincere hope that this support will continue.

Attached to this letter is a report on The Smith Trust for Charitable Purposes Scholarship recipients at Methodius College. This accounting covers grants in 2020 and 2021, and brings us up to date in all respects. Should you wish to receive further information about these scholarship funds, please contact me.

Methodius College maintains a nationally-recognized academic program, and we are committed to providing financial assistance to students who have chosen health care as a profession. Private support such as grants from The Smith Trust for Charitable Purposes has enabled us to fulfill that commitment. I ask that you look favorably on our request this year.

Sincerely,

This letter should be signed by your
chief executive officer.

Timothy Kachinske
President

Figure 4.14

volunteer and has some special credibility or influence at the foundation.

You may want to draft the cover letter as you begin the proposal, but the final draft that you recommend for the review of your chief executive officer will be presented at the point when he or she sees the final draft of the proposal.

Executive Summary

Executive summaries always appear at the beginning of a grant proposal. However, they are usually the last section you will write. It is very hard to summarize and introduce something that hasn't yet been written. Once the rest of the proposal is finished, the task of summarizing is simple.

> The executive summary must be cogent and complete. Write it last.

Even if your colleagues voice stylistic objections to placing the word *executive* before the word *summary*, you should use it. The first sentence of the executive summary should be something like, "[Your organization] requests support in the amount of $_____ from the X Foundation for _____."

What follows will be a distillation of the proposal. If it is written in sections, you may craft a sentence or phrase for each section to describe the purpose, need, scope, goals and objectives, timeline, and so on. The key is to be brief. Ideally, you are shooting for a third of a page of text. Every word must be carefully selected. The executive summary could be the only portion of your proposal that some people will read.

Introduction/Background

Following your executive summary, you may include a section introducing your organization. Over time, you will develop appropriate verbiage to describe your organization. Nevertheless, each time you submit a foundation proposal, you will need to tailor that verbiage to the audience receiving it and the project you are proposing to undertake.

> When describing your organization and its accomplishments in a grant proposal, make sure you highlight things that relate to your request.

For example, a university applying for a science research grant would emphasize that aspect of its history and reputation. That same university would emphasize its school of education if seeking support for an undergraduate teacher-training program.

This section of a proposal presents you with an opportunity to "sell" your organization. Don't hold back. Make it as persuasive and impressive as possible. Be sure to include any recent awards and public distinctions.

The body of your proposal will be composed of a variety of separate sections. You will, of course, include all sections required by the guidelines of the foundation. If you do not have guidelines to work with, you will want to consider breaking down your proposal into sections that will enable you to make an effective case for support. In the next few sections, you'll see examples.

Statement of Need

The statement of need is the reason you're writing the proposal.

This section is critical because it drives both your project and the foundation's motivation to support it. It is the reason you are writing the proposal. It describes the status quo and defines the problem you are proposing to address or solve.

For example, if you are working for a social service agency and you are proposing to develop a new program for people with disabilities, you would want to present facts, statistics, and perhaps vignettes or testimonials substantiating the pressing social need for your project.

If your proposal deals with an environmental issue, you would include expert opinions and all the factual information needed to persuade a reasonable person that the problem you wish to address is real and urgent. The statement of need must be compelling but accurate and truthful.

Project Description

The project description shows your solution to a problem that you've defined earlier in the proposal, most likely in the statement of need.

This section describes your proposed solution to the problem defined in your statement of need. It, too, must be compelling, accurate, and truthful. You will need to present a logical, convincing case for your project as a promising course of action likely to solve or mitigate the problem you have described. You will also need to show how your proposed solution is new and innovative.

Even if you are proposing to apply strategies shown through research to have been successful elsewhere, it will be essential to demonstrate that what you are proposing to do hasn't been done before in quite the way you are proposing to do it. Foundations tend to support either new ideas or the application of existing ideas in a new context.

Goals and Objectives

This section describes what you intend to accomplish, expressed in measurable terms. Measurability is essential because it establishes the quantitative framework for program evaluation. Sometimes you will see the two words used almost interchangeably, but in the development world, *goals* tend to be more general than *objectives*.

For example, if your overall goal is reduction in the dropout rate for high school students, you would need baseline data (to show what the dropout rate is currently) and objectives that express the expected improvement in quantitative terms. For example: By December 31, 2022, the dropout rate will have decreased from 15.2 percent to 8.0 percent.

Program objectives must be clear, measurable, reasonable, and attainable. A reader should be able to see a direct correlation between your project and the improvement you are trying to bring about.

Plan of Operation/Implementation

This is where you will describe the steps you will take to carry out your project. You will include a timeline, key personnel, and a description of the activities to be undertaken.

Sustainability

Generally speaking, foundations support projects for a specific period of time. They do not enter into support with the assumption that they will continue to fund your project so long as it is successful and needed. However, they do not want to support change that does not endure after the project has ended.

Your proposal will be greatly strengthened if you can demonstrate in a reasonable way how you plan to sustain positive change after the initial project is completed. Sometimes this section will be referred to as *future funding*.

Dissemination

Foundations like to support projects and programs that result in publicity of substance. You might issue news releases regularly during the course of the project. You might commit to feature stories on the project in your organization's magazine or newsletter. Successful completion could result in a video, article, or book.

Foundations tend to prefer projects that can result in publicity of substance. This might be a news article, a published report, a video, or a CD.

Your organization's key staff might make presentations about the project at professional meetings and conferences. Whatever you propose for dissemination, you should make it clear that nothing will be undertaken without the review and approval of foundation staff.

Evaluation

An evaluation section can have several useful purposes. First of all, it will structure how you determine whether your project is a success or a failure. Also, it presents an opportunity for you to demonstrate that you know what you are doing and have the ability to analyze and present results in a professional manner.

A fully developed grant proposal will describe a need or problem, strategies to meet or solve it, goals and objectives, and plans for implementation and evaluation.

Evaluation also gives you information that can be used to provide an occasion for further communication with the foundation, even beyond the life of the grant.

Budget and Budget Summary

Comprehensive, detailed budget information for projects or programs will usually be provided to you by program people after approval by the financial officer of your organization. You will not be expected to cost out exactly what your organization needs in order to undertake a program.

A proposal budget must lay out how much money your organization is requesting and exactly how it will be spent.

What you will be expected to do is communicate that information concisely and effectively. Your budget summary, like the executive summary, is a brief paragraph that will tell the reader exactly how much money you are requesting and how it will be spent. If it is an extensive project, you may need several paragraphs to describe the expenses, in which case you will write a budget narrative.

When writing a budget summary or budget narrative, make sure it links closely to your executive summary. The busy person who only reads the executive summary of each proposal will probably turn next to the budget if impressed with the executive summary. Therefore, plan your proposal to satisfy a reader who looks at these two sections and nothing else.

Post-Award Tasks

The awarding of a grant does not end your work as a foundation relations officer. Instead, it marks the beginning of a new phase. You will be involved in communication with the foundation following the award of the grant. You will also coordinate publicity associated with the award. Finally, you will coordinate any reporting required by the foundation.

Your work continues after a foundation grant is awarded.

Grant Acknowledgement Letters

Normally when a grant is approved (typically on a timeline that coincides with foundation board meetings), you will receive a letter stating the amount and purpose of the grant award. This letter might also tell you when the actual check will be released and information about reporting requirements.

The grant acknowledgement signed by your CEO serves as the letter of record.

If it is a multiyear award, there will probably be information about the planned release of the funds over the grant period, including the dates when you can expect to receive the funds. Sometimes a check is included in this letter, and sometimes it is sent at a later date.

Viewed positively and strategically, a rejection can mark the first step toward developing a future approach that will be successful.

Since the letter will be sent to your CEO, you will want to make sure that he or she involves you as soon as it is received. You will want to turn around a brief acknowledgement letter from the CEO, expressing your organization's gratitude for support and including any information about forthcoming reports that the foundation expects (see Figure 4.15).

This will serve as the letter of record. If there are personal relationships between the foundation and your organization's board members or staff, you might want to orchestrate additional thank-you letters with verbiage like, "I want to add my thanks to President Doe's letter…." Handwritten notes on the letters add a gracious touch.

Never send a grant acknowledgement as an e-mail.

If you get a rejection letter, there is no need for an immediate response from your CEO or whomever the letter was addressed to. However, you will want to determine your next step to find out what went wrong and what you can do in the future to improve your chances of funding.

If you get a letter of rejection, use this as an opportunity to cultivate the foundation further.

This might involve a variety of things in the coming months, including calling a program officer to discuss your unsuccessful proposal or perhaps even arranging a meeting. In most cases, a rejection letter will not give you detailed information but will simply reflect the decision made by the board of the foundation.

SAMPLE FOUNDATION ACKNOWLEDGEMENT LETTER

January 1, 2022

Ms. Jane Doe
Trustee
Doe Foundation
125 Park Avenue
New York, NY 10011

> Acknowledge the amount of
> the grant in your first
> sentence.

Dear Ms. Doe:

I write to thank you on behalf of everyone at the Fr. Meger Center for Social Justice for the grant of $50,000 from the Doe Foundation. Please know that we will endeavor to be good stewards of this important gift.

For more than forty years, the Fr. Meger Center for Social Justice has worked on behalf of people with carpal tunnel syndrome. Our efforts have been sustained by gifts from people who share our mission to lead through innovation so that people with carpal tunnel syndrome can continue to work.

Sincerely,

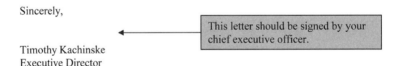

> This letter should be signed by your
> chief executive officer.

Timothy Kachinske
Executive Director

Figure 4.15

Press Releases

It is a good idea to do a press release when you receive a significant grant, because it provides a public document that you and
others will find useful even if it doesn't find its way into print or
onto a web publication (see Figure 4.16). Any press release needs
to be coordinated with foundation staff, including information on
the grant as well as the verbiage used to describe the foundation.

Your organization may have someone internally (a public
information officer, for example) who produces and disseminates
press releases, in which case you will need to be the conduit of
foundation-approved information about the grant award even if
you are not the final author. You should also make sure that your
grant is publicized in your own internal publications, such as
newsletters, magazines, and annual reports. Copy for this type
of publicity should likewise be vetted by the foundation before
publication.

If your organization does not have public relations staff, you will
need to produce and distribute the releases yourself. The *Chronicle
of Philanthropy* publishes a "New Grants" list in each issue. Some
foundations will announce grant award lists in press releases that
are submitted to the *Chronicle* and other philanthropic and educational publications. If you want your foundation grants noted
in the *Chronicle*, you can submit them yourself to make certain
they have a chance of being noted.

Other publications you contact will vary according to your locale,
your organization, and the nature of the project to be funded. As
you gain experience, you will develop contacts in local media,
electronic media, and trade publications. It is a good idea to nurture these relationships in order to increase the likelihood that
your news releases don't end up in a wastebasket or recycle bin.

Always give founda-
tions the opportu-
nity for advance
review of news
releases and other
publicity about a
grant award. You
don't want your
well-intentioned
efforts to put you in
damage-control
mode.

Grant Reports

You are the point person for any reports that must be filed as a
condition of a foundation grant award (see Figures 4.17 through
4.19). You will be responsible for making sure that all deadlines
and requirements are met.

You will need to have a good handle on these activities because
in many cases you will be depending on other people (for example, financial, program, and executive staff) to provide you with
information. The availability of your CEO to sign off on reports
is another consideration. All of this requires that you have a grasp
of calendars and schedules other than your own.

As a foundation
relations profes-
sional, you will be
responsible for
coordinating
all aspects of
foundation grant
reporting.

SAMPLE FOUNDATION GRANT PRESS RELEASE

FR. MEGER
CENTER
FOR SOCIAL JUSTICE

**Fr. Meger Center for Social Justice receives grant to
build volunteer support for people with arthritis in King County.**

For Immediate Release
January 1, 2022

Contact: Jane Doe
Phone: (direct) 301-555-1224
(main) 301-555-1200

The Jim and Jane Johnson Foundation has awarded a grant of $135,000 to Fr. Meger Center for Social Justice for a new model of support for people with arthritis in southern King County.

This grant will enable Fr. Meger Center for Social Justice to develop a model community living partnership, and an interfaith network of volunteer supports to help close the gap left by insufficient federal, state, and county services.

"In southern King County, people with arthritis and their families have a great need for basic help," said Timothy Kachinske, President of the Fr. Meger Center. "It is critical that we develop a volunteer core of support now."

Volunteers will be recruited and trained specifically in the following areas of need: transportation, respite, case management, and advocacy.

The Jim and Jane Johnson Foundation, based in New York, NY, is the nation's largest philanthropy devoted exclusively to health care for people with arthritis. The Arthritis Action program is based on the ideal of community volunteerism and neighbors helping neighbors.

The Fr. Meger Center for Social Justice provides life-span educational and human services in the King County region in support of people with all types of disabilities.

Figure 4.16

SAMPLE FOUNDATION REPORT

January 1, 2022

Ms. Jane Doe
The John and Jane Doe Foundation
125 Park Avenue
New York, NY 10011

Dear Ms. Doe:

It was good to talk with you on Friday. Thank you for setting aside some time to meet with me when I will be in Indianapolis on Friday. It will be a pleasure to give you a personal update on The Meger Academy and our new Principal, Jim Johnson. In the meantime, I would like to provide you with a report on The John and Jane Doe Foundation Endowment for The Meger Academy newsletter.

I would like to report that the market value of The John and Jane Doe Foundation Endowment Fund was $256,334 as of October 1, 2021. This is the most recent audited figure that is available. Our audited endowment figures for the financial year that just ended will be available in a few weeks, and I will be pleased to provide you with updated figures then.

I am pleased to enclose a copy of this past academic year's final issue of The Meger Academy's newsletter for the 2020-2021 academic year. The issue caries articles about our new headmaster, as well as information about our students' college placements.

Again, thank you for your continued support of The Meger Academy.

Sincerely,

This letter should be signed by your chief executive officer.

Timothy Kachinske
Principal

Figure 4.17

SAMPLE FOUNDATION REPORT & REQUEST LETTER

January 1, 2022

Ms. Jane Doe
Executive Director
The Jim and Jane Johnson Foundation
125 Park Avenue
New York, NY 10011

> Acknowledgement of your previous grant and request for continued support should be in the first paragraph.

Dear Ms. Doe:

I am writing to thank The Jim and Jane Johnson Foundation for its grant of $30,000 to Methodius College. I ask that the Foundation consider making another scholarship grant for the 2022-2023 academic year.

I would also like to report on how The Jim and Jane Johnson Foundation's grant this past year has benefited the young men and women who have been selected as recipients of the Johnson Scholarships at Methodius College. In my request last year, I proposed that Johnson Scholarship be awarded to undergraduate physics students of high academic promise. The attached report provides some basic information about this year's Johnson Scholarship students.

Once again, please extend my thanks to all trustees of the Jim and Jane Johnson Foundation for their support of Methodius College.

Sincerely,

> This letter should be signed by your chief executive officer.

Timothy Kachinske
President

Figure 4.18

SAMPLE FAMILY FOUNDATION REPORT ATTACHMENT

Methodius College

> Ideally, this report should be a one-page attachment to your letter.

TO: Timothy Kachinske, President

FR: Dr. John Smith, Dean

RE: Johnson Scholarships at Methodius College

DATE: January 1, 2022

It is my pleasure to provide you with information about students who have been awarded Johnson Scholarships for the 2021-2022 academic year. All of these students are presently enrolled in Methodius College's undergraduate program.

As you know, this is a highly competitive program, and the grade point averages noted in the table below attest to the high academic quality of our students. I am also pleased to note that all of these students intend to pursue careers in business and industry.

All of them will have participated in an industrial internship by the end of next year. As you know, this grant has been awarded to Methodius College to develop special programs that will promote the entry into business and industry.

Should you require further information about the recipients of the Johnson Scholarships, please let me know. I would also like to extend gratitude to the Jim and Jane Johnson Foundation on behalf of the young men and women who have received this scholarship support.

Student Name	Grade Average	Class Year
Jane Gates	A	Freshman
Jim Biltmore	A-	Sophomore
Robyn Goodall	B+	Sophomore
Anastasia Jivkov	A-	Sophomore
Mita Roberts	B	Freshman

Figure 4.19

The complexity of reporting requirements tends to depend upon the size of the grant award and the nature of the project. Matching requirements necessitate detailed financial information. A large grant involving many people outside your organization can also increase the effort you may need to expend in order to satisfy reporting requirements.

The ideal report is short and easy to understand.

If the foundation requires no reporting beyond an official acknowledgment of receipt of the funding, it is still a good idea to provide the foundation with a report once the program has been completed and the funds fully spent. Assuming that the program was successful, this is an additional cultivation step that you otherwise would not have. At the point that you are awarded a grant, your research and strategy should begin on your next approach for funding.

Normally, you can't approach a foundation until the program is completed. If it is a scholarship program or a project that will last a year, you can't approach the foundation for another 12 months. Still, you should be thinking 12 months ahead to formulate your strategy for the next grant cycle.

Your Professional Action Plan

In your new position as a foundation relations professional, you will want to have a plan to track and report your progress at fundraising for your organization. Such a plan will also help you to develop your skills and expertise.

Create a Proposal Log

Your proposal log will serve to document your productivity as a foundation relations professional.

The best method for tracking your progress is probably one that you devise yourself. You know what matters to you and to your organization, and you also know your own preferences for organizing information. A complete, chronological record of the submission of foundation proposals during your employment is the single most important tool for assessing your productivity.

You should start your proposal log your first day on the job. It may be some time before you are actually sending out proposals. But after some research, you will very soon be able to enter potential submissions and their deadlines on your log. More than likely you will be asked for some kind of report on foundation support prior to each board meeting of your organization. Your proposal log could be part or all of that report. A proposal log is a succinct document that will help others to gauge your productivity. It will also help you to analyze and document your own work.

It is possible to develop an activity report based on your foundation research and other activities related to communicating with foundations and developing proposals. If you are working with contact relationship management (CRM) software, as discussed in detail in Chapter 8, "Fundraising Software," you can easily track and print out reports on your day-to-day activities from your software's calendar.

You need a proposal log for yourself to keep on top of your proposal submissions.

Even if you are not required to submit detailed activity reports to your supervisor, you should still maintain some kind of activity report for your own information. Activity reports will enable you to analyze your work and how you spend your time. Research can be very time consuming, and you will want to be able to balance research time strategically against activities that directly relate to getting proposals out the door.

Regardless of the audience for your proposal log, it should always be considered and treated as a confidential document. The log you keep for your own purposes can be a simple Word table or Excel spreadsheet. The log you prepare for presentation to your supervisor or board should go on official paper and show your name and title (see Figure 4.20). Be sure to include summary information that shows the dollar totals for grants submitted, grants pending, and grants awarded during the period of the report.

You will likely need to present your proposal log to your superior and perhaps to your Board of Directors. This is an important part of your job.

The main part of the proposal log is a series of columns—for example, foundation name, amount requested, purpose of request, submission date, anticipated decision date, and outcome in dollars.

Develop Your Continuing Education Program

As a new foundation relations professional, you should take charge of your career right away by devising your own continuing education plan. Begin by making a list of outside reading. To learn about current issues and happenings, study every issue of the *Chronicle of Philanthropy*. Knowledge of the past is invaluable as well.

You can broaden your knowledge about the foundation world through reading, workshops, seminars, and conferences.

You will need a frame of reference about foundations that goes beyond the specific books and online material you encounter on

SAMPLE FOUNDATION PROPOSAL LOG

CONFIDENTIAL

University of the United States

Report to the President from
Timothy Kachinske, Director of Foundation Relations

Proposal Log

Proposal totals Dec 2020-Nov 2021

Submitted	Pending	Awarded
$2,200,000	$1,100,000	$1,100,000

Proposal totals current fiscal year

Submitted	Pending	Awarded
$2,000,000	$1,000,000	$1,000,000

Foundation	Amount	2020-2021 Purpose	Submission Date	Decision Date	Outcome
The Jim and Jane Johnson Foundation	210,000	Scholarship	8/15/2020	1/1/2021	Declined
The General Foundation	45,000	Medical Research	8/15/2020	1/1/2021	Hiatus
The Jim and Jane Johnson Foundation	67,000	Scholarship	8/15/2020	1/1/2021	50,000
The General Foundation	5,000	Engineering Chair	8/15/2020	1/1/2021	5,000
The Jim and Jane Johnson Foundation	6,000	Scholarship	8/15/2020	1/1/2021	6,000
The General Foundation	15,000	Politics Conference	8/15/2020	1/1/2021	15,000
The Jim and Jane Johnson Foundation	454,000	Medical Research	8/15/2020	1/1/2021	Declined
The General Foundation	125,000	Scholarship	8/15/2020	1/1/2021	Declined
The General Foundation	53,000	President's Discretionary Fund	8/15/2020	1/1/2021	53,000
The General Foundation	100,000	Scholarship	8/15/2020	1/1/2021	100,000

Continued…

Figure 4.20

a day-to-day basis. Books about the great philanthropists of the 20th century are a great place to start. As you read your list will undoubtedly grow quickly, since the field is fascinating and much has been written.

Workshops, seminars, and conferences especially designed for foundation relations professionals will constitute another important area of continuing education. You should aim to attend at least one national conference a year on foundation relations. Regardless of whether you work at an educational institution, CASE (*Council for Advancement and Support of Education*) conferences are a must.

Visit the Council for Advancement and Support of Education (CASE) at www.case.org.

Every year CASE has a national conference on corporate and foundation relations. Even if you work in healthcare or social services, you still should attend. This CASE conference brings together the largest concentration of your professional peers anywhere. CASE also offers a number of regional conferences that are worth looking at, especially if you won't need to travel far or get a hotel.

The Foundation Center publishes information about other conferences available around the country, specifically on the topic of foundations. You can search for these conferences on the Foundation Center's website.

Scrutinize this information regularly for special topics. A special seminar on family foundations or new foundation tax laws might be worth your travel, and you could conceivably plan a foundation cultivation trip that includes a day for a seminar. Every area has its own associations. Find yours, join, and get connected. If you have a limited budget, webinars may be a very helpful option. However, webinars should only serve as a supplement to attending conferences and meetings, not as a substitute.

Develop a Mentoring Plan

From this point forward, start thinking of people you know and meet as potential mentors. Of course, it is helpful to have a mentor within your organization to teach you the ropes and put forward a positive word when you need it. You will also need mentors outside your organization. Involvement in professional associations, conferences, and seminars is invaluable because it will put you in touch with other professionals who understand exactly what is involved with your job.

Look for mentors both inside and outside your organization.

Conferences provide a collection of such people with the experience and inclination to be available when you need advice. Actually, it is a good idea to have potential mentor goals for every conference and seminar you attend. For example, at a large, multiday national conference devoted to foundation relations, such as the annual CASE conference on corporate and foundation relations, it would be reasonable to set a goal of meeting at least three people who might be potential mentors.

At a smaller regional seminar, you might have a goal of meeting just one. The point is, you must intentionally reach out and build relationships. If you do reach out, you will find your mentors.

90-Day Foundation Relations Checklist

✓ You understand your employer's expectations for foundation support.

✓ You have both digital and traditional structures in place for managing the results of your research on foundations.

✓ Your proposal log shows several foundations you have identified that have upcoming deadlines for which you are eligible.

✓ You have identified at least three volunteers as potential advocates for your foundation approaches.

✓ You have registered for CASE's annual conference on corporate and foundation relations.

✓ You have attended at least one free seminar offered by the Foundation Center.

✓ You have met at least one person whom you have identified as a potential mentor outside your institution, and you have written or called that person.

Chapter 5

Corporate Relations

- What Is Meant by Corporate Relations?
- Methodology
- Matching Corporate Priorities and Interests with Your Needs
- Categorizing Potential Sources of Corporate Support
- Corporate Giving Research
- Involving Others in Your Efforts
- The Solicitation Process
- Your Professional Action Plan
- 90-Day Corporate Relations Checklist

What Is Meant by Corporate Relations?

As a fundraiser focused on corporate relations, you will manage relationships with corporations that are prospective sources of support for your organization.

Like foundations, corporations are an important source of support for the not-for-profit sector. Early manifestations of corporate support were often efforts of "enlightened" corporate self-interest related to the benefit of the workforce of a company.

For example, in the first half of the 20th century, the great iron mining companies in northern Minnesota built magnificent schools on the Iron Range for the children of their huge, multinational immigrant workforce. In Duluth, the U.S. Steel Corporation built an entire town for their workers. Morgan Park was a planned community, complete with steel-reinforced concrete housing, community centers, and public buildings. These amenities were available only to employees of U.S. Steel's massive concrete and steel production plants.

You will be an important point person for your organization's contact with the corporate world, and you will involve staff and volunteers in your contact.

Today, a living example of this tradition of corporate philanthropy is manifested in Columbus, Indiana. Over the past 50 years, corporate philanthropies of the Cummins Engine Company have directed and funded a remarkable architecture program in Columbus. This small town in Indiana, site of the Cummins Engine Company's corporate headquarters, boasts buildings by giants such as Eliel Saarinen, Eero Saarinen, Richard Meier, Cesar Pelli, and I.M. Pei. No other town with a population of less than 40,000 has such a collection of 20th-century architecture.

There can be little doubt that a certain amount of corporate philanthropy is simply good business and works for the long-term benefit of the investors.
—John Mackey, Founder and CEO of Whole Foods Market

As a fundraiser focused on corporate relations, you will be dedicating your efforts toward matching the specific needs of your organization with companies that are likely to be interested in funding those needs. You will be the point person in your organization charged with managing the relationships with corporations considered to be prospective sources of support.

Large nonprofit organizations typically have corporate and foundation relations as separate positions and often as separate multiperson departments that coordinate but do not do the same work. However, more often than not the roles are combined into one position. In a small organization, a director of development might have both corporate and foundation relations in addition to other responsibilities.

In terms of methodology, many of the things you do in corporate relations are similar to what is done in foundation relations. This chapter deals basically with the differences. If you are charged

> **MYTHS AND MISCONCEPTIONS**
>
> **Myth:** Corporate giving plays a major role in American philanthropy.
>
> **Reality:** Corporate giving represents on average 5 percent of all charitable gifts in recent years.
>
> **Misconception:** Corporate philanthropy is motivated by altruism.
>
> **Reality:** Corporate giving programs ultimately serve corporate business interests.

solely with corporate relations responsibilities, you will want to refer to the previous chapter on foundation relations for guidance on topics such as proposal development and communication.

Methodology

Identifying your organization's needs for restricted and unrestricted corporate funding calls for the same methodology you would use in foundation relations. If your organization separates corporate and foundation relations, you will want to coordinate the identification and prioritization of needs with foundation relations staff. There are cases where needs will be appropriate to both the corporate and foundation audience, but you cannot assume that what might appeal to a foundation would appeal to a corporation.

Most corporate giving programs focus on specific areas, such as education or the environment.

Understanding How Corporate Philanthropy Works

Like foundations, many corporations have specific giving interests and areas that they support. Unlike foundations, corporations are not always looking to fund programs that are new and innovative, but rather to fund programs that support the corporation and its community in some way.

Corporations tend to support programs that further their business objectives.

You may be able to find a corporation that gives unrestricted support to categories of organizations you happen to fit. More often than not, a corporation will focus on a specific area of program support. For example, over the past 20 years, the Exxon Corporation has supported mathematics education in a variety of ways. Outdoor retail giant REI supports environmental stewardship. American Express supports projects that help to preserve tourism sites.

If you have noticed a link between what these companies support and the types of business activities they are engaged in, you are on your way to understanding corporate philanthropy.

Matching Corporate Priorities and Interests with Your Needs

Finding that all-important match between your needs and a corporation's funding priorities involves processes very similar to those you read about in Chapter 4. You will need a very thorough and up-to-date knowledge of the philanthropic history and profile of every corporation you look to for support. Even though you are working at a nonprofit organization, you will have to think like someone working in the private sector in order to be successful at corporate fundraising. Corporate giving involves business decisions. The only way to position your organization with corporate donors is to understand their motivation.

Building Your Knowledge Base

To understand the corporate world, become a regular reader of national business publications, such as The Wall Street Journal, Forbes, and Fortune.

If you are new to corporate relations, a helpful way to begin building your knowledge base is to do some reading. If you are not yet a reader of *The Wall Street Journal*, you should get a subscription and read it front to back every day. Do that for six months, and you will have a good start on understanding the corporate world.

Business periodicals should also become part of your required reading. You will want to read *Fortune* and *Forbes* as a start to get a handle on the country's most important public and private companies. If you have online subscriptions to these periodicals, you will be able to download lists and articles as you work on your corporate research. There are many other good business magazines. You should be aware of all of them and consistently read the ones you find are relevant to your work.

It is important to start out and keep up with general reading on current business affairs so that eventually you will be able to carry on conversations with corporate people on their terms. There will be times when you may be one of the few persons—or the only person—in your nonprofit organization who can do this, which will make you an invaluable resource to your colleagues.

Local and regional business journals, usually tabloid-format weeklies or monthlies, are also required reading because they will bring you up to speed on the business environment surrounding your organization. These journals often sponsor breakfasts or luncheons on business issues of particular interest to area executives. You should aim to begin attending such events in order to build relationships in the local business community. Business journals publish lists, such as the "25 largest manufacturers" in your area, which will help you both in your research and in your understanding of the environment.

It would also be good for you to read at least one business book a month. Autobiographies and biographies of industry leaders are the best place to start. Books on business management strategies and organization are also helpful. If you are in an area where particular industries are concentrated, such as paper manufacturing or automobile manufacturing, it would be good to bone up on those industries.

To get in touch with your local corporate community, seek out local and regional business publications and organizations.

This is not to suggest that a crash MBA course is needed in order to be successful at corporate relations. However, a personal reading program will help you understand the culture of business and be good at your job. An English major who reads the right stuff can be very successful in corporate fundraising.

Identifying Corporations That Fit Your Organization in Terms of Eligibility and Interest

Your first step in identifying corporations of potential support will be to read everything you can about the history of corporate support for your organization. All corporations that have supported your organization in the past should be on your watch list. Even if you find a reason for ineligibility, keep past corporate donors on your list of prospects.

Learn all you can about past corporate donors; they should be on your list for potential future support.

Talk to anyone in your organization who has any firsthand or secondhand knowledge of past corporate support. Previous donors are always a good starting point for someone new on the job. What you learn about unsuccessful applications for corporate support will be as useful as the success stories. If you are lucky, you may find files that explain the reason for a denial of support. However, it may be up to you to discover through your research what went wrong.

Research the eligibility requirements and philanthropic profiles of both national and regional companies to develop your list of potential corporate prospects.

Your appointment gives you a reason to propose a visit to recent corporate donors. You can introduce yourself, have a conversation about your organization, and establish the beginnings of a relationship. You will have researched the prior relationship to the point that you can give an update on the results of recent corporate support, and perhaps even extend an invitation for a visit to your organization. Take along your business card and current information about your organization.

Figure 5.1

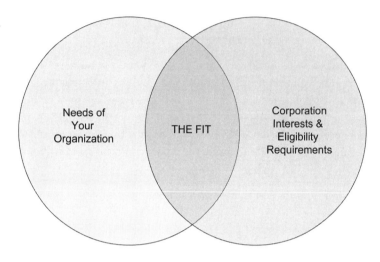

Study Your Competition for Potential Corporate Supporters

If you know yourself but not your enemy, for every victory gained you will also suffer a defeat.
—*Sun Tzu*, The Art of War

If you don't already know who your competitors are, you will learn about them early on from conversations with your colleagues. You will want to read your competitors' newsletters, annual reports, and magazines for any donor lists or stories that recognize corporate support. Keep your colleagues informed about your interest in competing organizations, because they will often be able to pass on publications that wouldn't otherwise come to your desk.

If you have enough competitors to merit organized, sustained scrutiny, it will be helpful to establish a system to organize and retain this information for occasional analysis. Private schools, colleges and universities, social service agencies, public policy organizations, and hospitals all have formal competitive leagues or associations that will make it easy to identify who you should be looking at.

Private schools, colleges, and universities have natural competition groups in athletic leagues and academic consortia. Most social service agencies, public policy organizations, and hospitals have regional as well as national membership groups. By their nature, such groups set up members for comparison and competition where funding is concerned. Once you have established a working knowledge of your competitors, you may want to do online research on their grant support.

Categorizing Potential Sources of Corporate Support

You can assume that most corporations have some kind of geographical or program area of interest. These will be major criteria for you to use to determine whether a company is a likely prospect.

There are countless private corporations in the United States— far more than you can research as potential supporters. Your task as a corporate relations professional will be to narrow the numbers to tease out a list of those corporations that are worth your investment of time and effort on research and cultivation.

Maintain a list of major corporations that are possible donors.

Public Corporations of National Significance

If you are starting fresh, you should always take a look at the *Fortune* lists, because not every company has a geographical restriction, and these are the largest companies in the country and therefore presumably will have the greatest resources available for corporate giving. Even in difficult economic times, companies will have various reasons to maintain corporate giving programs.

Even when times are tough, most large companies will continue their corporate giving programs.

Regional and Local Companies

You will glean information on regional and local companies from your business-journal reading. Since companies normally restrict their giving to localities where they have business operations, these regional and local companies will be very important to you. Business journals will give you lists of companies in various industries ranked by size. These rankings will provide names of companies to consider for your list of potential corporate supporters.

You will also want a list of local and regional companies that might be interested in supporting the work of your organization.

Colleagues can be helpful, too, in adding to your list. They may know of companies that should have been cultivated but for one reason or another have not been approached. Colleagues may have spouses or other family members who work at companies that otherwise have a low profile locally, but which may be good prospects for your organization because of the relationship.

Privately Held Companies

Personal connections are important in cultivating the support of privately held companies.

A few privately held companies (sometimes called *closely held companies*) are large and national in scope, such as Cargill and Koch Industries, and have the assets of a Fortune 500 company. Most privately held companies are smaller and more difficult to identify and research. They are important, however, because ownership is vested in a few individuals. Power and decision making are concentrated in these individuals. Due to this, relationships far exceed any other factor when it comes to the philanthropic activities of privately held companies.

If at all possible, it is good to be able to rely on connected board members or other people close to your organization who have an intimate knowledge of business in your area and who will be acquainted with the directors of local privately held companies. Ideally, your list of privately held companies will come from these connections.

If you are taking a position in corporate relations at a large university, you will likely have a prospect research staff in the development office to help you with identifying and researching privately held companies. The *Forbes* list of America's Largest Private Companies will be a resource if you have no other means of identifying privately held companies that may be prospects.

Small Businesses

The support of small businesses can provide valuable evidence that your organization is valued in the community.

Small businesses are vitally important to the American economy, so it should not be surprising to learn that they can be a critical source of support for nonprofits. Their gifts tend to be small, but they also tend to be unrestricted—which is always the most valued type of gift support. The support of small businesses can provide evidence to other larger prospective donors that your organization has sustaining community support. It can also help in meeting a challenge grant.

Small businesses often will provide very welcome in-kind support.

Small businesses often provide in-kind support to provide resources that would otherwise have had to have been purchased outright. For example, a local restaurant might feed all of your volunteers during a phone-a-thon, or a local hotel might agree to provide a free room for your invited speaker.

In your role as a corporate relations professional, you will need to develop and maintain a list of small-business prospects for your organization. Your local Chamber of Commerce will likely be the best source for doing a quick study on small businesses in your organization's area. Colleagues will also be an important source of information about small businesses.

Corporate Giving Research

Like foundation research, corporate giving research is available in print and online. A vast array of research tools is available. In general, your methodology will be similar to that used in foundation research. You will search, read, analyze, and store your information, all with the goal of making a match between a company's interests and your organization's need for support.

Corporate Foundations

Corporate foundations are an excellent place to find important information on corporate giving. Not all corporations have a foundation. In fact, there are fewer than 3,000 corporate foundations out of a total of 80,000 foundations. Nevertheless, these corporate foundations are significant and worth researching because almost 30 percent of all corporate contributions are given through corporate foundations.

Some corporate foundations have an endowment that provides additional income for their corporate giving program.

Corporate foundations file the same annual tax return as private foundations—the IRS 990-PF. The 990-PF for a corporate foundation will yield exactly the same important information that you would find for a private charitable foundation. See Chapter 4 for help in finding and analyzing 990s.

Like private charitable foundations, a corporate foundation may have an endowment. Such endowments are usually comprised of real estate or securities. At the end of the year, all assets are added up, and the foundation is required to spend at least 5 percent of the assets on grants and administration of the foundation. Corporate foundations with endowments are dependent on their investment market, and in years of good return they can increase their grant award dollars. An endowment can enable a company to maintain corporate giving even when the company itself has had a difficult financial year.

Other corporate foundations are set up to receive funds transferred from the company and passed through the foundation to grant recipients.

Other corporate foundations are pass-through foundations, which means that each year the company transfers funds from the corporation to its foundation. These funds, less any administrative expenses, comprise the total grant dollars available in the forthcoming year. The amount of funds transferred will depend on the company's financial success in the previous year. Some companies will maintain a foundation with an endowment and also transfer funds in good years, thereby maximizing the ways in which their foundation can receive funds.

You can get a good sense of potential future grant dollars available to a corporate foundation based on the previous year's income and grants awarded. All of this information is available on the 990.

If your corporate prospect has a corporate foundation, then that would be a good place start your research. The dollar grant amounts on a 990 are cash grants, whereas in corporate publicity about corporate support, the dollar amounts noted could include in-kind contributions as well. Many corporations have giving programs that extend well beyond the grants of cash awarded by their foundations, giving cash from marketing budgets, services, materials, and equipment in total amounts well beyond their foundation's annual total grant awards.

Corporate Grants or Giving Programs

Learn everything you possibly can about the corporate giving programs of your prospects.

Sometimes large corporations have a dedicated corporate giving staff that maintains web pages and publishes reports and magazines detailing corporate giving program activities. It's important to collect and update this information. No two corporations will have an identical corporate giving program. As you do your research, you will be collecting the information needed to determine whether your organization is eligible for funding and of possible interest to the company.

Procedures for contact and applications will be a routine item to collect in your research on corporations. In some cases, you will find that all corporate giving is centralized in one office with direct contributions being made through grant programs in this office. Other large corporations with facilities and offices across the country may centralize some basic information about corporate giving in guidelines and other publications, but require that all steps taken to seek support take place at a local facility or office level. Decisions about grant proposals would then be made at the local level.

Often in medium-sized companies, a corporate giving program, including the administration of a corporate foundation, is assigned to an office that also has other significant corporate responsibilities. Most often these offices are human relations or public relations.

Knowing where a corporate giving program is housed can be crucial to your strategy because it will give you important clues regarding corporate motivation. For example, a program administered out of human resources may be designed to ensure continued availability of a highly trained workforce able to meet the company's hiring needs. If you are working for a college or university that has a reputation for turning out first-rate engineering graduates, you may be of interest to the company. A program administered out of a public relations office may exist to generate publicity and goodwill. Understanding that, you will make certain that your approach for funding includes substantial "incentives" in terms of such things as press coverage, signage, and public acknowledgement.

Where a corporate giving program sits on the company flowchart can give you important clues as to its purpose.

Occasionally a corporate giving program will be administered out of a company's executive offices. In such cases, corporate giving is a relatively small responsibility mixed in with myriad other executive functions. When executives involve themselves personally in a corporate giving program, you can assume that it is very closely tied to the company's overall strategy. This placement puts corporate giving in close proximity to the board. If anyone at your organization has connections, he or she may be able to assist you.

Reference Resources on Corporate Giving

Most of your resources for information on corporate giving will be online. The one indispensable reference book you will want to purchase is the Foundation Center's annual *National Directory of Corporate Giving*, which is the most comprehensive directory in print. You may prefer to subscribe to the online version, called *Corporate Giving Online*, to take advantage of the Foundation Center's continuous updating of this information. Both resources will give you information on nearly 4,000 corporate foundations and corporate giving programs as well as details on more than 250,000 recent corporate grants.

The Foundation Center is not just a resource for information on foundations. It also will provide you with a wealth of information on corporate philanthropy.

From time to time, regional, state, and local directories of corporate giving are published as books, which you may find at a Foundation Center affiliate library. But mostly, you will be doing your corporate giving research online. Go to www.foundationcenter.org (see Figure 5.3). Company websites will give you application guidelines and information about recent grants, as shown in Figures 5.2a and 5.2b.

Most of your research on corporate giving will be done online.

Figure 5.2a

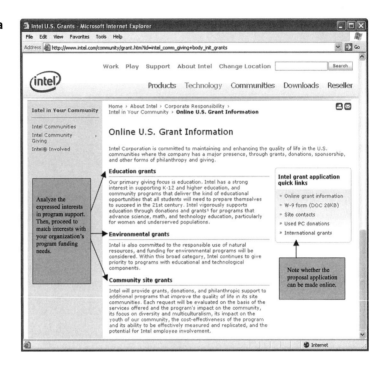

Figure 5.2b

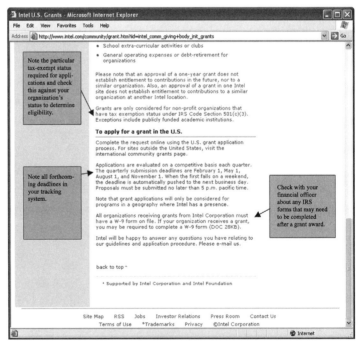

Figure 5.3
The Foundation Center's webpage for corporate giving describes various search services available.

Managing the Results of Your Corporate Research

As you do your research on corporate giving, you will be collecting information on grants made to other organizations that might serve as a model for your own approach for support. This may be a list of grants from a website or more detailed information, such as a press release. You will also want to search for specific information about a company's areas of philanthropic interest, eligibility rules, application procedures, deadlines, contact information—any other details you can glean.

Organize the results of your corporate research in both electronic and paper filing systems.

As a matter of routine, you will save the results of your web research in electronic files, but at some point it will be helpful also to set up paper files for each prospective corporate donor. You will want a place to put clippings from print journals and copies of company publications so that they are available for quick reference when you need them.

A database will not only help you to organize information, but also will enable you to generate reports on your productivity.

Beyond these files, you will also need a way to organize your corporate giving research so you can both document your efforts and analyze the vital information that you are amassing. Start out with a simple Excel spreadsheet to track basic information, such as companies' areas of interest in giving, eligibility requirements, and deadlines for submissions (see Figure 5.4). Eventually, you should put this information in a database.

Chapter 8, "Fundraising Software," will provide you with plenty of information about your software options for tracking corporate research, contacts with corporate representatives, and proposal submissions. If possible, it's a good idea to set up your corporate database early on so that you will be able to produce reports for your own use and also for your supervisor.

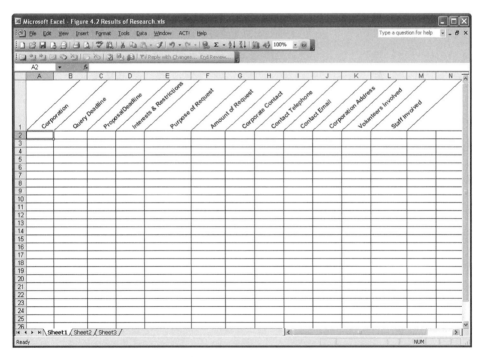

Figure 5.4 *Sample spreadsheet for tracking corporate giving research.*

Involving Others in Your Efforts

Although you will be the point person for your organization's relations with corporations, you should not be working in isolation. Other staff members and volunteers can add credibility and substance to your efforts, and often they can do things that you could not do alone. Initially it may seem as though involving others just adds to your workload, but over time you will find that seeking corporate support is often more successful when done as a team effort. As the corporate relations professional, you will be leading that team.

Staff Involvement

It is important to seek out colleagues who are doing work that is potentially of interest to corporate donors. At a college or university, the career development people will have a wealth of knowledge to share related to their recruiting experiences with companies. In a social or community service organization, program staff involved in workforce development or employment training programs will be keyed in to the corporate scene. If you are working at a healthcare organization, you should meet with anyone who regularly sees representatives of medical manufacturing companies or pharmaceutical companies.

Your colleagues may be able to tell you a lot about your organization's experience with companies. Look for ways to collaborate with them.

In general, you should seek out anyone at your organization who is working directly with companies in order to learn everything you can about existing relationships. Eventually this interaction will often lead to some kind of collaborative effort to increase corporate support of your organization.

Volunteer Involvement

You will also want to develop volunteers to help with corporate fundraising. If your organization has alumni or members, seek out any who are employed by companies on your list of prospective donors. At first you may only be looking for "inside" information. But as your relationships strengthen, you may be able to have employees endorse and support a proposal submission.

Volunteers can provide advice that is helpful in formulating an approach. They can also help you to leverage an approach.

Corporate Advisory Groups

Upon taking a new position in corporate relations, a development officer will often be given the responsibility of assisting with managing an existing volunteer advisory group. You may find yourself charged with this duty. Or as you grow into your new position, you may find yourself able to help form such an advisory group. Typically, corporate advisory groups are comprised of people with connections or experience in the business world. A large nonprofit organization might have several such groups. A small nonprofit might not have a corporate advisory group, in which case you may be able to truly advance the mission of your organization by making that happen.

As is explicit in the name, a corporate advisory group does not exist to develop policy or make leadership decisions. Those are tasks for your governing board. Instead, corporate advisory groups can offer advice, bring greater credibility to your cause and the work of your nonprofit, and identify new sources of corporate support to your organization.

Many such groups have a volunteer membership scheme similar to dues, and member volunteers ask for an annual corporate donation. If your group is seen as an industry-related effort of direct benefit to a company, it is possible for a volunteer to convince the company to make a donation. Policy-, scientific-, engineering-, and marketing-oriented nonprofits can reasonably expect these annual donations from the companies of such volunteers. Many corporate advisory groups are formed without any immediate expectation of a donation, but rather with the hope that eventually the work of the group will result in new gifts and grants.

Getting to Know Your New Corporate Advisory Group

If one of the responsibilities of your new position in corporate relations is to administer a corporate advisory group, you will want to become fully acquainted with its history before engaging the volunteers. First, you will read every file available on recent activity. Then you will want to talk with all professional staff, including the CEO of your organization, about past involvement and what is expected in the future from this group.

You will also want to learn about any gifts or other support your advisory group members have made to your organization. If they have leveraged previous corporate support, that will be essential information for you. Talk to any support staff involved in planning past meetings or managing correspondence. They can give you an entirely different—and very helpful—perspective on both the personalities and the accomplishments of the volunteer advisory group.

Sidenotes:
A corporate advisory group can provide advice, credibility, and new ideas as you build your corporate relations program.

If your organization does not have a corporate advisory group, it will be worth your while to organize one.

If your organization has an established corporate advisory group, learn as much as you can about its history and the strengths and connections of each member.

Next you will want to have some contact with the chairperson of the group. Depending on distance and availability, your communication may be entirely via e-mail prior to any scheduled meeting. But if the chairperson is local or lives in a city where you will be traveling, you should try to meet in person before you meet with the whole corporate advisory group for the first time.

In both your communications and your meetings, you will want to be focused and organized. Ambiguity about the purpose of the group and expectations for involvement will cause the group to flounder. A narrowly defined purpose is ideal. For example, focusing solely on potential sources of support might be preferable to trying to assist with public relations, special events, and programmatic design. Meeting agendas should be crisp and organized and should result in a clear plan of action. You will plan all meetings well in advance, in consultation with a volunteer chairperson.

> Clarity of purpose is vital to the success of a corporate advisory group. The minute volunteers feel that their time is being wasted, you have lost them.

Forming a New Corporate Advisory Group

Because corporate advisory group members can influence private support, they can, when managed carefully, serve as a resource for you to increase your bottom line with new corporate support.

Creating a new advisory group can be challenging. But in the right circumstances, a corporate advisory group can help to increase funding in ways you and your colleagues simply cannot do by yourselves. If you can enlist talented and connected people to help publicize and solicit financial support, you will have developed an important resource.

> Some corporate advisory groups are formed to support specific fundraising initiatives.

So what type of scenario might prompt you to create a corporate advisory group at your organization? Say you work at a research university, and the Dean of the School of Engineering tells you that she is launching a new biomedical engineering initiative focusing on home healthcare. You might want to work with her first to identify any alumni or parents working for home healthcare service companies or medical manufacturers in home health technology. Then you might want to review all alumni and parent contacts who have significant corporate connections of any kind.

This would be a starting point for thinking about people for a corporate advisory group that could help you to secure new resources for the initiative. You could then branch out to look at other volunteers who may not have such a direct connection to your university, but who are interested in the initiative and work for a company that could benefit from the publicity or advances in home healthcare that are certain to result from the initiative. These people could become good prospects to work with as you develop a fundraising plan for your initiative.

A corporate advisory group composed of influential individuals can do a lot to increase your bottom line.

A corporate advisory group is not only useful for major, complex initiatives involving huge dollar amounts. Say you are working for a social service agency that has a new program to help homeless people to secure employment in clerical jobs. You may want to talk to your chief executive and the director of the new program about setting up a corporate advisory board to help place your clients and also approach companies for in-kind or direct dollar support for the program.

The Solicitation Process

At the point where you have identified a potential fit between a corporation and your organization, the methodology moving forward is similar in almost every respect to that used with foundations (described in Chapter 4). You will need to think strategically, communicate clearly, prepare thoroughly, and document every step of the process.

A cultivation plan should precede proposal submission.

Before You Submit a Proposal

Your research into corporate support possibilities will have proposal submission as its ultimate goal. Before you actually submit a proposal, you will want to develop a cultivation plan—perhaps in consultation with a member of your corporate advisory board. See Figure 5.5 for a sample corporate cultivation letter.

Often, personal visits are an important part of a cultivation plan because they can enable you to forge relationships that will work in your favor at decision-making time.

If a company visit is part of your plan, you should dress the part and arrive armed with background knowledge about the business. Company executives may be interested in supporting environmental cleanup projects, but they probably will not feel comfortable if you turn up in jeans and work boots. Wear business attire and bring pictures of yourself in jeans and work boots, pitching in as a volunteer. You need to be perceived as professional, knowledgeable, interested, and committed.

If a visit to your organization is part of your cultivation plan, keep in mind that workforce development and community improvement are likely to be issues you will showcase.

SAMPLE CORPORATE CULTIVATION LETTER

FR. MEGER CENTER
FOR SOCIAL JUSTICE

January 1, 2022

John Doe
Human Resources Manager
Moose Lake Stores, Inc.
225 Pike Road
Moose Lake, MN 10011

> When possible, do your corporate cultivation visits with staff or others involved in the substance of a program you know to be of interest to the company.

Dear Mr. Doe:

Thank you for setting some time aside next week to meet with Jane Smith, our program manager in Moose Lake. It will be a pleasure for me to join the meeting and provide you with an update on the Fr. Meger Center for Social Justice program initiatives in Pine County that benefit the lives of people with disabilities and their families.

In the meantime, I enclose a copy of our annual report for the year 2021. I also enclose a release about an exciting new workforce development initiative headed by Ms. Smith and recently funded by the Jim and Jane Doe Foundation. With this support, the Fr. Meger Center has launched a concerted effort to build a model of employment supports for people with mental retardation and other disabilities in Pine County.

You are no doubt aware that public services are woefully lacking in the greater Pine County area. Ms. Smith's program addresses transportation, education, and other services that are of a critical need.

We look forward to meeting you next week.

Sincerely,

Timothy Kachinske
Director of Corporate and
 Foundation Relations

> Keep your colleague fully informed. Take the initiative for any communication and transportation arrangements.

cc. Jane Smith

Figure 5.5

Proposal Submission

When it comes time to submit a proposal, don't take any liberties with the company's published guidelines. Do exactly what the instructions tell you to do. If that means completely redoing a proposal previously submitted elsewhere, redo it.

Like foundation proposals, corporate proposals should scrupulously follow published guidelines. Make your proposal succinct; corporate readers tend to be even less inclined than foundation readers to wade through mounds of verbiage before arriving at the points you are trying to make. Don't lose sight of the corporate motivation for support; wherever appropriate, highlight links between the company's interests and what your organization is proposing to do.

Post-Award Responsibilities

The rules for appropriate gift acknowledgement and publicity are universal. Be prompt and sincere with your private expressions of thanks and obtain prior approval from appropriate corporate staff for all public acknowledgements. Press releases, magazine articles, published reports, and media events all must be coordinated with the donor to ensure that your efforts are perceived in a positive light. Corporations, much more so than foundations, have well-oiled PR offices that can be a tremendous help in getting out the word about a grant. They will often be glad to help, and asking them to do so helps avoid the damage-control issue. A company that has to do damage control over ill-conceived publicity is not likely to support your organization twice.

To avoid missteps, all post-award publicity should be coordinated with the corporate donor.

Grant reporting for corporate support is usually less elaborate than it is for foundations. Each company has its own requirements; all you need to do is follow them.

Your Professional Action Plan

As a new person at your nonprofit organization charged with the responsibility of raising financial support from corporations, you will benefit greatly from a personal plan to develop your skills and experience. Such a plan will not only support your professional growth but will also reap immediate and long-term rewards for your organization.

Creating Your Proposal Log

A proposal log is essential for tracking your progress (see Figure 5.6). Everything you read in Chapter 4 about creating foundation proposal logs applies to corporate proposal logs. If you are responsible for both corporate and foundation relations, you will

SAMPLE CORPORATE PROPOSAL LOG

CONFIDENTIAL

Civil Policy Association

Report to the Vice President of Development
Timothy Kachinske, Director of Foundation Relations

Proposal Log – Current Fiscal Year

Proposal $ Amount Totals Since Jan 1, 2020			Number of Proposals		
Planned	Submitted/Pending	Awarded	Planned	Submitted/ Pending	Awarded
$2,200,000	$1,100,000	$246,000	36	24	6

Corporation	Amount	Purpose	Submission Date	Decision Date	Outcome
Alpha Corporation	25,000	Immigrant Studies	1/15/2020	3/1/2020	Declined
Beta Company	45,000	Medical Costs Policy	2/15/2020	1/1/2021	Hiatus
Gamma Corporation	67,000	Recycling Survey USA	2/16/2020	3/1/2020	67,000
Delta Corporation	5,000	Env.Engineering Conf.	3/1/2020	1/1/2021	5,000
Epsilon Corporation	6,000	Undergrad. Internships	8/15/2020	1/1/2021	6,000
Zeta Company	15,000	New Soil Regengeration	8/15/2020	1/1/2021	15,000
Eta Corporation	454,000	Downward Econ Mobility	7/15/2020	1/1/2021	Declined
Theta Company	125,000	Publication: Env. Handbook	8/15/2020	1/1/2021	Declined
Iota Corporation	53,000	K-12 Social Studies Curr.	7/15/2020	1/1/2021	53,000
Kappa Company	100,000	State Capitol Measurements	8/15/2020	1/1/2021	100,000
Lambda Inc.	33,220	New Congress Conference	7/23/2020	3/15/2021	Pending
Mu Corporation	12,000	Graduate Fellowships	7/15/2020	2/1/2021	Pending
Nu Company	25,000	Book: Current Env. Policy	7/25/2020	3/15/2021	Pending
Xi Corporation	39,560	Laptops for Teachers Prog.	7/26/2020	2/1/2021	Pending
Omicron Inc.	27,990	Health Equality Study	7/30/2020	3/15/2021	Pending
Pi Company	62,500	Animal Rights Conference	8/1/2020	3/15/2021	Pending
Rho Corporation	33,110	Manufacturing Survey	8/2/2020	4/1/2021	Pending
Sigma Inc	25,000	Corporate Advisory Group	8/8/2020	2/1/2021	Pending
Tau Company	10,000	Winter Conference	8/16/2020	3/15/2021	Pending
Upsilon Inc	25,680	Winter Conference	8/23/2020	4/1/2021	Pending
Omega Corporation	14,200	Graduate Fellowships	8/27/2020	2/1/2021	Pending

Continued…

Figure 5.6

want to keep separate logs for each area, both for your own personal use and for reporting purposes.

Your corporate proposal log will enable you to track your productivity and growth.

If you are a corporate and foundation relations officer, it may be helpful in certain situations to create additional logs that combine corporate and foundation proposals supporting a particular initiative. For example, if you are working on securing support for a major bricks-and-mortar project, you might want to maintain an additional proposal log combining both corporate and foundation proposals for quick reference.

Developing Your Continuing Education Program

The CASE conference on corporate and foundation relations is a major annual event you should attend if at all possible.

The annual Corporate and Foundation Relations Conference sponsored by the Council for the Advancement of Education (CASE) is a must. Whether you are charged solely with corporate relations or with both corporate and foundation relations, you need to attend this event if at all possible. The Association of Fundraising Professionals (AFP) has local chapters that occasionally run corporate and foundation fundraising programs at a reasonable cost.

You will want to seek out other training opportunities during the year as well. The Foundation Center and its affiliates sponsor free or low-cost seminars and workshops on various aspects of corporate fundraising. Try to coordinate your travel so that it coincides with these opportunities.

Local gatherings of business professionals provide an easy way to network within your community.

In your reading of regional and local business journals, you will see announcements for business breakfasts, luncheons, or roundtables that are open to the public. Usually these events feature a speaker on a business-related topic of special interest. Make a point to find out about these events and aim to attend at least one a quarter. Such gatherings will help you to learn about the issues and concerns of executives in your area. Even more important, they will give you opportunities to meet businesspeople outside the immediate circle of your nonprofit organization.

Develop a Mentoring Plan

In addition to attending professional and business conferences and workshops, you will also want to build a network of professionals in the area of corporate fundraising whom you can call upon when you want to try out a new idea or when you are facing a challenge. The ideal person for this role is a peer who has more experience than you and is willing to share his or her knowledge in a noncompetitive situation. If your predecessor has moved to another development position in your organization, you may call on her from time to time with questions.

You will also want to consult people outside your organization. Your best pool of potential mentors will be found at the annual CASE conference on corporate and foundation relations. It would be reasonable for you to set a goal of meeting 10 new people in corporate relations at this conference. It will be up to you to break the ice, get acquainted, and obtain contact information. It will also be up to you to nurture the relationship after the conference, with follow-up correspondence.

It is important to have mentors who are experienced in corporate relations and can give you advice when you need it.

Even though the area of corporate fundraising is highly competitive, professionals engaged in this work have so much in common that they enjoy talking shop. Most are sharp enough not to reveal information that would jeopardize their own corporate relationships, but they are usually happy to share what they know as long as you aren't in direct competition.

Whenever you attend a conference, you should be on the lookout for potential mentors.

90-Day Corporate Relations Checklist

✓ You understand your employer's expectations for corporate support.

✓ You have both digital and traditional structures in place for managing the results of your research on corporations.

✓ Your proposal log shows several corporations you have identified that have upcoming deadlines for which you are eligible.

✓ You have identified at least three volunteers as potential advocates for your corporate approaches.

✓ You have registered for CASE's annual conference on corporate and foundation relations.

✓ You have attended at least one free seminar offered by the Foundation Center.

✓ You have met at least one person whom you have identified as a potential mentor outside your institution, and you have written or called that person.

Chapter 6

Major Gifts, Planned Giving, and Endowment

- What Are Major Gifts?
- What Are Planned Gifts?
- Determining Your Major Gift Needs
- Planning Your Major Gift Program
- Working with Staff and Volunteers
- Cultivating Major Donors
- Soliciting Major Gifts
- Acknowledgement and Stewardship of Major Gifts
- Positions in Major Gifts Abound
- 90-Day Major Gifts Checklist

What Are Major Gifts?

From a donor's perspective, a major gift is quite different from a contribution to an annual fund. Gifts to an annual fund are usually cash and come from the disposable income of the donor. Little planning or consulting is involved in making an annual fund gift. A typical annual fund donor will take a phone-a-thon call, make a quick decision, and write a check. Donors who make major gifts, on the other hand, will take their time. Not only are they making a larger than normal contribution, but they are most likely making this substantial gift from their assets as opposed to from disposable income.

Major gifts are more complicated than annual fund gifts, not only because of their relative size but also because of the time and planning involved in making the decision. Usually the donor will need to consult with relatives and professionals, such as a financial planner and an attorney. Often the actual gift is not cash, but property or appreciated securities. It may be a planned gift that is deferred until a later time. Some preparations for a major gift can involve complex tax strategies. The consultations surrounding a donor's decision to make a major gift can take months or years.

Major Gifts Are Important to Donors and to Nonprofits

Belief in a nonprofit organization's mission and trust in its leadership must be present in order for a donor to consider making a major gift.

Major gifts tend to represent a major life decision. Typically, a major donor has had a long relationship with the recipient organization before committing to a major gift. Usually that relationship has involved long-serving staff members and volunteers whom the donor has known for some time. Donors need to have complete trust in an organization's mission as well as its leadership and staff before deciding to make a major gift.

From the perspective of the recipient organization, major gifts likewise represent a significant investment in time and planning. Because of their size, major gifts tend to be the most important gifts that a nonprofit organization receives. Many colleges, schools, and other institutions were founded by a single large gift and owe their existence today to the generosity and vision of that donor. Well-established nonprofit organizations usually owe their longevity to an endowment that has made it possible to survive during particularly difficult times. Organizations with substantial endowments have received many major gifts from donors over time.

Major gifts count for more than a nonprofit's survival, however. They provide resources for expansion and improvement. Sometimes they make possible that which seems impossible. Major gifts have funded everything from medical research to the delivery of primary medical care, from the construction of new buildings to the preservation of historic ones, and from undergraduate scholarships to endowed professorships. American society has benefited in countless ways from the foresight and benevolence of major donors. Much of the dynamic intellectual and physical growth of the nonprofit sector is due to major gift funding.

> Major gifts are vital to a nonprofit organization because they provide resources that make it possible to transform a vision into reality. Endowments created and nourished by major gifts can be the key to stability—and sometimes even survival.

How Big Is a Major Gift?

Major gifts tend to be larger than the gifts typically made to a nonprofit. How much larger is difficult to say, because it is not always easy to define a major gift strictly by amount. Each nonprofit organization will have its own definition of a major gift in terms of a minimum dollar amount. There is tremendous variation among nonprofit organizations with respect to how this is determined.

> It is difficult to define major gifts in terms of dollars because nonprofit organizations tend to define major gifts using their own criteria.

In advertisements for major gift officers, you will sometimes see a minimum dollar amount incorporated into the position description. At a private school or small college, it could be $25,000. At a research university or a large international relief organization, the amount could be $100,000. For one of the country's top universities engaged in a $1 billion-plus capital campaign, it might be $1 million. At a small nonprofit with a modest fundraising operation, anything more than $5,000 might be considered a major gift. Sometimes position announcements for major gift fundraising positions will not include a threshold dollar amount. In such cases, the leadership of the organization undoubtedly has a figure in mind but chooses not to publicize it.

> Major gift positions often include a dollar range in the job description. For example, a major gift officer might be responsible for gifts ranging from $50,000 to $500,000.

What Do Major Gifts Support?

Major gifts differ from annual fund gifts not only in size but also in the kinds of needs they address. Most major gifts are capital gifts; that is, they fund part or all of an expressed one-time large need that is not part of the nonprofit's operating budget or part of its normal course of work during the calendar year.

Major gifts can fund capital needs, such as building construction or renovation, infrastructure, or endowment.

Construction of new buildings or renovations of existing buildings are typical examples of capital needs. Infrastructure expenses, such as new heating or air-conditioning systems or new computer network systems, can also be significant capital needs. New programs can also be capital needs, provided that they are above and beyond programs funded in the annual budget and are dependent on new funding.

Endowment can represent another type of capital need. Major gifts can be used to create an endowment or add to an established endowment. Gifts for these capital needs are considered restricted capital gifts when they are restricted to a specific purpose, such as scholarships, building maintenance, or faculty or staff position support. Even when an endowment gift is not designated for anything in particular, its use is still restricted to the endowment.

Most major gifts are restricted with respect to their use because donors usually have particular programs or projects in mind that they wish to support and sustain.

A major gift can also be unrestricted, meaning that it is not designated specifically for a given purpose. This would be the ideal major gift. Such gifts are rare. Most major gift donors will want to see their gift going to support something specific that they believe in or care about.

Who Makes Major Gifts?

Because major gifts usually come from assets, the decision to make a major gift sometimes involves not only the donor and spouse, but also other family members.

Major gifts are given by individuals who have substantial assets. Sometimes only the donor and possibly a spouse are involved making the final decision to give. However, because major gifts so often come from assets, other family members may also be involved in the decision. Major gifts can be outright gifts of cash or securities. A major donor could also choose to make a "planned gift," which might be a deferred gift or tangible property.

Donors who have family foundations may choose to make major gifts through the family foundation.

When a family has a family foundation, a major gift of cash could come from the family foundation. (In this situation, the distinction between major gifts and foundation relations is blurred.) Ultimately, most major gifts from family foundations turn on the support of a single family member who is committed to a particular nonprofit and advocates for that cause among the board members of the family foundation.

Training in Major Gifts

It is unlikely that your previous education has prepared you to be a major gifts officer. It is therefore important to take advantage of training delivered by professionals who have a thorough grounding in major gift philanthropy. CASE (*Council for Advancement and Support of Education*) offers a wide range of conferences and online seminars geared toward development officers at colleges, universities, and independent schools. Their Summer Institutes are designed specifically for newcomers to the field. AFP (*Association of Fundraising Professionals*) offers an annual conference and a year-long menu of web conferences and online courses, including "essentials" courses for beginners. AHP (*Association for Healthcare Philanthropy*) offers a slate of trainings specifically designed for professionals engaged in healthcare development.

Major gift development is not something you want to learn by making mistakes. Take advantage of specialized training opportunities designed specifically for major gift development officers.

For comprehensive major gift training, you would do well to familiarize yourself with the offerings of Advancement Resources, a private training organization that utilizes a research-based corporate training model (see Figure 6.1). Advancement Resources offers training for a variety of audiences on a range of fundraising topics. Their courses on donor development are a good place to start your training in major gift fundraising.

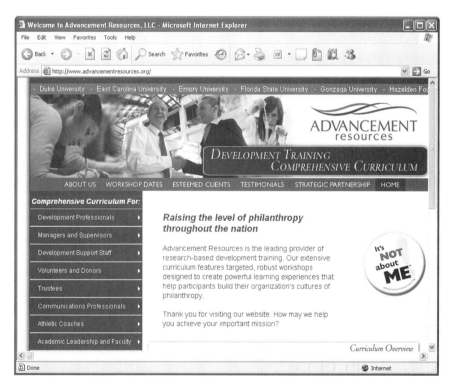

Figure 6.1 *The website of Advancement Resources (advancementresources.org).*

What Are Planned Gifts?

Planned gifts are not actually received at the time the donor commits to the gift. If the planned gift is a bequest, it will not be received until the donor dies and the estate is settled.

In a sense, all major gifts are planned gifts, since no donor can make a gift from assets without some personal planning. In development circles, outright major gifts of cash or appreciated securities are not usually considered planned gifts because they are relatively easy to accept. They require no special planning on the part of the nonprofit. A gift of cash by check is simply deposited in the nonprofit's bank account the day it is received. Gifts of publicly traded securities can be sold for cash as soon as a donor transfers the securities to the nonprofit organization.

In the parlance of development officers, the phrase *planned gifts* typically refers to deferred gifts, such as bequests, trusts, and annuities. The nonprofit organization does not actually receive this type of planned gift at the time of the donor's decision and commitment, but rather at a later date. That date could be undetermined, as in the case of bequests, which are not received until the death of the donor. Or the gift could be deferred for a specified term of years, as in the case of a trust that specifies the nonprofit will receive the gift at the end of the term of the trust. Considerable time can lapse between the moment when a donor commits in writing to make a deferred gift and the moment the nonprofit organization receives that gift.

Major gift officers facilitate the planned giving process, ensuring that both the donor's charitable intentions and the nonprofit organization's needs are met.

Planned gifts can be highly complex for both donor and recipient. A planned gift may involve the sale of a privately held company or large parcels of property or buildings. Works of fine art can also be given as planned gifts, necessitating independent valuation and documentation. Substantial planning with legal and financial advisors on the part of the donor is required for such gifts, and the nonprofit's own financial officers, advisors, and attorneys need to be involved as well. For a donor, there are often significant tax implications associated with planned gifts.

The major gift development officer is at the center of this planning process, taking on the role of helping to ensure that the donor's charitable intentions will be met while simultaneously ensuring that competent experts are addressing the nonprofit organization's financial needs and legal obligations. Planned giving officers work with a variety of professionals during the course of their daily interactions. Important among these are the nonprofit's attorneys and the host of charitable tax and estate attorneys in private practice who serve the nonprofit world.

Some major gift positions include planned giving responsibilities because oftentimes major donor prospects must resort to a more complicated planned gift than cash or securities in order to make a major gift to a nonprofit organization. Planned giving is important in major gift fundraising because for many nonprofits, most major gifts—certainly most of the largest ones—are in fact planned gifts.

Wills and Bequests

Bequests are the most common planned gift. A bequest is a gift that a person has provided for in his or her will. The gift could be cash, securities, or tangible property, such as fine art, real estate, or books. The recipient of a bequest gift is called a *beneficiary*. Individuals or nonprofit organizations can be named as the beneficiary of a gift in a will.

> Most planned gifts to nonprofit organizations are bequests of cash, securities, or tangible property.

When the donor dies, the estate is settled, and at that point the nonprofit can receive a bequest gift. Among nonprofit organizations, the preponderance of planned gifts received are gifts from a bequest. Bequests are by far the most commonly promoted planned gift because they require fewer resources and less legal expertise than other planned gifts. Bequests are also the most cost-effective planned gift to promote and administer. Most nonprofits can afford a bequest promotion program.

> A bequest can be altered or cancelled at any time up to the death of the donor if the will is changed.

Bequests are revocable. A donor who has told you that your organization is a beneficiary of her will can change her mind at any time before her death.

Gift Annuities, Trusts, and Other Planned Gifts

Some nonprofits encourage "life-income" planned gifts, such as charitable gift annuities and charitable remainder trusts. These instruments offer income to an older donor over his or her lifetime. Upon the death of the donor, what remains of the original gift goes to the charity. Charitable gift annuities and charitable remainder trusts can offer tax savings to a donor as well as income for life, but they are primarily a means of making a larger gift than the donor would otherwise be able to make in his or her lifetime. Both of these life-income gifts are irrevocable. When the donor makes this type of gift, he cannot change his mind and have his money back.

> A "life-income" planned gift instrument will provide income to the donor, with the remainder going to the nonprofit organization after the donor's death.

Planned gifts that provide a donor with life income take a considerable amount of financial planning and management on the part of the nonprofit as well as the donor. While most large universities and the largest nonprofit organizations have these planned gift opportunities in place, most small nonprofits cannot easily take on the financial and legal burden of promoting and managing these gift instruments.

Planned gifts make it possible for a donor to make a much larger contribution than would be possible otherwise.

There are a number of other instruments that enable a donor to make a major gift that would not be possible otherwise. Life insurance policies, pooled income funds, and charitable lead trusts are some of the means that can be used to make planned gifts.

Small nonprofits can sometimes offer life-income gifts through an umbrella charity. The Episcopal Church Foundation (ECF) is an example. Any church, school, or other nonprofit affiliated with the Episcopal church can use the ECF's planned giving services to encourage charitable gift annuities, charitable remainder trusts, and other life-income planned gifts. The ECF takes on the legal and financial burdens of administering and managing the gift. Upon the donor's death, the ECF gives 90 percent of the gift to the local Episcopal charity named by the donor. Many churches, schools, and social service agencies that could not afford to promote and manage life-income gifts use the ECF to secure these planned gifts.

Training in Planned Giving

Although major gift officers engaged in planned giving must never give legal or financial advice to donors, they must have training in the complexities of planned giving in order to facilitate the process and provide appropriate information to donors and their advisors.

Major gift officers with planned giving responsibilities need specific training in order to cultivate and promote planned gifts. Planned giving requires a development officer to work with his or her own institution's financial leadership and legal counsel as well as a donor's legal and financial advisors. A major gift officer never serves in the role of financial or legal advisor to a donor. However, an effective major gift officer must know enough about tax law and philanthropy to be able to seek competent legal counsel and to provide donors and their advisors and attorneys with appropriate information.

Unless you are a financial planner or an attorney hired as a major gifts officer specifically because of your expertise, you will need training in planned giving. Most new major gift officers are not familiar with the complexities of planned giving. Major gift officers with planned giving responsibilities are continuously educating themselves and updating their knowledge of changing laws regarding planned giving and new methods of promoting planned gifts for the benefit of nonprofit organizations.

There are a number of competent legal practitioners who offer public workshops and custom training sessions in planned giving. Three stand out as having national reputations among fundraising professionals. These three write consistently on philanthropic tax law and how to encourage donors to make a planned gift. They hold regularly scheduled workshops for development officers. If you are considering working in planned giving, you should be familiar with the services of all three. If you are taking a position that involves planned giving, you should sign up for at least one workshop in your first 90 days.

A new major gifts officer should begin attending planned giving workshops as soon as possible.

- Conrad Teitell; www.taxwisegiving.com; see Figure 6.2
- Winton Smith; www.wintonmith.com; see Figure 6.3
- Jerry McCoy; www.mccoylaw.com; see Figure 6.4

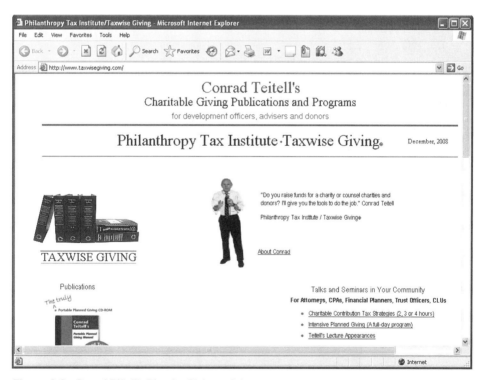

Figure 6.2 *Conrad Teitell's Taxwise Giving website*

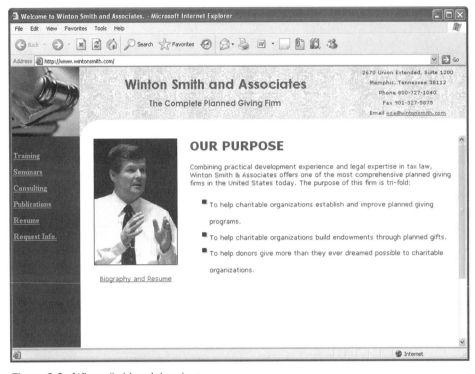

Figure 6.3 *Winton Smith and Associates*

Figure 6.4
Law Office of Jerry McCoy.

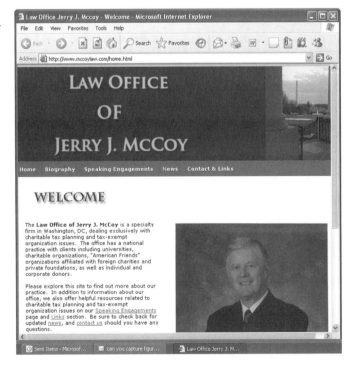

Determining Your Major Gift Needs

Major gift fundraisers work closely with the leadership of a non-profit organization. Leadership in this context usually means the chief executive officer. At a social service organization, it will be the executive director. At a college or university, it may be the president, or if you are a major gifts officer in a constituent school, it may the dean. At an independent school, it will be the CEO, whose title could be president, headmaster, or principal. Major gift needs arise out of the vision an organization's leader has for the future of the organization. Annual fund and other areas of fundraising deal with the day-to-day needs that keep an organization functioning and fulfilling its purpose during the year. Major gifts fund what your leadership determines is needed to move forward beyond the current year.

Major gift needs spring from leadership's vision for the future of the organization.

Knowing Your Institution and Its People

Major gifts turn on relationships between a donor and the organization. Ideally, your prospective major donors have strong relationships with people in your organization. And ideally, other people in your organization—such as board members and senior staff—have bought into your leadership's vision for the future and the capital needs associated with this vision. Much of your work as a major gift officer is to encourage and enable relationships to develop to the point that a prospective major donor feels comfortable making a decision. To facilitate this, you will need to know your colleagues as well as you know your prospective donors.

As a new major gifts officer, you will depend on the knowledge and support of colleagues who have relationships with your major donor prospects.

Determining and Articulating Major Gift Needs

If you are a major gift officer working on a capital campaign, your work in determining, organizing, and articulating major gift needs will be done within the context of planning that capital campaign. If the campaign is well along in the planning stage when you assume your responsibilities, a capital campaign case statement will be in draft or final form, and that is where you will begin to learn the details of your organization's major gift needs.

If your nonprofit is in capital campaign mode, the case statement will frame your major gift needs.

Of course, not all major gift officers are working on a capital campaign. Whenever needs are not defined clearly, the major gift professional must consult with leadership to define the vision and the needs that go with it. Governing board buy-in for these needs is critical. Your purpose as a major gift officer will be to draw out the vision for the future of your organization in terms of capital programs and projects that have time and dollar details. Then you will need to articulate these needs so that you can communicate them effectively to prospective donors.

If your nonprofit has not defined and articulated major gift needs, you will need to work with your CEO to develop a vision that translates into compelling needs.

Your financial officer can assist, but articulation of major gift needs is ultimately dependent on the vision of your CEO. If leadership lacks such a vision, a major gift officer's job is draw that vision out to the point that needs are compelling to potential major gift donors.

Planning Your Major Gift Program

Knowing your major gift needs and being able to articulate and document them is essential preparation for the process of matching needs with donors. Next, you will identify and cultivate your major donor prospects.

Creating and Managing Your Portfolio of Prospects

The group of prospects a major gift officer is responsible for managing is referred to as a portfolio.

Major gift officers often speak of a "portfolio" that begins with a list of prospective major donors who are the responsibility of a specific development officer. At any given time a major gift officer will have the individuals in his or her portfolio at some stage of cultivation for a major gift.

If you are not given a portfolio of prospects when you assume your new major gifts position, you will need to create one.

The number of major gift prospects in a portfolio varies. Some larger institutions have a set number of prospects required in each major gift officer's portfolio. The number can vary from 50 to 100—or reach absurd numbers, such as 500. Some institutions are more interested in the number of major gift decisions made over a year than in the number of prospects each major gift officer manages. Regardless, if you are not given a portfolio in your first major gift position, you will want to create one so that you have a basis for strategizing and documenting your activities related to bringing prospective major donors to the decision to make a gift.

Identifying Prospective Major Donors

If you are at a large institution, you may have development infrastructure supported by a prospect research team that will provide you with prospective major donors for your portfolio. If your institution does not have such infrastructure, you will need to support yourself.

Your first step will be to look at the leadership of the organization—members of your governing board and senior staff—for ideas about prospective major donors. You will be keeping them in mind as prospective donors themselves, also.

Past donors should always be considered possible future donors. You will want to review all past major donors, paying particular attention to the relationship they have had with your organization since their last major gift. Next, you will want to review all other donors of record who have not yet made a major gift. Try to identify those who might be capable of making a major gift. Internal sources, such as files and staff knowledge, will help you to identify donors with the potential to give substantial support.

Your annual fund records will be invaluable in your efforts to identify prospective donors. It is very unusual for a major gift to be a first-time gift. More often, a major gift comes after years of contributions to an annual fund.

Going beyond your organization's internal records and Internet resources to do prospect research is a budget issue. There are services that will take your donor list and provide you with detailed research on assets, contributions to other nonprofit organizations, and political contributions.

If you are getting started in major gift prospect research, you should join the Association of Professional Researchers for Advancement (see Figure 6.5). APRA offers symposia, online virtual seminars, and an annual conference.

> If your organization has a prospect research team, you will have a great deal of support for identifying prospective major donors. If not, you will need to do your own prospect research.

> Always look at past donors as possible future donors. Join APRA if you're new to prospect research.

Managing Prospect Research

The methodology for managing prospect research for major donors is similar to that used for corporate and foundation prospects. You will need to have a paper filing system and an electronic filing system. A spreadsheet will help you to get started, but as your prospect list grows, you will need a database to manage this information. (See Chapters 4, 5, and 9 for further discussion.)

> Both paper and electronic filing systems are essential for managing prospect research.

Figure 6.5 *Homepage of APRA (aprahome.org).*

Working with Staff and Volunteers

Staff and volunteers are important to anyone working in fundraising, but in major gifts they take on an extreme importance. Because major gift decisions turn on strong relationships, you will be counting on people who have a longer association with your organization than you do yourself.

Board Members and Other Friends

The assistance of board members and other volunteers is critical to success in major gift fundraising.

Board members and other volunteers who have been associated with your organization for a considerable amount of time are likely to have relationships with many of your major donor prospects. Consult with these individuals for information about your prospects. Ask them to do things that will help to move your prospects toward making a major gift. You may even involve these volunteers in strategy discussions about people they know and ask them to meet with or host major donor prospects.

Always be prepared to take on the responsibilities of managing every aspect of what you ask your volunteers to do. They may be capable of setting meetings, writing correspondence, and sending information on their own. However, they may not have the time, and in any event you want to maintain some element of control so that your strategy does not veer off track. Make the process of assisting as simple as possible for your volunteers so that their efforts are focused on the relationship, not the arrangements. If you take on the burden of any work that they prefer not to do, your volunteers will have a positive experience.

When you involve volunteers in major gift work, make certain that you take care of all arrangements so they can concentrate on relationships.

Staff

Much of your work in cultivating major donors will consist of strategizing with executives or other staff who have invaluable firsthand knowledge and experience with your prospects. You will ask staff with the closest relationship with your prospective major donors to do things that will help to move your strategy forward. A spirit of teamwork is essential, as is respect for donor confidentiality.

Teamwork is fundamental to successful fundraising. Major gifts work is no place for prima donnas.

As a last resort, you may be the person contacting or meeting with a major donor prospect. However, it is always better to have the actual contact made by someone who has an existing relationship with the prospective donor. Here again, you will be responsible for doing all or most of the work behind the scenes. This could mean drafting a letter for another staff person's signature or making arrangements for a meeting you may or may not attend.

As a rule of thumb, you always want to involve staff members who are close to your major donor prospect.

Cultivating Major Donors

When a farmer talks about cultivation, he is talking about the process of preparing the land for growing crops. When a development officer talks about cultivation, she is talking about the process of preparing a prospective donor to make a gift. Once you have a portfolio of major donor prospects and have identified the volunteers or staff who will assist, you are ready to begin donor cultivation.

You need a database to manage major gift prospects because the process typically involves keeping track of the correspondence and activities of a number of individuals.

Managing Your Contacts

You need more than a pocket calendar to manage major gift cultivation because the process involves more than just managing your own activities. You will also be managing the phone calls, visits, correspondence, and reports of the staff and volunteers assisting you with major donor cultivation. This really needs to be done in a database.

Both calendar and activity tracking are important in managing the donor cultivation process.

If your organization has development software that includes a calendar and activity tracking, you will need to learn that software. If your organization does not have development software, or if you would prefer to use software specifically designed for contact management, you should consider looking at ACT! or Microsoft-CRM. (See Chapter 8, "Fundraising Software.")

Methodology of Cultivation

Veteran development officer David Dunlop provides major gifts officers a methodology with a long record of success.

There are many books and articles on major gift fundraising, and it is worthwhile to read them all. But if you are new to the field, or if you need to focus due to time constraints, start with David Dunlop.

A retired Cornell University development officer, David Dunlop has been producing articles and chapters of books on major gift fundraising for 30 years. He frequently presents on the subject at national and district CASE conferences and various other development conference venues. Do a web search to read about him and to find his next public presentation. One thing you will discover is that countless successful major gift officers credit him with providing them with a methodology for success. Do a search for Dunlop's writings and purchase every book available that contains a chapter written by him on major gifts.

SELECTED WRITINGS ON MAJOR GIFT FUNDRAISING BY DAVID R. DUNLOP

David R. Dunlop, "Major Gift Programs," in Michael Worth (ed.), *New Strategies for Educational Fundraising* (Westport, CT: Praeger, 2002), pp. 89–105.

"A Conversation with David Dunlop," *Give and Take* (Robert F. Sharpe & Company), January, 1998.

David Dunlop with Ellen Ryan, "Thirty Years of Fundraising," *Case Currents*, November/December, 1990.

David Dunlop, "Strategic Management of a Major Gift Program," in Roy Muir (ed.), *Developing an Effective Major Gift Program* (Washington, DC: CASE, 1993).

Dunlop, D.R., "Special Concerns of Major Gift Fund-Raising," in W. Roland (ed.), *Handbook of Institutional Advancement* (San Francisco: Jossey-Bass, 2000), pp. 322–336.

David R. Dunlop, "Major Gift Programs," in Michael J. Worth (ed.), *Educational Fund Raising: Principles and Practice*, (Phoenix: Oryx Press, 1993), pp. 97–116.

Dunlop is often credited with inventing the "moves management" major gift fundraising methodology. If you hear Dunlop speak on the subject, you will find that he always credits his mentor, G.T. "Buck" Smith, a three-time college president, with developing the model.

In Dunlop's own words, "moves management" is just common sense. Don't be deceived by his humble and modest demeanor. What David Dunlop says is profoundly important for any aspiring or practicing major gifts officer because he gives you a time-tested framework for success.

Soliciting Major Gifts

If you have done a thorough job of cultivation, you will have a good sense of when a major donor prospect is ready to become a major donor. You will also know the appropriate person to do the asking. It could be your CEO, a volunteer, or a long-time staff member. It might even be you.

It is important to make your solicitation when the donor is ready and the time is right.

The "ask" should be carefully worked out in your strategy sessions. A major gift solicitation is rarely successful if done on the spur of the moment. However, major gift solicitation is an art, not a science. In certain circumstances, there might be a perfect unplanned moment for making a request. Don't count on it, for such moments are the exception, not the rule.

Encouraging Planned Gifts

Every nonprofit organization should have procedures in place and literature available for encouraging bequests. A bequest program requires a minimum budget investment on the part of the nonprofit. If you are starting a bequest program from scratch, you will need to get the assistance of your organization's finance officer and legal counsel for the proper wording of a bequest intention to your organization. That wording can then be furnished upon request to donors' attorneys.

A bequest program is relatively simple and inexpensive to set up. Consult your organization's finance officer and legal counsel if you do not have a bequest program in place.

If you have no budget for special publications, you can promote your bequest program through letters and your organization's existing publications and fundraising appeals. For example, every annual fund donation card should include a check box for requesting information about making a bequest to your organization. If you do have a budget, there are companies that can assist you in producing simple or elaborate planned giving newsletters, mailers, and booklets customized to your organization's look and feel. Such companies can also customize materials for life-income gifts. Cultivating planned gifts helps people come to a decision. Sometimes it will prompt planned gifts, and sometimes it will prompt outright major gifts.

When encouraging planned gifts, a major gifts officer must be very careful not to offer legal or financial advice to a donor. That is a job for a planner or attorney hired by a donor.

The "ask" for a planned gift is a little different than for an outright gift in that you must be very careful not to overstep ethical boundaries. A donor may tell you that she has included your organization in her will and leave it at that. She may say that she has left a specific dollar amount or percentage of her estate for your organization. She may say she has left your organization the residue or a part of the residue of her estate. Whatever your donor chooses to reveal about her estate is her business. A major gift officer is never an advisor—financial, legal, or otherwise. Advisory duties are performed by professionals hired by the donor, not by anyone associated with the nonprofit.

Encouraging Endowment Gifts

Board-approved policies regarding investment, distribution of income, and the kinds of restricted endowments that can be established should be in place as a framework for endowment fundraising.

Endowment refers to funds that an organization invests in perpetuity. Only a part of a year's interest is spent annually, so ideally the endowment will grow from year to year.

A sizeable endowment equates to stability, so endowment gifts are very important. Many institutions dedicate planned gifts to endowment. An endowment can have both restricted and unrestricted funds. The income from restricted endowment funds must be spent for a specific purpose, such as scholarships for needy students. Income from an unrestricted endowment fund can be spent on any organizational needs. Organizations that seek endowment gifts will have board-approved policies on investment, distribution of income, and the kinds of restricted endowments that can be established, as well as the minimum amount of money needed to establish a restricted endowment fund.

In order to give an endowment gift, a donor must believe in your mission and trust your leadership to manage assets wisely.

Often donors are not familiar with endowment gifts, so it will be your job as a major gift officer to explain what they are and why they are needed. Endowment gifts probably require a greater level of donor trust than any other type of gift. Donors need not only to believe in your mission but also to believe in your organizational capacity to carry it out indefinitely. Trust in your organization's capability to manage its investments is critical.

In promoting endowment gifts, you may be asked to discuss details of your existing endowment and how it is managed. Your financial officer can tell you what information can be shared and what must remain confidential. Endowment management for the most part is confidential territory. Information about endowment size is sometimes available to the public. For example, *The Chronicle of Higher Education* publishes an annual survey of the market value size of the endowments of colleges and universities.

Encouraging Gifts of Stock

Gifts of appreciated securities can provide tax benefits to a donor as well as a major gift to your organization. You should develop verbiage to encourage these gifts and use this verbiage in letters and publications. Seek the advice of a professional because tax laws change frequently.

Acknowledgement and Stewardship of Major Gifts

With each major gift comes an obligation to provide an immediate acknowledgement. Although you will send a thank-you letter and recognize the donor in a published list of donors (just as you would do in the case of an annual fund gift), you will want to do more than that to acknowledge a major gift. Treat every major gift as an opportunity to continue your cultivation with stewardship of that gift. You may not get another major gift from every major donor, but with good stewardship you may get some. As a development officer you have a moral obligation to steward each gift, but you also have a built-in incentive because good stewardship can lead to additional gifts.

Gifts of stock can provide benefits to both donor and recipient. The donor must always consult his or her own tax professional when considering a gift of stock.

Major Gift Acknowledgement and Recognition

Like an annual fund gift, a major gift must be acknowledged with a letter that serves as a gift receipt. Typically, this letter will come from the CEO. It should not be a form letter. It should be crafted in the voice of the CEO specifically for the major donor. Personalize it as much as possible, and leave space for a handwritten note. Additional notes or letters of thanks might be appropriate if staff or volunteers were involved in the solicitation of the major gift. These should be secondary to the executive's letter. Coordinate the mailings to make certain that the executive's letter arrives first.

Gift acknowledgement refers to the provision of a receipt for tax purposes. Recognition goes way beyond that, often involving media coverage, public events, and celebrations.

Group recognition is a standard way to recognize donors who have contributed at a certain level or to a particular project. You might, for example, organize a group recognition event for donors who together have contributed the funds used to create or renovate a building. At such an event, it would be appropriate to unveil a plaque recognizing the contributions of this group of donors. Planned gifts also are often given group recognition. An organization might have a planned gift society to recognize any donor who has made a bequest or other planned gift. This enables donors to be recognized during their lifetime for gifts that will not be received until after their death. You can generate goodwill by holding an event, such as a planned gift society luncheon or reception at which you recognize new members who have made planned gifts over the previous year. You may also want to have a plaque for your planned gift society that updates your list of donors each year.

Always tailor major gift recognition to the needs and wishes of the donor.

You should also recognize major donors individually. What is appropriate will depend on the size and importance of the gift and the proximity of the donor to your organization. You might, for example, create a special event to recognize a major donor. A multimillion-dollar endowment for a new professorship might prompt a ceremony to unveil a plaque and an inaugural lecture given by the first chair holder. There are many ways of creating a recognition event or visit for a major donor. Use your creativity to tailor the recognition in such a way that your donor takes pleasure and pride in having made a major gift to your organization.

Major Gift Stewardship

Good stewardship paves the way for additional major giving in the future.

Good stewardship is an obligation of a development officer that goes beyond the immediate recognition of a major gift. When entrusted with money, a good steward manages it in such a way that it grows. A development officer entrusted with a major gift will take advantage of every opportunity to show a donor that her gift has helped the organization and the people it serves. Good stewardship of a gift can prepare the way for additional major gifts in the future because it strengthens the relationship between a donor and an organization. Stewardship involves continuing to build trust over a period of years.

Donors of major gifts should continue to receive reports long after making their gift. These reports need not be complicated. They can be letters containing facts and descriptions related to the gift. For example, if someone endows a scholarship, you should provide that person with a report on the performance of the scholarship endowment fund and the amount of income used during the year for scholarships. You can check with administrators to see what information might be revealed to a donor about the students who benefited from the endowment. If a donor has made a gift to endow a chair, you should prepare an annual report about the activities of the chair holder and any publications by or about the chair holder. Major donors to a new program should receive periodic updates on the progress of that program. Letters with enclosures would suffice for these reports.

Major donors should receive regular updates about good things made possible by their generosity.

Major donors to building projects should receive letter reports on the anniversary of the grand opening. Published stories about activities or people in the new or renovated building would serve as excellent enclosures. Such a letter report should be written specifically to the major donor. Form letters are never acceptable for stewardship purposes.

Positions in Major Gifts Abound

Every week new major gift positions arise. When you search for major gift openings, you will notice that "until filled" is often noted as the deadline for filling the position. There is only one reason for an advertised position remaining unfilled: No suitable candidate has accepted it.

Major gift fundraising is essential to the vitality of the nonprofit sector, so it is an area where jobs are likely to be available regardless of economic conditions.

Major gifts often take on a special importance for an organization entering a capital campaign. Large private universities engaged in $1 billion-plus capital campaigns will launch into hiring mode and take on dozens of new major gifts officers at a time. These positions tend to end with the culmination of the capital campaign.

However, there is no need to feel sorry for these major gift officers. Anyone who has worked in a successful $1 billion-plus capital campaign will be in demand and consequently will have many choices about where to work next. Most college and university capital campaign veterans feel free to take full advantage of the possibilities for advancement presented by a mobile profession because they can take their TIAA-CREF retirement plan to their next position.

Organizations usually take on additional major gift officers for the duration of a capital campaign. This experience is invaluable for a major gift professional.

A small liberal arts college or a social service agency entering a capital campaign may add just one or two major gift officers to its development team for the duration of the campaign. In decades past, colleges and universities would carry out a capital campaign for three or five years, and then undergo a hiatus in campaign activity. Today, virtually every private institution and most large public institutions of higher learning are in a perpetual capital campaign mode, meaning that if a campaign has not been announced to the public, the development staff is nevertheless working on a campaign in a "silent stage."

Other kinds of nonprofits have not yet entered the perpetual campaign mode, but most engage in capital campaigns. A private school, a large social service agency, a large Catholic or Episcopal diocese, or a national membership organization will hire one or more major gift officers for the duration of a capital campaign. At the same time, there are plenty of new major gifts positions at these and other kinds of nonprofit organizations that are not prompted by a capital campaign in progress. The need for major gifts is a universal in the nonprofit world, and therefore opportunities abound for the aspiring or experienced major gift officer.

DIALOGUE WITH A PROFESSIONAL: RICHARD MEISTERLING

Richard Meisterling has been a development officer and fundraising executive for more than 25 years. During this time he has had many successes in major gift solicitation. In addition, he enjoys an excellent reputation among his peers in fundraising for having shared his expertise and experience with other development officers as an instructor and workshop leader.

For the past 12 years, Meisterling has served as Vice President for Advancement at Coe College. A private selective liberal arts college, Coe is located in Cedar Rapids, Iowa. Meisterling leads an advancement team of 16 at Coe and is currently well into his second major fundraising initiative there—the Defining Moment Campaign for Coe, a capital campaign with a goal of $80 million. In 2004, Coe College concluded its One By One Campaign, raising $63 million and exceeding the campaign goal by $13 million.

Previously, Meisterling served in several development positions at Ohio's Wittenberg University, a selective liberal arts college affiliated with the Evangelical Lutheran Church. Hired as Wittenberg's Director of Planned Giving, Meisterling expanded the program and eventually directed all fundraising activities as Executive Director of Development.

Meisterling is a founder and President of Advancement Resources, the country's leading provider of research-based training for fundraising professionals, nonprofit executives and managers, and development support staff. Though no longer involved in the day-to-day operations, he participates in strategic decisions and plotting the long-range vision of Advancement Resources.

So, how did you get interested in fundraising? Where did you go to college, and how was that experience influential on your career path?

I graduated from Xavier University. I received my MBA from the American Graduate School of International Management. Then I returned to my hometown of Chicago, where I worked as an executive recruiter, eventually starting my own firm.

Curiously, I think those experiences prepared me well for a career in fundraising. Not only did I learn the inner workings of the corporate world, but as a recruiter, my success was often determined by how well I could inspire a candidate to share his or her inner feelings about ambition, ability, vision, and passion. Much of that was relationship building, a skill I can only describe as indispensable for the successful fundraiser.

What did you do to get your first development position? How did that job lead you to major gift fundraising?

Moving into the development world was, as is so often the case, driven by serendipity. A casual meeting with a fellow who was the Chancellor of Purdue University Calumet led to his suggesting that I help him build a development program for that 12,000-student campus. I agreed, worked with him for four years, and, as they say, the rest is history. Again, had it not been for the creation of a strong relationship, little would have happened.

My interest in major and planned giving was immediate, for rudimentary data clearly indicated that not only do a few give the lion's share of the dollars, but that was obviously where the action was, and that's what I pined for. Because I was essentially a one-man shop at the beginning, I had a great deal of flexibility in establishing my *modus operandi*, so although we established an annual fund program and worked with local corporations and foundations, I became enmeshed in the world of planned giving. Eventually, I pursued a ChFC [Chartered Financial Consultant] and started a local chapter of NCPG [National Committee on Planned Giving] when I moved to Ohio.

Planned giving and major giving go hand in hand. Developing relationships with those who had a passion for my organizations was something I enjoyed tremendously. Part of the joy was knowing that my work with these people could make a difference in their lives and the organizations for which I worked.

You've been very successful. What sort of skills are most important for success in capital gift fundraising?

The world of capital and major gift fundraising is an immensely fulfilling career arena. Tantamount to one's success is the ability to deeply understand the objectives, strategies, and mission of the institution. Learn to easily articulate that vision. Hone your writing skills to better describe your mission when the written word is needed. Prepare well for each conversation you have with prospects. And learn how to uncover their passion for your organization. Merge those passions with the institution's activities and objectives. Help your donors to internalize the reality of how their contribution can make a difference.

Ultimately, the key to successful major gift fundraising is developing meaningful relationships between yourself—as a representative for your institution—and the donor. Recognize as a fundraiser that, "It's not about me." No—it's about the donors, and your job is to help them to understand their own passions and how their gifts can make a real difference in the fulfillment of the charitable organization's mission.

What kind of experience helps to make a person competitive for a major gifts position?

When hiring senior development officers, I always look for bright, articulate, and aggressive folks who know how to develop relationships. Good relationships also mean good follow-up and stewardship, so diligence in those areas is important. Finally, just as we, as development people, seek to bring out the passion in our prospects, we must also be passionate about our mission. If ambivalence exists in that area, success is unattainable.

What would be the most important things to accomplish in your first few months as a major gifts officer?

Completely understand and be able to articulate the mission. Learn who among your prospect base has the ability and interest to make a difference. Establish a strong relationship with your organization's leadership, and clearly understand his/her vision for the future.

Are there any major gift management theories or methodologies that you would recommend to a new major gifts officer?

I'm deeply biased, but the philosophies, skills, and methodologies taught in Advancement Resources' workshops are the culmination of my years of experience and extensive research by our team of experts.

What do you find most rewarding about major gift fundraising?

Knowing that my work has made a difference in the institutions I serve and that I have helped to bring real fulfillment and joy to those individuals with whom I've worked.

Have there been any challenges?

Any work has its challenges, and careers in philanthropy are no different. Curiously, the essential challenge of nonprofit institutions—that they depend on the largess of others—is also the foundation upon which success in the industry is built.

You're considered a fine educator among your fundraising executive peers. Looking beyond your formal education, what have you done or what would you recommend to a person looking for training or updating skills and knowledge in major gift fundraising?

Again, I am prompted to bring up Advancement Resources as a primer for anyone interested in major gift fundraising. Though the industry is replete with various training schools, workshops, and seminars, the company's utilization of corporate training techniques, formats, and research have proven to me to be helpful. Many other professionals have endorsed this training, too.

90-Day Major Gifts Checklist

✓ You understand your employer's expectations for major gift support.

✓ You have a good grasp on your organization's capital needs, and you are comfortable discussing those needs with people outside your organization.

✓ You have created a one-year timeline for major gift cultivation and solicitation that you feel comfortable with.

✓ You have assembled a portfolio of major gift prospects, and you have had some communication via e-mail or letter mail with at least 20 prospects.

✓ You have had face-to-face meetings with at least five major gift prospects in your portfolio.

✓ You have identified at least one staff member or volunteer for each major prospect in your portfolio, and you have five of these people committed to assisting you with cultivation.

✓ You understand your organization's endowment needs, and you are able to discuss your organization's current endowment and the purposes it is used for.

✓ You are able to discuss with a prospective donor why a gift of stock might be advantageous to the donor as well as to your organization, and you can explain to the donor how to go about making this gift to your organization.

✓ You are familiar with all aspects of your organization's bequest program, or if one does not exist, you have convinced your organization's leadership that one must be created now.

✓ You have signed up for a CASE major gifts conference this year, you have started an AFP online course, and you are looking at other major gift training conferences scheduled this year.

✓ You have met at least two persons as potential mentors outside your organization and working in major gift fundraising.

✓ You have called or written both potential mentors after your initial meeting.

Chapter 7

Capital Campaigns

- What Is a Capital Campaign?
- Gearing Up for a Capital Campaign
- Teamwork Involved in a Capital Campaign
- Donor Recognition
- 90-Day Capital Campaign Checklist

What Is a Capital Campaign?

Capital campaigns extend beyond a single year. They differ significantly from the annual fund in that they encompass a multiyear timeline and seek capital rather than annual gifts. A nonprofit organization can engage in a capital campaign to raise funds for a single capital project, such as a new building or an endowment-building effort. More commonly, organizations engage in comprehensive capital campaigns that encompass such things as brick-and-mortar needs (new buildings and renovation), new program development (above and beyond what the annual operating budget underwrites), and endowment funds.

> Capital campaigns extend over a period of years and raise funds for capital needs that go above and beyond what a nonprofit organization's annual operating budget is able to support.

A capital campaign has a distinct beginning, middle, and end. It has a planning phase, a quiet phase, and a public phase. Development staff will be aware of the phases that each capital campaign goes through, even if the public is only aware of the public phase.

Capital campaigns require substantially more resources, human and otherwise, than are allotted to the routine development operation of an organization. Years ago, capital campaigns took place on an occasional basis, and there was often a multiyear hiatus between capital campaigns. This still is probably true for many small nonprofits today. However, many large nonprofits and universities are now in a perpetual campaign mode, although members of the public might not know this.

> Capital campaigns offer opportunities for professionals who are willing to work hard because they involve growth and expansion.

The ultimate aim of every capital campaign is to make the organization something it is not by increasing capital resources. Capital campaigns offer rich growth potential for professionals because they tend to stretch an institution.

The majority of funds raised in any capital campaign come from a small number of donors. For this reason, major gift fundraising is an important aspect of any capital campaign.

When Does an Organization Undertake a Capital Campaign?

A nonprofit organization should engage in a capital campaign when it is ready for dynamic growth. There are only two good reasons for not engaging in a capital campaign. One is a financial crisis on the part of the nonprofit organization. If a nonprofit cannot demonstrate financial stability, there is little likelihood that the major gifts needed for a capital campaign will come through.

> When a nonprofit organization is poised for dynamic growth, it is ready for a capital campaign.

No major donor wants to invest in a sinking ship. The second reason for not engaging in a capital campaign would be a moral scandal. If your university president has just been arrested, it is not the time to launch a capital campaign. Other than such extreme cases, there is no good excuse for avoiding a capital campaign. The record demonstrates clearly that countless nonprofit organizations owe their financial stability, prestige, and ability to adapt to changing times to successful capital campaigns.

Unless your nonprofit is embroiled in a financial crisis or a moral scandal, you should be thinking about a capital campaign.

Phases of a Capital Campaign

Each capital campaign has a planning phase (that involves relatively few people), a quiet phase (that involves at most people who are potential major donors or who are in volunteer leadership), and a public phase. These three phases could be subdivided. For example, the planning phase could initially just involve a handful of people in the development office, the executive of the nonprofit, and the chairman of the board. Later on in the planning phase—as human resources are marshaled for capital campaign planning—the entire board would be involved, as well as the executive cabinet and everyone in the development office.

Capital campaigns typically have a planning phase, a quiet phase, and a public phase. At least half of your goal should be met before announcing a capital campaign to the public.

It is generally considered ideal to have 50 to 60 percent of your capital campaign funds committed at the point the campaign is announced to the general public. Most work takes place out of the public eye. Often, by the time a capital campaign is announced to the general public, an organization has a fairly good idea of where the remaining gifts are going to come from. This is worked out in advance, because capital campaigns are so important that no organization wants to risk failure.

A capital campaign involves meticulous planning. Nothing should be left to chance, because it is vital that goals be met.

What Is Involved in a Capital Campaign

From a development point of view, a capital campaign means carrying out some fundraising efforts on a more intensive level than usual. A campaign involves doing business in new ways, as well. Staff are often added due to the intensity of the work.

Capital campaigns involve new job opportunities, because existing staff rarely are able to assume all of the duties of a campaign.

Capital campaign work requires a firm conceptual grasp of the future of the organization as well as the reality of its present. At the same time, it requires an encyclopedic knowledge of all of the details associated with individual major donor prospects. The successful capital campaign staffer must have passion for the work, effective communication skills, and a willingness to commit a great deal of time and energy to the cause.

Gearing Up for a Capital Campaign

Board commitment is essential for a successful campaign.

In order for a capital campaign to move forward, the leadership (in other words, the executive and governing board) must be fully committed. Their vision must be clear.

Often an organization will commence a capital campaign upon the conclusion of an external review or an internal long-range planning study.

Many organizations engage in a capital campaign after substantial external review or long-range planning. For example, if an independent school, college, university, or hospital has just completed an accreditation review, there is often enough momentum, planning, and analysis to provide the beginning framework for a capital campaign. Likewise, if an institution has just engaged in a multiyear internal long-range planning effort, the conclusion of that planning effort is a logical place to commence a capital fundraising effort.

Planning the Capital Campaign

The goal of a capital campaign must stretch the organization beyond what it is currently capable of accomplishing.

It is very important that capital campaigns have a goal that stretches an organization. One simple rule of thumb is that a capital campaign goal should be at least 10 times the annual fund goal. However, many capital campaign goals now greatly exceed this amount.

Capital campaign staff must be prepared to extend themselves for the duration of the capital campaign. Hard work, long hours, and travel are to be expected. Rewards are commensurate with the effort expended.

At all times, capital campaign planning must be done mindful of the annual fund. An organization never wants to have a decline in the annual fund in the midst of a capital campaign. Annual fund staff must be involved in capital campaign planning from the outset and should never be alienated from the campaign or given the idea that the annual fund is secondary in importance. Even in the heat of a capital campaign, it is critical that annual fund goals and operating needs be met.

It is also necessary to plan for staff and volunteer involvement that will go above and beyond what anyone is accustomed to in the daily course of business outside of campaign mode. Capital campaigns are intense. Everyone involved must be prepared for that intensity.

Increased Fundraising Resources and Budget

Development staffing and budget usually increase during a capital campaign.

Capital campaigns require staff and resources beyond the normal staffing and operating budget of a development office. It is not reasonable to expect that capital campaign goals can be met without increased resources.

Fundraising Counsel

Capital campaigns are usually undertaken with the assistance of external fundraising counsel. Services provided by consulting firms can be anything from studies and analysis to data on donors, assistance with publication production, and even in some cases provision of temporary fundraising officers.

Feasibility Study

Every capital campaign is preceded by a feasibility study. These studies are normally done by external fundraising counsel. Their aim is to measure the fundraising potential of the organization, with specific reference to achieving capital campaign goals. Consultants collect data, quantitative and qualitative, from the nonprofit organization's development staff. They also usually interview the leadership of a nonprofit organization and major donor prospects during the course of the feasibility study. Some also will include focus groups in their methodology.

> Before a capital campaign begins, external fundraising counsel is usually called upon to do a feasibility study.

The conclusions of a feasibility study are made by the consultant based on evidence indicating that the organization can or cannot make its campaign goals. There are three options that a consultant might recommend:

1. Delay the campaign and work on any issues that need to be resolved.

2. Revise the original goal downward but move ahead with the capital campaign.

3. Move ahead with the capital campaign and the original goal put forward at the time of the feasibility study.

> Upon completion of a feasibility study, a consultant might recommend that a campaign be delayed, revised, or carried out with the goals set by the board and executive staff.

The Case Statement

The case statement is the document that communicates an organization's capital needs and the reason these needs are compelling and worthy of support.

> The case statement communicates the capital campaign vision and needs.

The case statement can contain building plans, descriptions of new programs, and details about endowment needs. It grows out of consultations with leadership, typically the chief executive officer and perhaps his or her cabinet. Buy-in of the governing board for these needs is essential. The case statement articulates the vision for the future of your organization in terms of needed capital programs and projects that have time and dollar details. In draft form, the case statement can be a working document, but eventually (before the public phase) it will be prepared as a glossy pictorial suitable for communicating campaign needs and discussing solicitations with prospective major donors. A case statement prepared for major donors normally will not be mailed, but rather personally delivered by a volunteer solicitor or staff person.

Toward the end of a campaign, an updated version of the case statement is usually produced for mailing, showing progress toward the goal and information about major gift commitments to the campaign. This version of the case statement is usually mailed, in an effort to attract major donors who have not yet been personally solicited.

DIALOGUE WITH A PROFESSIONAL: DAVID WILLIAMS

David Williams has been a development officer and fundraising executive for more than 33 years. Throughout his career, he has been very successful at leading or participating in capital fundraising efforts. His reputation extends beyond our shores to Europe.

Presently, Williams serves as Vice Chancellor for University Advancement and Marketing at the University of Wisconsin-Stout, one of 13 universities in the University of Wisconsin system. As Wisconsin's Polytechnic University, UW-Stout focuses its educational mission in 32 technically oriented degree programs. Previously, Williams served as Vice President for University Advancement at Minnesota State University, Mankato, and as Vice President for Development at Ripon College.

At Minnesota State, Williams led a 23-person staff in annual and capital fundraising efforts. During his tenure, annual giving increased from $2.7 million to more that $4 million, and capital giving was increased dramatically as the University launched a capital campaign. The 2007–08 fiscal year resulted in more than $14 million in new capital pledges and gifts for the University's endowment.

At Ripon College, a private liberal arts college in Wisconsin, Williams led a successful capital campaign of more than $40 million and began another campaign with a goal of $50 million. During his final year at Ripon College, Williams served as interim president.

A graduate of Beloit College, Williams earned an M.A. at the University of Wisconsin before embarking on his development career. From his early work, first as a development officer at Ripon College, followed by a development position at University of Wisconsin-Stout, Williams has been engaged in capital fundraising. Williams launched UW-Stout's first capital campaign in the early 1980s and set the stage there for subsequent campaign work after he departed for Ripon, where he successfully brought the College's $40 million campaign to conclusion.

Williams has been called upon for his expertise by many professionals in the United States and elsewhere. He traveled to Britain and Germany on a sabbatical focused on comparative fundraising in the late 1980s and in 2007 was the recipient of a Fulbright award directed at sharing U.S. higher education administration and fundraising expertise with German universities.

So, you have a bachelor's degree in German from Beloit College and a master's in German from Wisconsin. How did you get into fundraising?

I have always known that I wanted to work in the field of education, which I personally believe can be the singular most important tool for an individual to improve their life and society, but I quickly found that teaching German would not be the best way for me to make a difference. I landed a position directing the annual fund at Ripon College through an acquaintance who had moved there as Vice President for Development, and I quickly found my niche.

Fundraising work allows me to work with people to help them realize their dreams and hopes through their philanthropy to support an institution we both admire and appreciate. I found I enjoyed learning people's stories, and then tying those stories to their need to do something of significance in their life, which often is through helping the institution I serve. While I don't use the German degrees I have very often, the discipline of learning a language and the time on a college or university campus prepared me well for my work in higher education. And it was a tremendous help on the Fulbright Program to Germany recently.

How would someone get experience in capital fundraising if he or she is a recent college graduate?

Simply being part of an advancement office during a campaign provides great exposure to the mystery of how capital campaigns work. I was fortunate to land in the annual fund director's chair and could watch how the prospects I worked with for annual support became involved with capital projects. I watched the communication unfold, saw how I could contribute to prospect identification, research, and cultivation, and then tried to learn from my vice president how he had approached the prospect for a major capital gift. A new graduate should consider all the "peripheral" positions in a campaign, whether it's gift processing, or communication, or special events, or the alumni program—all get involved in a well-run campaign.

What would you recommend for persons who are looking for a career change?

The world of higher education and the world of advancement are wonderful places if you truly care about people and ways to help them maximize their philanthropy. The first assessment would have to be whether you truly have that interest in people, whether you can enjoy meeting new people, gently questioning them to learn what is important to them, and building their confidence and trust in you. It means some travel, and it means considering things from the prospect or donor's perspective.

But the rewards are phenomenal. I've helped donors honor a loved one with a scholarship gift that will continue the life values of the loved one through the students who receive that scholarship. I've watched donors who believe passionately that the world needs more ethical training endow an ethics center that will help every student to a better understanding of how ethics play out in our lives—and those donors pleasure in making that gift completely anonymously.

What are some important skills for someone who might want to work in capital fundraising?

Anyone interested in capital fundraising has to first understand the institution they serve, its history, and its needs. The aspirant must also have that love of people and their stories noted previously, a willingness to travel to visit the prospects (often multiple times), some understanding of personal finance to help them structure a gift in a way the donor is comfortable making, and enough attention to detail to make sure follow-up happens and is timely and appropriate. I'm a solid list-maker, jotting down the tasks I need to do to make sure I've responded to prospects in a way I'd want to be.

What would you need in your background to successfully lead a capital campaign?

I believe it is important to be able to generate trustworthiness as quickly as possible with a prospect. I've stayed at the institutions I've served for relatively long stretches because I think some of that trust comes from the commitment I show a prospect with the time I've committed to the institution I serve. I've managed to return to two institutions I've served in my career, working at Ripon College and UW-Stout twice. I think the reputation I left behind at each of these made it easy for them to rehire me, in each case for a more responsible position. I also need prospects to know that I support the cause I'm asking them to provide their resources to, through annual, capital, and planned or legacy gifts. And sometimes just plain old determination is in order—to keep calling for that appointment until you connect—I've had prospects thank me for my persistence in trying to connect with them.

What in your formal education has helped or prepared you for a successful career in capital campaigns?

My formal undergraduate and graduate education gave me a good sense of the flavor of life in the academy, of the richness of a higher education environment. It allows me to talk with authority about how higher ed works—often seen as quite different from the business world. My degrees are essentially the admission card to this world—from there it's up to me through personal character, or work ethic, or persistence, and through the learning I've done on the job to be successful. I'd encourage anyone considering the field to take all the seminars you can, join a group such as the Association for Fundraising Professionals, take grantsmanship training, and watch successful practitioners in the field. If you work for one of those, ask questions, look at the letters or proposals they draft, listen in on prospect meetings or strategy sessions. All of these are great—if not formal—learning occasions.

How do volunteers fit into a successful capital campaign?

Campaigns are usually such huge undertakings that we need all the help we can get. I've heard of major universities adding scores, if not hundreds, of additional development officers when entering a campaign, but most organizations don't have that luxury. So extending our reach through volunteers is an important way to get our work done. Recruiting them, then training them and supporting them in their work takes a great deal of time. But they can bring solid gift results to any campaign, especially if they have made their own commitment first. Volunteers can be a priceless addition to a campaign leader's arsenal, but they do take much care and feeding. That includes regular communication, phone calls, and often taking the time to join them on some calls.

What do you find most rewarding about capital fundraising?

It is the singular joy of watching a donor realize a dream or accomplish something with their resources they might never have considered, but for the campaign I serve or my efforts. For most institutions, campaigns provide the resources they could never realize through annual budgets or state appropriations, so it's the chance to bring these special opportunities to the table that is also rewarding. Some gifts are complex and require bringing multiple people to the same table, negotiating, and helping everyone walk away feeling good about the final gift—those are incredibly meaningful. I was honored to be a key part of helping a donor and his son honor their deceased wife and mother through an endowment for the arts, which had been dear to her. With the gift, the donor and his son created amazing creative opportunities for years to come, all of which would benefit students in her name. It was a powerful moment.

Teamwork Involved in a Capital Campaign

Teamwork is important in all development efforts. In a capital campaign, it is crucial. Capital campaigns offer a tremendous opportunity for growth in experience and knowledge for volunteers and staff alike.

Role of the Board

Unanimity of board support is required for a successful capital campaign. This broad statement specifically means that every board member must not just vote to support a capital campaign, but must also make a personal financial commitment in the earliest stages of the campaign. Not every board member can make a million-dollar commitment, but the contribution made must represent relative commitment.

If a campaign is to be successful, it must enjoy the support of the board.

Board members must be donors themselves before they can effectively ask others to support a capital campaign.

Board members will need to be involved as solicitors of major gifts in the capital campaign, and they will have no credibility if they have not already committed to a contribution of their own. If a board wants a staff-driven capital campaign, it is probably a sign that the campaign will not achieve ambitious goals.

Role of Volunteers

Volunteers play an important role in any successful capital campaign. If they have a passion for the cause and know what to do, they are likely to be very effective at soliciting major gifts.

Board members and other volunteers are critical to a capital campaign's success, not only as donors themselves but also as actively involved participants in the campaign. Successful campaigns rely on volunteers to perform services or duties that staff are not in a position to perform. For example, volunteers are often asked to "rate" prospective major donors' ability to make major gifts. They are asked to do this because their knowledge of prospective donors either through personal relationships or business relationships puts them in a position to judge an individual's interest in making a gift and ability to do it out of assets. (Additionally, consulting firms can be contracted to produce data on your major gift prospects that your organization might not have from donor records or research. This is a very sensitive area.)

Teams of volunteers are developed specifically for soliciting major gifts. At colleges and universities, they could be clustered around decades or class years. Likewise, at independent schools, parents may also be grouped by class and involved in soliciting major gifts. Volunteers who are committed and well trained tend to be far more effective at soliciting major gifts than staff.

Role of Staff

Everyone in a nonprofit organization has the potential to grow and develop professionally as a result of the capital campaign experience.

A capital campaign offers an opportunity for growth and new experiences, not just for the development staff, but for all people involved in the advancement effort. Professionals supporting the effort through strategic planning, fiscal planning, public relations, college relations, alumni relations, patient relations, or parent relations will also be critical to the success of a capital campaign.

Capital campaigns typically have a unique name, a unique logo, and a unique style and format in publications. A capital campaign provides a budget and a reason to expand an advancement operation's publications. Therefore, professionals involved in producing publications will also have opportunities to undertake new and exciting work.

Identifying and Rating Prospective Donors

The process of identifying major donors is supported by prospect research. Frequently, a capital campaign will provide the budget to start up a prospect research operation and hire new people or supplement an office already in place.

Identifying a significant number of major donor prospects is critical for a capital campaign because a majority of the funding of the capital campaign is going to come from these donors. Various benchmarks are used. For example, you might hear that 90 percent of the dollars raised in a capital campaign come from 10 percent of the donors. You might also see claims that 80 percent of the dollars raised in a capital campaign come from 20 percent of the donors. Various consultants and theoreticians have designed gift pyramids and gift charts to demonstrate the number and amount of gifts needed for a successful capital campaign. They all show that in terms of amount, the significant gifts are coming from a relatively small number of donors.

Once prospects are identified and researched, capital campaign officers organize volunteer groups to rate these prospects. These are usually organized as peer group ratings using a list of criteria and personal knowledge to match a donor with the largest reasonable amount and the most likely need of interest.

> The majority of the funds raised in any capital campaign will come from a relatively small percentage of major donors. For this reason, it is very important to identify prospective major donors.

Timeline

A capital campaign starts when the leadership and staff of an organization begin to conceptualize and plan it. A capital campaign is launched after a certain number of major gifts have been committed.

Frequently, capital campaigns are announced to the public after 50 or 60 percent of the funds needed for the goal have been secured with commitments. A capital campaign will be divided into a silent phase and a public phase. The early days of the silent phase are sometimes called the *leadership phase*, which concentrates on solicitation of the very large gifts needed to move the capital campaign ahead to the point of announcement.

Generally speaking, at the point of announcing a capital campaign publicly, campaign staff have done sufficient research and planning to have confidence in where the remaining gift dollars are going to come from.

> Capital campaigns typically have a silent phase followed by a public phase. By the time the campaign is made public, the potential for success is usually assured.

Campaigns are carefully planned to ensure success and to avoid public disappointment.

Managing Capital Campaign Pledges

The annual fund must be carefully coordinated with the capital campaign to make certain that it does not decline.

Whatever system a nonprofit development office uses to track annual fund pledges must be adapted to coordinate with capital campaign pledges. The two cannot be run separately. There must be careful coordination when producing pledge reminders for each. If the annual fund is folded into the capital campaign, you want to make sure that it isn't neglected. It is important to make certain that the annual fund does not suffer as a result of capital campaign efforts. Clear communication and coordination of all pledge reminders is critical. The sample letter of intent in Figure 7.1 provides a form with ideas for incorporating capital and annual pledges into one pledge document.

Donor Recognition

The close of a successful capital campaign gives everyone involved many reasons to celebrate. It is important to make certain that celebrations are meaningful to staff and donors alike, for together they have accomplished what could never have happened without their hard work and generosity.

At the end of a capital campaign, it is important to celebrate. Volunteers who have worked on a capital campaign need to have special recognition for their efforts. Major donors will be recognized in individual ways, but they also should be recognized for their part in making the team effort of the capital campaign a success. Receptions, celebration dinners, open houses for brick-and-mortar projects, and special celebratory or commemorative publications are all appropriate ways to mark the end of a successful capital campaign.

90-Day Capital Campaign Checklist

✓ Your organization is planning a capital campaign, and you understand your role in the planning process.

✓ You organization is engaged in the "silent phase" of a capital campaign, and you understand and feel comfortable with your role in this phase of the campaign.

✓ You have met individually with at least three important volunteers involved in your capital campaign.

✓ You are well aware of the services available from fundraising counsel contracted for your capital campaign.

SAMPLE LETTER OF INTENT

University
of the United States

Letter of Intent

To demonstrate my support and appreciation for the educational experience provided by the University of the United States and to insure that it flourish in perpetuity, it is my desire to pledge a total of $_____ to capital needs of the university. This total amount will be paid over a period of _____ years. Payments will be made on or about _____ each year. Of this total, $_____ should be allocated to the annual fund campaign during this period.

My gift is:

> Remind the donor that his capital support should not deter him from his regular annual support over the term of your campaign.

☐ Unrestricted

☐ For capital needs and improvements _____

☐ For endowment_____

☐ Unrestricted

My gift will be made as follows:
☐ Cash   ☐ Securities
☐ Trust   ☐ Bequest ◄——
☐ Insurance   ☐ Real Estate
☐ Tangible Personal Property

> A check in the Bequest box makes this letter an important planned giving document.

Name (s) _____

Address_____

City, State, Zip Code_____

Signature (s)_____ Date_____

Figure 7.1

✓ You are comfortable discussing the capital campaign case statement with individuals outside your organization, or if a case statement does not yet exist, you have completed a first draft for internal planning only.

✓ You have identified five people outside your organization who have worked on a capital campaign and are potential mentors.

✓ You have met with two potential mentors and have followed up with a phone call or a letter to each.

✓ You have signed up for a CASE conference in capital campaign fundraising, and you have completed an AFP online course in capital campaign fundraising.

Chapter 8

Fundraising Software

- Essential Software
- Automating Tasks with Fundraising and CRM Software
- Microsoft Dynamics CRM and Microsoft Dynamics CRM Online
- ACT! by Sage
- Outlook Business Contact Manager (BCM)
- Salesforce.com
- Raiser's Edge (Blackbaud)
- DonorPerfect
- 90-Day Fundraising Software Checklist

Essential Software

You won't be able to manage your fundraising efforts effectively with pen and paper alone. Today, there are hundreds (maybe thousands) of computer programs that can help you track your work. In this chapter, we'll focus on two major types of software you should be aware of: customer relationship management applications and fundraising-specific applications.

Customer Relationship Management (CRM) Software

CRM applications enable you to track names and contact information. You can also generate your own reports easily and create custom tables.

While not specifically written for fundraising professionals, CRM software is seen by many to be an indispensable tool because it enables you to manage contacts. CRM applications give you a relational database that you can use to track names, addresses, and other key contact points. Beyond that, all are flexible in their ability to add custom fields, reports, custom tables/entities, and custom scripting. In general, CRM applications—because they have a wide market appeal—have better integration with Microsoft Outlook and Microsoft Word and better web interfaces than fundraising applications.

CRM software will enable you to organize the history of your relationships.

One of the most important qualities of a successful fundraiser is the ability to keep track of (and report on) contacts with others. CRM software is ideal for this purpose because it allows you to organize the history of a relationship effortlessly. Although the CRM programs discussed here are not specifically designed for fundraising, all can be customized to adapt well to serve the fundraising professional's needs.

Reasons to Consider CRM

General customer relationship management software is often the best solution for companies looking to integrate existing systems, automate correspondence, and link with Outlook.

What are some of the reasons you might choose to use a generic CRM application over a fundraising-specific vertical application? CRM applications are generally cheaper, more customizable, and offer a wider range of general contact management features—such as integration with Outlook.

CRM applications were developed for the for-profit world and are primarily used by sales and marketing professionals. CRM software is as close as you can get to state-of-the-art software for contact management. Because sales is such a profitable area, CRM's capabilities are superior to most other proprietary programs, especially in terms of mail merging, reporting, dashboards, and information retrieval.

The disadvantage of using a CRM product to manage your fundraising operations is that most of the custom fields, entities, reports, and features found in fundraising software will need to be customized from scratch in your CRM applications. It's really a tradeoff.

I have written in considerable detail about most major CRM applications, including Microsoft CRM, Outlook Business Contact Manager, Salesforce.com, and ACT!. Go to Amazon and search for Kachinske (my last name) to see a full list of my books.

The most popular CRM applications are Microsoft CRM, Salesforce.com, ACT!, Outlook Business Contact Manager, and SugarCRM.

Fundraising-Specific Software

Applications written specifically for fundraising professionals typically include the base field structure and reporting for development officers and related staff. They usually don't require a lot of customization to track donations and pledges, but they sometimes lack the ability to easily track letters, e-mails, and activities that customer relationship management software generally provides.

The most popular fundraising-specific software programs include Raiser's Edge, DonorPerfect, Convio, eTapestry, Sage Fundraising, GiftWorks, ebase, and Telosa Exceed!

Automating Tasks with Fundraising and CRM Software

The whole point of implementing software is to automate tasks that you would otherwise have to perform manually. Automation makes it possible for fewer people to accomplish more in a given span of time, an important consideration if your organization, like most nonprofits, is on a tight budget. The right software combined with the right training can reduce the need for staff positions. It can also enable you to be organized at all times, a vital skill for successful fundraising.

A Centralized Contact Database

All CRM applications have a database component that lets you track names, addresses, categories, and other relevant information (see Figure 8.1). Tracking all of this in a central database helps keep your mailing lists up to date.

As a fundraiser, one of the most important things you will need to coordinate is your list of contact records. If possible, try to keep your contact list in one centralized database to avoid duplicates.

Here's a possible scenario: A member of your board suggests that your organization run an annual telethon. You've never run a telethon before, but with help from a loyal volunteer, you have assembled a group of staff and volunteers to conduct the event. The first thing you will need is a list of people to call—with phone numbers.

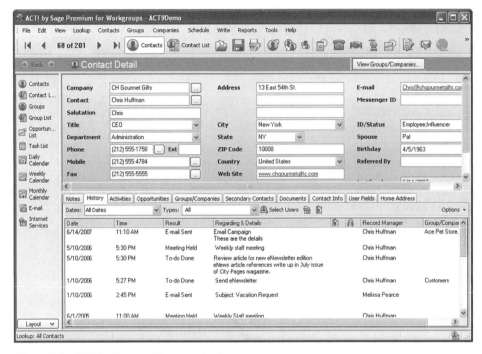

Figure 8.1 *CRM software with contact database component.*

Avoid storing electronic records in multiple systems.

Because CRM software has a database component that lets you track names, addresses, phone numbers, and so on, you will be able to go to your CRM software and generate a phone list for each volunteer with a minimum expenditure of time and effort.

It's important that this information is all housed in a central location within your organization. Using the telethon example, let's say you didn't have a central database of donors, prospects, and friends of the organization. Let's assume instead that you have contact information stored in your accounting system, on individual database systems on each staff member's computer, and in a set of paper files stored in the back room. In this scenario, putting together a call list for your telethon would be a nightmare project that would necessitate combining all of these sources into a central list and then de-duplicating the list to ensure that your prospects don't get multiple phone calls.

Automated Correspondence

Mail merges, mass e-mails, and other correspondence can be automated with CRM software. Do you need to contact everyone who contributed to your annual fund last year but has not yet contributed for this year? Just look them up in your CRM database and send a mail merge.

Here's a possible scenario: At the end of the year, you need to send a gift acknowledgement letter to all of your donors noting the amount of the gifts received during the year. This fulfills your legal obligation, and it is also a great way to keep the relationship with your donors active, plus it gives them a handy document for tax filing. It might also be a good way to put your organization in the minds of donors who might need a last-minute year-end tax deduction.

There are two ways you can send these letters: You can either write them manually one at a time, or you can automate them with a mail merge process. Especially if you are writing to a large number of donors, you will obviously want to automate this process. Each CRM application discussed in this section integrates with Microsoft Word for writing letters (see Figure 8.2). For this function, ACT! is probably the most user friendly, and Salesforce.com is probably the weakest, since the mail merge feature in Salesforce is turned off by default, and integrating the online Salesforce application with the offline Office products requires excessive security checks.

If you write a lot of letters in your fundraising role, make sure that the CRM application you use makes it easy to mail merge into Word. ACT! gets our best marks for this. Salesforce is probably the hardest application to use for mail merging.

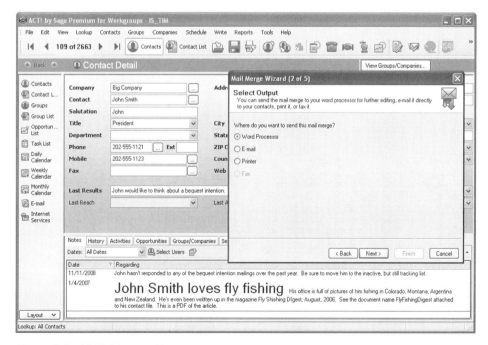

Figure 8.2 *ACT! doing a mail merge.*

Activity Tracking

Most CRM and fundraising applications have some sort of activity tracking feature. Need a reminder to follow up with a major donor about a pledge? Forgetting to make that call could potentially cost your organization a lot of money.

It's hard to use two calendars at once. If you use Outlook for your calendar, make sure the application you choose syncs with the Outlook calendar.

Keeping track of activities related to specific donors is important. In the course of your work, you will come into contact with a large number of donors, prospects, board members, alumni, volunteers, and others. Keeping track of what you have done with each of them is an important part of building relationships.

Here's a possible scenario: John Smith calls you on the phone. Two years ago, you met with him to discuss a bequest that he was considering. For whatever reason, he dropped off your radar screen, and the opportunity didn't come to fruition. It's Friday afternoon, and you have been working 12-hour days all week preparing for an upcoming board meeting. You vaguely remember dealing with Mr. Smith, but the context escapes you.

If you use a CRM application, all of the activities on your calendar are tied to specific contacts in the database (see Figure 8.3). While you are making small talk on the phone with Mr. Smith, you can click on his name in your CRM database and instantly pull up the entire history of your relationship with him. This history will include every phone call, meeting, and letter you have

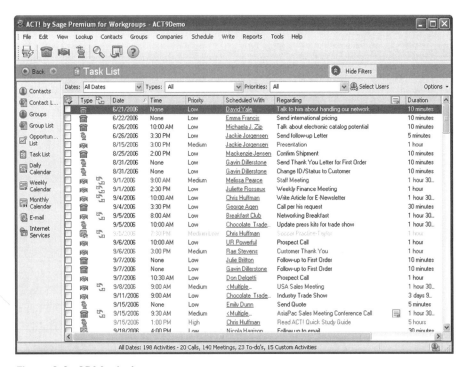

Figure 8.3 *CRM calendar.*

sent him, including a copy of a bequest intention letter that you sent him last year. Mr. Smith will never know that when you first heard his voice on the phone, you couldn't remember anything much about him. Thanks to the software, you can pick up right where you left off.

Gift Tracking

All CRM applications can be customized with additional fields to track information such as gift amounts. At the most basic level, you can customize CRM software with a custom field to track the amount of money a donor has given. Then, if you need to create a holiday card list at the end of the year for all of the people who have donated money, you'll be able to search for all contacts where this gift amount field is greater than $0.

Microsoft CRM, ACT!, and Salesforce all have the ability to create custom entities, which are sometimes called *custom tables*. It's a good idea to use custom entities to track gifts because with custom entities, you can create a one-to-many relationship between your gift records and your contact records.

General CRM applications can be customized to track gifts and pledges. Make sure your application can create custom entities, as most general database programs won't have a gift tracking component out of the box.

In the scenario where you just create a single field in the database to track the amount of money donated, what happens next year? Do you wipe the data and start over with the same field? What happens if a donor gives twice within the same year? What if a donor gives $50,000 in restricted funds and $10,000 in unrestricted funds? If you create a custom entity, you can enter each gift separately, and then all gift records are linked back to the contact record.

Here's an illustration: Your CEO has a brainstorming session with a few newly appointed board members. They express concern that you are not bringing in enough money in your annual fund, and they think that the annual fund goals for the upcoming year should be set higher. They think you'll be able to triple your revenues if you just focus more attention on the annual fund.

Here's another scenario: You are charged with managing corporate and foundation grants at your organization. You started out with a simple Word table to track proposals. Then you moved that information into an Excel spreadsheet because you needed to start filtering by date for your reports. The spreadsheet now has become cumbersome.

If you move to a CRM product and create a custom table or entity, you will be able to filter and sort previous and forthcoming proposal opportunities. You will be able to have dashboards on your desktop that show automatically updated live reports, such as forthcoming grant deadlines, proposals submitted this year and pending, grant awards this year versus last year, and top 10 forthcoming projects.

CRM applications are also useful to track corporate and foundation grant efforts.

If you track gifts in your CRM application, you'll be able to bring up a list of all gifts received in the last X days, months, or years. Sort that list of donations by source type, and you may be able to easily send back a report that shows exactly where all of your annual fund gifts have come from. This detailed data will enable you to make reasoned, strategic judgments about next year's annual fund goals. You will be able to analyze patterns and trends. You will have the solid information you need to move forward on the basis of hard data rather than hunches.

Notes

CRM applications have a notes feature that allows you to enter and search for random but important information about donors.

Development work in general involves managing details. Many times during the course of a day you will get random information about prospective donors that may be significant or even vitally important at some point in the future. How can you keep that information at your fingertips? Yellow sticky notes or even well-written notes on a piece of paper placed in a file will not serve you over time. A CRM database is an ideal solution for the problem of storing randomly acquired information in notes.

Keyword searches can lead you to very specific information about donors.

For example, you hear that a prospective major donor enjoys fly fishing. You are told that this is his passion in life. Where do you put that information so that you will have it when you need it? CRM applications have a notes feature that not only enables you to store the information but also to retrieve it easily. Months later, when you are trying to remember the name of that prospective donor and all you can remember is that his passion in life is fly fishing, with a CRM application you can do a keyword search on "fly fishing," and you will find your prospective donor (see Figure 8.4).

Reporting

If you use CRM software to track all of your correspondence, activity, and gift records, you will be able to generate a variety of useful reports quickly and easily.

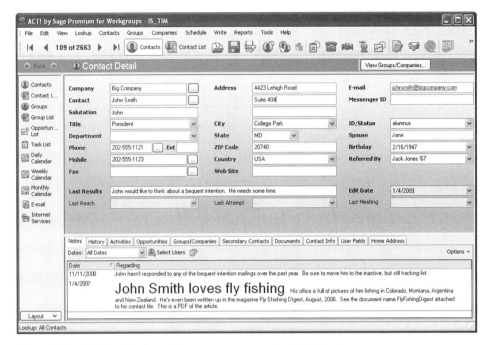

Figure 8.4 *CRM applications allow you to store notes about individuals.*

Here's a possible scenario: Your 90-day performance evaluation is coming up next week. You've heard rumblings that some of your colleagues—who aren't familiar with fundraising methodology—are grumbling about your job performance. They expected vast sums of money to begin rolling in the minute you were hired, and that hasn't happened yet.

The reality is that you have been doing intensive work behind the scenes to establish contacts and nurture relationships with an identified group of high net worth donor prospects. Within 12 to 18 months, your organization stands to benefit significantly from this work. However, you do not yet have cash in hand to produce as evidence of your effectiveness.

In this scenario, there are a couple of things you might do. You could make a presentation in which you rely on your powers of persuasion to reassure your review committee that you are working on a number of hot prospects that will come to fruition over the next year or so. Or you could present a detailed report that lists each prospect you have been working on, together with a chronological listing of all of the phone calls, appointments, tasks, letters, and e-mails you have undertaken in relation to each one.

If reporting is one of your most important functions, you might consider choosing a fundraising-specific software application, such as Blackbaud, DonorPerfect, or Sage Fundraising. You'll usually pay more for these applications, but they include many fundraising reports out of the box.

Most reports can be generated in Excel. If you can export your data to Excel, you can create charts, graphs, lists, and subsets of your contact list easily.

Having a concrete report instantly ready to show your progress with prospects can be a great way to justify your time because it gives hard evidence of the work you are doing on behalf of your organization. If someone should inquire about what you do all day, you can print out a report and show them in great detail that you are engaged productively. Especially if you work in a confrontational work environment, CRM software can be an essential tool for professional survival.

Microsoft Dynamics CRM and Microsoft Dynamics CRM Online

Microsoft Dynamics CRM is the fastest-growing CRM application on the market today. That's mainly due to its seamless integration into Outlook. Microsoft Dynamics CRM is a web-based CRM solution, but all of the features available in the web client are also available right from within Outlook.

Website: crm.dynamics.com

Price: Microsoft Dynamics CRM Online: $44/month

Microsoft Dynamics CRM On-Premise: $2,000–$5,000 per server plus $1,000 per workstation

Pros

- Integrates with Outlook contacts and handheld devices.
- Extremely customizable.
- Inexpensive hosted offering.

Cons

- On-premise solution requires IT infrastructure and knowledge.
- Heavy reliance on Outlook and Exchange Server (only a con if you don't use Outlook).
- Extensive product features can be overwhelming for someone with limited needs.

Product Overview

If you want to track gifts, send e-mails, track appointments and tasks, generate reports, and maintain a centralized list of contacts, you can do so right from within Outlook with CRM.

Microsoft Dynamics CRM is the big-brother version of Outlook Business Contact Manager, which is discussed later in this chapter. CRM is infinitely more customizable than Business Contact Manager, and it is definitely better suited to a multiuser environment.

Don't let the high sticker price scare you away. Microsoft Dynamics CRM is available to most nonprofits at a fraction of the suggested retail price through TechSoup. The Professional Server for Microsoft Dynamics CRM lists at more than $2,000, but the TechSoup price is less than $100. Workstation licenses through TechSoup can run less than $50.

Even at this highly discounted price, you should consider opting for Microsoft Dynamics CRM Online, the Microsoft-hosted edition of CRM. With Microsoft Dynamics CRM Online, you pay a monthly fee—usually around $44/month—and Microsoft takes care of the administration of your database. With the hosted version of CRM, you won't have to install on your server, maintain the database, manage your backups, and so on.

Microsoft CRM Online is often the ideal solution for nonprofit groups because the hosted offering requires very little existing infrastructure or IT help. You don't need a server or even a network to connect everyone in your office to the centralized database. All you need is an Internet connection and computers running Outlook or Internet Explorer.

Key Features

- Fully integrated into Outlook.
- Track e-mails sent through Outlook back to contacts, accounts, or even individual gift records.
- Track activities on your Outlook calendar back to contacts.
- Produce reports using SQL Server Reporting Services.
- Easily share contacts in Microsoft Dynamics CRM with contacts in Outlook/Exchange and handheld devices.
- Create custom entities to track gifts, prospects, pledges, and so on.

ACT! by Sage

Used by more than 2.8 million people worldwide, ACT! has held the top slot in the contact management category of software for more than 20 years. There's a reason for that: ACT! is really easy to use.

Website: www.act.com

Price: $99–$430. Available in multiple editions, including ACT! by Sage, ACT! by Sage Premium, and a version of ACT! by Sage Premium that includes your SQL Server Standard licenses.

Pros

- Intuitive user interface.
- Best mail merge features of any product reviewed.
- Inexpensive solution.

Cons

- Limited web client.
- Customization required to track gifts within the product.
- Lacks ability to automate processes with workflow.

Product Overview

Add water: instant database. That's the motto for most ACT! users. After purchasing the software, which can be done on the ACT! website or through most retail stores that sell software, you can be up and running within hours. Without a huge investment or IT infrastructure, ACT! will allow you to keep track of your donors and other contacts together with all the relevant information for each one.

ACT!'s strong point is its ability to manage relationships with individuals. Any fundraising professional looking to cultivate relationships with donors should look at ACT!.

Many development officers whose organizations have invested in enterprise systems such as Blackbaud still use ACT! to track relationships with individual high net worth donors. Sage Software Senior Vice President and General Manager of ACT!, David van Toor, says, "ACT! has always been embraced by nonprofit fundraising professionals because of its focus on managing relationships. Whether you're writing a letter in Word, sending an e-mail in ACT!, scheduling an activity, or just keeping relevant notes on a prospective donor, ACT! provides a quick and cost-effective way to keep everything organized."

If you are running ACT! 2009 or newer, you can create custom tables in ACT!. This feature allows you to create custom entities, such as gifts. You can track multiple gifts per contact and report on all gifts that were received within a specific range. You can also use the custom table feature to track pledges, prospects, and other development-related activities.

For more detailed information on ACT! and its features, take a look at my book on ACT!, *Managing Contacts with ACT! 2006* (Course Technology PTR, 2005).

Key Features

- Add an unlimited number of fields to track information about specific donors.
- Only five clicks to perform a mail merge into Microsoft Word.
- Full integration with Outlook for tracking both incoming and outgoing e-mails.
- Track activities back to contact records.
- Quick lookups make it easy to generate a list of contacts that match the criteria you provide.
- Use groups to associate otherwise unrelated contacts.
- Generate instant reports with the Export to Excel feature.

Outlook Business Contact Manager (BCM)

Outlook Business Contact Manager is a free add-on for most Outlook users. It was introduced to the Outlook suite in version 2003 and has been included with all versions since. It ships with most editions of Microsoft Office and is usually included on the supplementary DVD included with your Office media.

Website: www.microsoft.com/outlook
Price: Free with most editions of Outlook

Pros

- Free for most Outlook users.
- Track Outlook activities back to contacts and report on your activity.
- Solution fully integrated into Outlook, so there's no extra software to open.

Cons

- Limited security. All users have administrative rights and can delete any data or make modifications to the database.
- Contacts in BCM are tracked separately from Outlook contacts.
- No automated backup.

Product Overview

Once you've installed Outlook on your computer, you will need to install the Business Contact Manager plug-in separately to enable contact management features within Outlook. With BCM installed, you will be able to categorize contacts, run mail merges, send mass e-mail, create reports, create a dashboard to show graphical representations of your work, and create custom fields to track specific information related to your contacts.

Outlook BCM will track contacts, accounts, opportunities, and activities. You can make minor field customizations to track extra information and produce reports that show what you've done with specific contacts.

BCM is ideal for single users but doesn't always work well in a multiuser environment. Limits on customization and number of users and an inability to add custom entities make this solution inadvisable for large organizations. That's not to say that BCM is bad software. It's just better suited for a single user.

Key Features

- Easily import contacts from Outlook by dragging them.
- Add an unlimited number of fields to track information about specific donors.
- Use categories to track donor types, donor levels, prospect sets, staff types, and so on.

- Track activities on your Outlook calendar back to individual contacts, making it easy to show—on a contact level—what you've done with a specific person.
- Send personalized mass e-mails for an extra fee using the included Microsoft e-mail service.
- Run mail merges into Word to create personalized mass correspondence.
- Use the search features to find specific sets of contacts.
- Run reports to show your work.
- Export data to Excel for easy reporting.

Salesforce.com

Salesforce.com is the most popular hosted CRM application on the market, with more than 1,000,000 active users across tens of thousands of companies. The feature set is very extensive, to the point where getting going with the product can require significant training and can sometimes seem overwhelming.

Website: www.salesforce.com

Price: Prices range from $0 for the Personal Edition to $195/user/month for the Unlimited Edition. Many nonprofit organizations can get some (usually 10) users at no cost.

Pros

- Very extensive set of features.
- Hosted solution requires little IT infrastructure.
- Many add-on products available through the AppExchange.

Cons

- Pricing structure may force you to upgrade as your database and needs grow.
- Many features are very click-intensive.
- Mediocre integration with Outlook.

Product Overview

Salesforce can be used to track your database of contacts, manage activities, run automated workflow, and carry out most tasks that have already been mentioned for other applications.

This program is ideal for organizations with large numbers of users or highly complex gift-tracking or reporting needs.

Many nonprofit organizations will qualify for Salesforce's software donation program. Salesforce has a companywide mandate, called the 1-1-1 program, where 1 percent of employee labor hours, 1 percent of software bandwidth, and 1 percent of profits all go to charity. If your organization is a charity, you might be in a position to benefit from this program.

Before you purchase Salesforce.com, be mindful of their pricing structure, which is generally geared toward up-selling existing customers. The Personal Edition is free, but it doesn't allow you to export your data or perform offsite backups. The Professional Edition, at around $65/month, doesn't include handheld access or offline access. Those features cost about $300/user/year extra. The Enterprise Edition, at around $125/month, only allows for 20 MB of storage space per user, including attachments.

User friendliness isn't Salesforce.com's strong point, but if you're looking for sophisticated reporting or management analysis tools, Salesforce will become your best friend.

Key Features

- Ability to maintain a centralized list of contacts.
- Free for single users.
- Create custom entities to track.
- Completely hosted solution, so there's no software to install.
- Links with handheld devices.

Raiser's Edge (Blackbaud)

Raiser's Edge from Blackbaud is the most commonly used fundraising software on the market. It integrates with other Blackbaud nonprofit management software modules—such as Financial Edge, Education Edge, and Patron Edge. It is feature-rich and is best suited for large nonprofit organizations that have significant IT infrastructure and staff. Watch out for maintenance fees, which are comparatively high with Raiser's Edge.

Website: www.blackbaud.com
Price: $8,000+

Pros

- Integrates with existing Blackbaud modules, including Blackbaud's accounting software.

- Feature-rich and very focused on development/nonprofit efforts.

- Significant continuing education resources available for learning the system.

Cons

- Requires significant internal IT knowledge to deploy and administer.

- Very expensive.

- Module-based system may force you to purchase an extra module to get specific types of functionality.

Product Overview

Raiser's Edge is sold with a base component that is supplemented by specific modules. You can perform many basic record-keeping activities in the base software, but you may find that for a specific purpose—such as a charity auction—you will need a component. These components can add significantly to the cost, so you will want to make sure that you perform a database assessment before jumping into a Raiser's Edge purchase.

If you can afford it, Raiser's Edge can be a great asset to your organization. It has the widest range of features of any fundraising software reviewed in this book, and the reports included out of the box will probably cover most of your requirements.

Key Features

- Record key activity that you have with constituents.
- Synchronize your database with Outlook.
- Integration with online giving sites.

- SQL or Oracle back-end database allows for database security and growth.
- Extensive library of built-in reports.
- Out-of-the-box ability to track gifts.

DonorPerfect

DonorPerfect offers many of the features of Blackbaud and Sage Fundraising, but at a significantly lower cost. It doesn't include all of the features of either of these, but depending on your needs, DonorPerfect may be a good fit. It is now offered in both an online and an offline offering. If you do not have extensive server and IT infrastructure, go with the hosted version.

> Website: www.donorperfect.com
> Price: $3,000–$5,000; $54/month hosted

Pros

- Built-in social networking tools.
- Inexpensive total cost of ownership.
- Extensive set of reports preconfigured for fundraising professionals.

Cons

- Limited add-ons to extend functionality beyond out-of-the-box offering.
- More expensive than Salesforce.com's free option.
- Backed by a small company.

Product Overview

DonorPerfect offers a suite of products that help fundraising professionals to manage donors, coordinate volunteers, track grants, manage contacts, coordinate special events, send mass e-mails, create letters, and manage pledges and donations.

DonorPerfect is an appropriate solution for most small development efforts. It may cost a bit more than Salesforce's free solution for nonprofits, but included in your total cost of ownership budgeting is staff time. If you need an inexpensive solution for tracking donor pledges, for example, DonorPerfect can do most of what you'll need out of the box. Salesforce would probably require customization to perform that task.

DonorPerfect also links to WebLink online donation pages. WebLink pages are easily customized, so you can use them to manage general donations, donations for a specific event, tickets for a gala, or just about any other situation where you would want to collect money via credit card online.

Key Features

- Create user-defined fields for organization-specific information.
- Manage campaigns and track their results.
- Track grants.
- Events tracking component.
- Collect donations online.
- Automated pledge reminders.
- Constituent reporting.
- Export reports to PDF, Excel, or Word.
- Multi-currency support.
- Create relationships between contacts.

90-Day Fundraising Software Checklist

✓ You have looked into at least four CRM software applications for the purpose of tracking your activities, proposals, gifts, and reports.

✓ You understand the advantages and disadvantages of these four applications and how each might improve your productivity.

✓ You have taken a 30-day trial copy of two CRM applications and have practiced using the contact and calendar features of each.

✓ You have practiced automating your correspondence with two CRM applications, and you know how to perform letter mail and e-mail merges to single contacts and multiple contacts.

✓ You have identified the best CRM application from your perspective, and you have practiced customizing the application in one of the following areas: grant proposal tracking, event invitation management, individual gift tracking, planned giving mail campaign, major gift cultivation and solicitation.

Chapter 9

Fundraising with Social Media and Web 2.0 Technologies

- The New World Wide Web
- Social Networking
- Social Networking Sites
- Multimedia Hosting
- Online Fundraising Tools
- Online Auctions
- Blogging
- Webinars
- Your Website
- 90-Day Web 2.0 Checklist

The New World Wide Web

The World Wide Web started out as a set of single, static web pages. In the beginning, most organizations had small sites with at most a few hundred pages of information. The web was basically an online bulletin board. With the introduction of Web 2.0 technologies, however, the web has taken on a whole new—and very interactive—role.

Web 1.0

In the era generally known as Web 1.0, websites were mainly one-directional. Information was posted on sites with little feedback from readers.

When you hear people refer to Web 1.0, they are generally referring to the period when the World Wide Web consisted of static web pages. Organizations created websites as a one-way communication method to get information out to the general public. In the Web 1.0 world, there was little communication back to the organization from the reader.

In a Web 1.0 world, your website probably would have contained:

- An "about us" page
- A calendar of events
- A page with a history of your organization
- A page with contact information

Web 2.0

Web 2.0 technologies include blogs, podcasts, social networking sites, and other web services that offer readers the option to post content and contribute to the online discussion.

Web 2.0 is the term that refers to web technologies that are dynamic and provide two-way communication between your organization and people within your community. With Web 2.0 technology, your audience can actually be involved in creating content. The primary focus of your web page is to facilitate a conversation between your organization and someone who is reading your website.

In a Web 2.0 world, your web presence might contain:

- Interactive cause-related groups on a social networking site
- Podcasts with a message board for comments
- A blog where your CEO regularly posts updates
- A video page with clips from your recent events
- An online polling module on your site

This chapter focuses on Web 2.0 technologies that you can integrate into the greater fundraising plan for your organization. As you read through this chapter, keep in mind that the web can complement your existing fundraising activities, but nothing described here should replace the traditional activities discussed earlier in this book.

Social Networking

The primary goal of social networking is to boost and organize your group of supporters. There are many social networking sites available, and you should consider creating a presence on a few of them.

Without a sense of community, no fundraising can exist.

Without a community, no fundraising efforts can exist. A college or university has a community of students, alumni, parents, and faculty. Similarly, an independent school has a community of students, alumni, parents, and teachers. A social service network has a community of people who have been touched by its services, as well as relatives and friends of such people. A hospital has a community of patients, allied health professionals and physicians, and also friends and relatives who have seen people helped by the hospital. Their day-to-day operations provide such nonprofit organizations a built-in structure for growing their community.

Other nonprofits must build their community from the ground up with a continuing effort to increase membership and involvement. An animal rights group builds its community by contacting people who love dogs, cats, and other animals. Environmental organizations seek members and friends who support protection of parks, forests, trails, bodies of water, and various wild animal species. Scientific and other professional associations recruit members from the greater society by promoting and enhancing the professional interests of members.

Social networking sites extend traditional networking events into an online environment.

Without a sense of community, most of these organizations would not be able to raise funds. If you work for an autism research fund, you will probably tap into the network of people who have children or grandchildren with autism or who have a close friend or relative with an autistic child. People with personal experience with autism are your community.

As long as fundraising has been around, professional fundraisers have spent a good share of their time supporting their communities. Colleges and universities have periodic reunions for a reason. Membership organizations have annual meetings and other organized events for a variety of reasons, one of which is to enhance the fundraising capabilities of the organization. By consistently engaging their constituencies—whether an alumni base, a membership, or a group of people in a community—nonprofit organizations increase the likelihood that people will make contributions.

Social networking sites make it possible for you to create an online community that mimics your offline community. They give you the framework to keep track of your potential donors, and they provide a great way to organize lists of volunteers.

Following are some examples of situations where your fundraising efforts could benefit from a social networking presence.

Annual Fund

Social networking sites can be an integral part of your annual fund. In addition to letters, phone calls, and other correspondence, you might send out a solicitation to all of your friends on MySpace or Facebook.

Event Invitations

Your annual charity auction is coming up in three months, and you need to invite people. Every social networking site includes the ability to invite people to an event, so you can invite all of your Facebook, Bebo, and Friendster friends to the auction. Sending the invitation through a social networking site has a viral effect. When members of your community get the invitation, they can invite all of their friends on the social networking site.

Volunteer Solicitations

If you are an organization that provides disaster assistance, you could put out a call for assistance and donations in the event of a natural disaster that requires extra funding, in-kind contributions, or emergency volunteers. An environmental organization might alert members and friends of an unforeseen impending threat to a trail, forest, or animal species and make a special appeal for public action and funds to address this sudden threat.

Maintaining a Mailing List

One of your primary responsibilities as a development officer will be to maintain a list of potential donors. Social networking is perfect for this. When people move, their Facebook account will probably remain unchanged, so even though you do not have their current mailing address, you can still get in touch with them online. Conventional methods of keeping mailing addresses current can be time-consuming and expensive, often involving lengthy delays during which current information is unavailable. It is still necessary to do this conventional work, but social networking can relieve some of the time, effort, and expense involved in keeping current on your people.

Finding New Prospective Donors

Through social networking sites, you can actually expand your potential donor base far beyond its current state. If you create a cause on Facebook, for example, you might have 20 people join that cause. The Facebook page of each of those 20 individuals will then display the cause. Instantly, 2,000 people see information about your cause. Even if only one percent of these extended friends join your cause, you've just doubled the size of your Facebook mailing list. But you're likely to get a much higher response.

This method of community-building is very different from purchasing mailing lists to seek new members or donors. Conventional mass-mailing lists cannot be systematically qualified for anything before you actually use the names in a mail or phone campaign. You attempt to do the qualification at the point of contact, whether by mail or by phone. Vendors may refine or segment a list for various factors, which may increase the odds of your success over a random list of people. But you basically buy a list, try using it, and hope that you are actually communicating with people who have some reason to be interested in your cause. If you get positive results, you have qualified some recipients as prospective new members or donors.

If you have people joining your cause through Facebook, they qualify themselves by showing an intrinsic interest in your cause, and to a certain extent they qualify the thousands of other people associated in their own online networks. You couldn't really purchase this kind of community-building potential with conventional mass-marketing lists.

Social Networking Sites

There are hundreds of social networking sites available today. This is both good and bad. It's good because each social networking site offers you an opportunity to actively market into a specific subset of society. It's bad because there are more social networking sites than you could possibly join.

In this section, I outline a few of the major players in the social networking community. You should pick a few of the top networking sites and create a presence on them. Unless you have staffing to devote specifically to social networking, you probably should limit your online presence to two or three of these sites. Most people have a presence on at least MySpace and Facebook.

Facebook and MySpace

Facebook was originally created as a social networking site for college students. It was widely popular on college campuses and within a year was opened to high school students, then businesspeople, then everyone. Today, Facebook has more than 120 million members worldwide.

In principle, MySpace is almost identical to Facebook. In looks, though, MySpace is radically different. MySpace allows users much more flexibility in designing individual pages. Your MySpace page might be a bright color with flashing elements scattered throughout. It might include videos, music, and other multimedia elements that aren't possible with Facebook. MySpace has more than 240 million members. For an excellent example of how extensively some nonprofit organizations make use of Facebook, MySpace, and other social networking sites, see Figure 9.1 for the Humane Society of the United States' Facebook page sample.

Between Facebook's 120 million and MySpace's 240 million members, you have a potential online friend base of more than 100 million people., even factoring in those people who may have pages with both services

Here is a short list of terms you will need to understand to use Facebook and MySpace:

- **Friends.** Facebook is designed so that only people marked as friends can see your profile. MySpace tends to be more open, unless you have marked your profile as private. Your popularity is judged by the number of friends you have, and this statistic is prominently displayed when you launch the application.

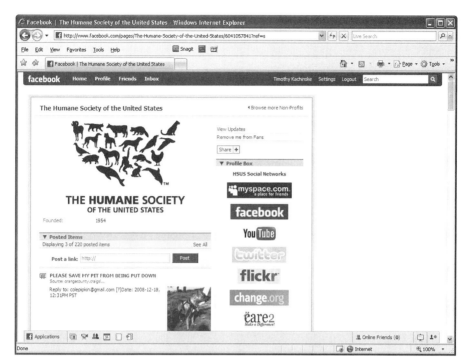

Figure 9.1 *Facebook page of the Humane Society of the United States.*

- **Fans.** If you join Facebook as an organization or a cause, users can add themselves as a fan. Fans are similar to friends. Once people become your fans, they will be able to see your photos, updates, and articles. More importantly (for you, at least), you will be able to easily send mass communications to your fans. As a development officer, your main goal will be to get as many friends and fans as possible, since you will only be able to see and communicate with your friends or fans.

- **Groups.** Any user can create a group of users. You might create a group for a particular cause, or you might have a general group. For example, if you are working for a college or university, you might have a group for alumni who are interested in volunteering in student recruitment. If you are an environmental group working to preserve a lake or river, you might have a group that volunteers to do watches or visits to the body of water, or you may have a group that wants to be mobilized for action when a proposed public policy or private development threatens the watershed. Any group can be approached for support.

- **Top Friends.** MySpace has a feature that lets you single out a few friends as your top friends. It's a good idea to put donors on this list.

- **Wall.** Each Facebook user has a wall. Friends can post to each other's walls, and the wall creates an online equivalent of the community bulletin board. You cannot put your organization and its efforts on the bulletin board. That must be done by your organization's friends.

- **Bulletins.** MySpace has a bulletin feature that lets you post relevant information, including links back to your website. You might send out a bulletin that simply says, "Go to www.yournonprofitname.com to promote social change." This bulletin can then be sent around to all of your friends. Be careful about sending too many bulletins, however. You do not want to annoy your friends, and you do not want to be seen as a spammer.

- **Blogs.** Both MySpace and Facebook have features that let you blog about recent developments within your organization. If your blog is interesting enough, users will subscribe to it, which will drive participation in your social networking site. If you have a blog, be sure to keep it up to date. Nothing looks sadder than a year-old blog with one posting.

- **Tagged Photos.** You can post photos to your site. Then, any of your friends or fans can tag individual people within the photos. Hover the mouse over a person's head in a picture, and that person's name appears. Go to a person's profile, and you can see all pictures in which he or she has been tagged.

- **Widgets/Applications.** Facebook includes the ability to create third-party applications. These applications can be installed onto any user's individual Facebook profile. You should definitely check out the "Causes" application, which allows any user to put an advertisement for a cause on his or her individual profile.

- **Events.** Facebook and MySpace users can create events. It's then easy to invite all of your friends to the events.

Twitter

Twitter is a simple service that allows you to update a status message that shows what you're doing. Other Twitter users can "follow" you on the service, and then each time your status changes, they will get notified, either by e-mail or through their own Twitter page.

If you have a celebrity who works with your organization, you might use Twitter to highlight what the celebrity is doing with your group. If you are college or university, your President should have a Twitter account. If 10,000 alums follow your President on Twitter, then you can use the service to showcase the great things your university is doing. If you are a cause-related non-profit, your executive director should have a Twitter account so that people can follow what he or she is doing on behalf of your cause. See Figure 9.2 for an example of the American Red Cross Twitter page.

Twitter lets you provide quick status messages to share updates about what you're currently doing.

Figure 9.2 *Twitter page of the American Red Cross.*

If your executive is not already a blogger who blogs all the time (including while sitting at the airport), you will want to designate a staff person to assist your executive in keeping a Twitter account current and interesting on a daily basis.

LinkedIn

LinkedIn is the most popular professional networking site (see Figure 9.3). You can post information about your education, current job, contact information, and past job history. Instead of

Figure 9.3 *Home page for LinkedIn.com.*

adding friends, as you would in MySpace or Facebook, you add other LinkedIn users to your LinkedIn network.

LinkedIn is a professional networking site. While you probably won't do much direct fundraising on LinkedIn, it can be a good professional resource and research tool.

The site includes the ability to create groups, so you could create a group for your cause on LinkedIn. LinkedIn probably won't be as powerful a fundraising tool as MySpace or Facebook, but if you are looking to target an older crowd, you may find that more of them will have LinkedIn accounts. LinkedIn's original membership was predominantly professionals working in high-technology careers, but that has changed. It now includes professionals of all sorts.

Change.org

Change.org is a social networking site geared toward nonprofit causes.

Change.org is a social networking site whose only goal is to connect volunteers with nonprofit organizations and causes (see Figure 9.4). *At no cost to your nonprofit organization*, you can join this site, accept online donations, and engage supporters. For $20 per month, you can purchase a premium account that will allow greater flexibility for creating a good-looking landing page on the site. Block out a couple of hours and sign up for a Change.org site.

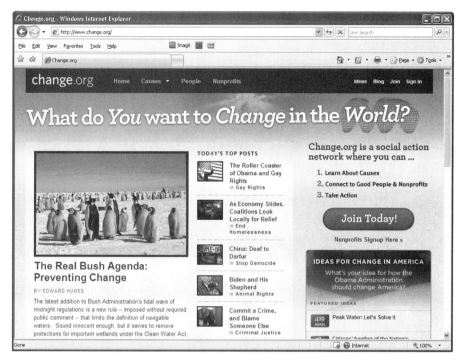

Figure 9.4 *Go to Change.org for social networking ideas and services.*

Other Social Networking Sites

There are about 250 major social networking sites worldwide, and so far we've discussed only a handful. You cannot have a major presence on all of them, so you should pick two or three for intense focus. If in doubt, Facebook, MySpace, and Change.org are probably the best picks to start with.

The social networking sites that you use will depend in large part on your target audience. If your constituency is largely made up of people from Brazil, for example, you will want to have a presence on Orkut, Google's social networking site. Orkut is the single most visited website in Brazil. It is quite popular in India as well. See Figure 9.5 for a page from the care2.com website that focuses on environmental and social issues and networking. The point is, ask around among your potential donors and see what networking sites they use. Consider conducting a survey. If you are working at a college or university, survey your alumni and friends who have an overseas address of record to learn which sites they frequent. If you are working at a nonprofit that has a membership roll, do a search of members or past donors and filter a report by country within the current mailing address of

Survey some of your donors to see what networking sites they use. Do some research to identify social networking sites that are specific to your nonprofit organization or cause.

247

record. Surveying these contacts will provide you with a basis for networking sites from an international perspective. You should focus on the most strategic sites.

Table 9.1 includes examples of sites that could be on your radar.

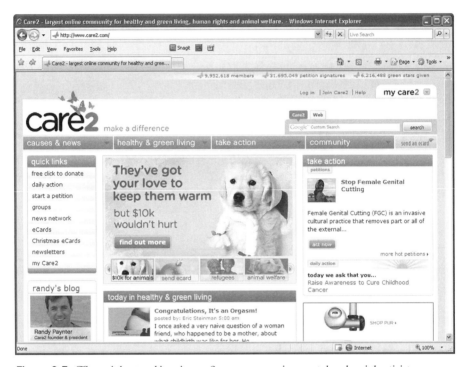

Figure 9.5 *The social networking site care2.com serves environmental and social activists.*

Table 9.1 Social Networking Sites

Site	Registered Users	Target Audience
Bebo.com	40 million	Young people in U.S., U.K., and Asia Pacific
Blackplanet.com	20 million	African-Americans
Care2.com	9 million	Environmentalists and activists
Friendster	80 million	General
Hi5.com	80 million	Eastern Europeans
Mychurch.com	150K	Christian churches
StudiVZ.com	8 million	German-speaking students
Xiaonei.com	15 million	China

Multimedia Hosting

Images and videos can play a big role in creating an online community for your organization. Always document fundraisers, galas, and other special events with pictures and video.

Posting the images on a multimedia hosting site can complement your social networking projects, since most social networking sites can integrate with these sites. Having a repository of online pictures and videos can also make your organization more prominent in search engine results.

Having a large repository of photos and videos can make your development materials sizzle. Postcards, brochures, appeal letters, annual reports, annual fund reports, and just about any other fundraising literature will be more effective if you use photos from your organization.

Multimedia Equipment

Your development office should invest in some basic multimedia equipment so that you have photos and videos to post to social networking and image/video hosting sites. At a minimum, this should include:

1. **Digital cameras.** Invest in quality digital cameras. You should have multiple cameras, and make sure you have enough in your fleet so that you can loan them out to volunteers at events. If you have an alumni reunion, for example, ask one of the attendees to volunteer to take pictures. Then, you can follow the event with an annual fund appeal and links to the pictures from the event.

   In your fleet of cameras, you should have at least one SLR camera with a professional flash. Pictures taken indoors will look much better when taken with one of these cameras. Expect to pay $1,000 for the camera, $1,000 for a wide angle lens, and another $500 or so for the flash.

   It is also a good idea to have a good point-and-shoot digital camera at every event. These are less cumbersome than an SLR, but they still have sophisticated settings. Learn how to set lighting, flash, and other settings in a variety of indoor situations. You can test a point-and-shoot, determine and set the proper settings for successful indoor pictures, and then instruct a volunteer to click off pictures at a specific distance from subjects for perfect photos of your attendees.

Invest in a set of good still and video cameras. Keep a good supply of memory cards on hand for your cameras. Use these cameras to document special events for your organization. Make sure staff and volunteers know how to take digital photos and how to submit them to you.

2. **Photoshop.** Invest in a copy of Photoshop and consider taking classes to learn its features. Photoshop is an invaluable tool for touching up and cropping images. It is the industry-leading picture-editing tool. No other software in this category comes close to Photoshop's feature set.

3. **Video camera.** Make certain that your video camera can interface with your computer. Most digital video cameras on the market today come with built-in FireWire ports, which make it really easy to transfer video from the camera to your computer. Not all computers come with FireWire ports, but you can get add-on cards that will add the functionality to any desktop or laptop.

4. **Video editing equipment.** Macs come with great built-in software to edit videos. iMovie is included with any Mac purchased today. For more complex video editing needs, check out Final Cut Pro. There are also a number of video editing suites available for PCs, including Adobe Premiere, CyberLink PowerDirector, and Roxio Easy Media Creator. If you can edit videos yourself, you will save a lot of money.

5. **CD/DVD duplicator.** Consider purchasing a mass CD or DVD duplicator. They're relatively inexpensive, and they can be a great way to create many copies of a multimedia CD or DVD for a fraction of the price you would pay to have them professionally mastered.

Some duplicators have a robotic arm that loads new CDs into the burning drive, so you can make hundreds of CDs or DVDs without babysitting the machine. Primera makes a line of duplicators that cost between $1,300 and $6,000. The lower-end machines can only make about 25 discs at a time, but they perform the same general function as the more expensive duplicators.

Flickr

Flickr is a picture- and video-hosting site.

Owned by Yahoo, Flickr is a picture-hosting site that currently hosts more than 3 billion images (see Figure 9.6). Free users can upload up to 100 megabytes per month, but for a nominal fee, you can upgrade to a professional account with no upload limits. Pictures are divided into albums and are accessible to anyone with access to the web. To sign up for a Flickr account, go to www.flickr.com.

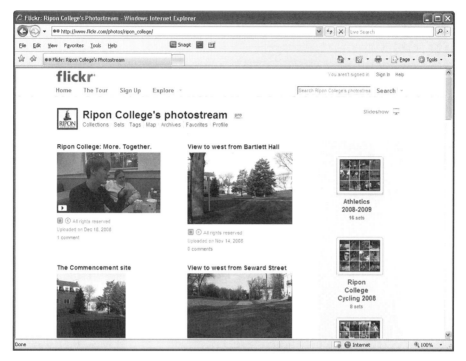

Figure 9.6 *Flickr.com is a website for uploading photographs.*

Picasa

Picasa is the Google-owned version of Flickr (see Figure 9.7). Online tools incorporated into Picasa include the ability to edit red eyes and do skin touchups. You can also crop pictures and perform some basic functions that would otherwise require a tool such as Photoshop. Picasa has a downloadable software program that makes it easy to bulk-upload images to the site. Images can then be tagged by album, event, or individual.

Picasa offers up to 1 gigabyte of picture hosting for free. Additional space is very inexpensive.

The online photo-sharing service offered for users of the Picasa desktop application is called Picasa Web Albums. Up to 1 gigabyte of free space is available with this service, but you can purchase additional space for between $1 and $2 per gigabyte per year, depending on volume. To sign up for Picasa, go to picasa.google.com.

YouTube

Unless you have spent the last few years under a rock, you have probably spent some time on YouTube (see Figure 9.8). Nearly 10 percent of all Internet traffic worldwide comes from YouTube

YouTube is the most popular video-hosting site worldwide.

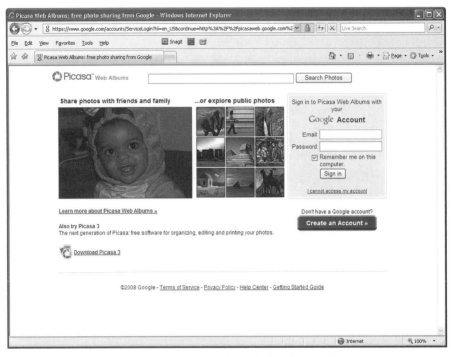

Figure 9.7 *Picasa is Google's version of Flickr for uploading photographs.*

Figure 9.8
*Sample YouTube
page showing
college video
postings.*

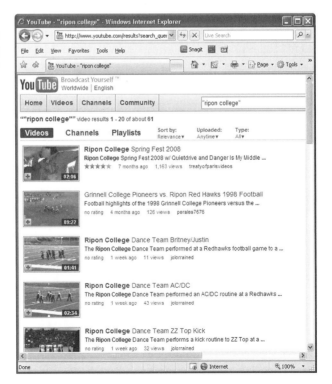

downloads. Create a YouTube account and post relevant videos from your organization on the site. Once the videos have been posted, you can embed them into your e-mail templates or website.

Online Fundraising Tools

Chapter 8 discussed customer relationship management (CRM) in detail. *Constituent relationship management* is the common term used to apply traditional CRM to the fundraising industry. The main difference between customer relationship management tools and constituent relationship management tools is that the constituent tools generally make it a lot easier to publish websites with online donation sites, blogs, and other Web 2.0 features. Constituent relationship management tools also generally have some level of built-in gift accounting with fundraising reports pre-built.

Convio

Convio is the market leader for online fundraising and marketing (see Figure 9.9). Through Convio, you can create an online list of donors. Convio can send HTML-formatted mass e-mails to these donors, and the site makes it easy to create web landing pages with online "Donate Now" buttons. The software is very easy to use. If you want a no-hassle solution for organizing your electronic communication with donors and prospects, you should consider Convio.

Convio is the biggest software-as-a-service online fundraising tool.

For more information, go to www.convio.com.

Firstgiving

Firstgiving is an online service that lets anyone create a web page for a nonprofit or cause (see Figure 9.10). To date, more than a million people have used Firstgiving to donate to charities, making contributions amounting to more than $67 million.

For more information, go to www.firstgiving.com.

Blackbaud Kintera

Kintera is Blackbaud's software-as-a-service platform for delivering online constituent relationship management tools to nonprofits (see Figure 9.11). Like most Blackbaud software, Kintera is sold in modules.

For more information, go to www.kintera.com.

Figure 9.9 *Home page for convio.com, an online source for low-cost fundraising services.*

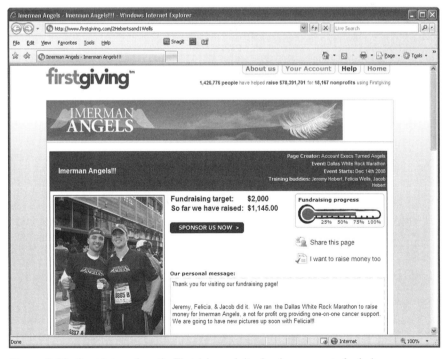

Figure 9.10 *Sample page from the Firstgiving website showing grassroots fundraisers.*

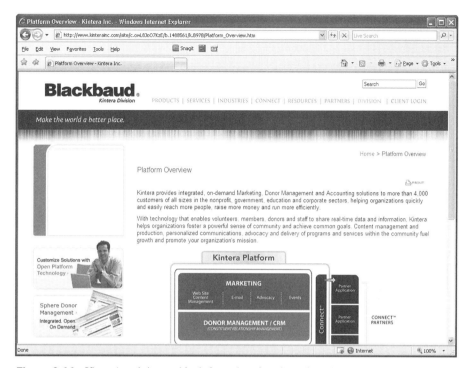

Figure 9.11 *Kintera's website provides information about its online relationship management software and services.*

Online Auctions

Holding your charity auction online can be the best way to have an auction. By holding the auction online, you reduce the need to advertise and publicize an onsite event, your production costs are minimal, and you can potentially reach a worldwide audience. You would never want to create the mechanics of an auction site from scratch. Instead, turn to one of the many Internet auction sites.

eBay Giving Works

eBay is the largest auction site in the world, and by placing your auction items on eBay, you will reach the widest audience possible. Make sure all of the items listed on your auction are listed through Giving Works, which is eBay's charity auction program (see Figure 9.12). Through Giving Works, you can encourage people within your community to post items for sale on eBay with a portion of proceeds benefiting your organization.

eBay Giving Works is the online charity auction site from eBay and is integrated into the main eBay site.

Figure 9.12 *eBay's Giving Works home page introduces you to its online auction to benefit charities.*

Giving Works auctions are listed on eBay specifically as charity auctions with a special ribbon icon. Any items sold through Giving Works also note the percentage of proceeds that go to the charity. More than 14,000 nonprofit organizations are currently enrolled in eBay's Giving Works program.

For more information, go to www.ebaygivingworks.com.

Auctionpay

Auctionpay is a charity auction site that can also automate your event registrations.

Auctionpay offers a suite of products that organize your auctions and gala functions (see Figure 9.13). You can use Auctionpay to create an online mechanism for receiving online donations. Auctionpay also has a comprehensive online auction tool that can automate the process of running your charity auctions. The event management modules offered by Auctionpay assist with managing the guest lists for events, RSVPs, event payments, and thank-you/follow-up correspondence.

For more information, go to www.auctionpay.com.

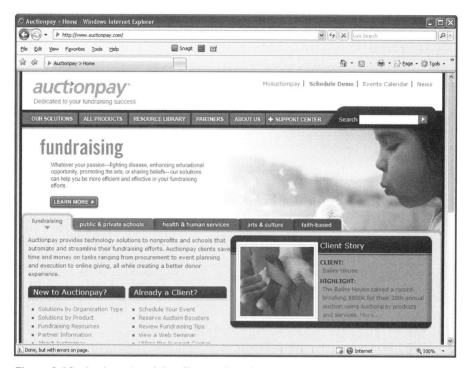

Figure 9.13 *Auctionpay's website offers a variety of resources and services for fundraising events.*

BiddingForGood.com

BiddingForGood.com is an online auction site that is similar in function to eBay, but BiddingForGood.com only offers charity auctions (see Figure 9.14). Bidders looking for a good cause can support their favorite nonprofits and get some cool stuff in the process.

> Biddingforgood is an all-charity auction site that only hosts non-profit auctions.

For more information, go to www.biddingforgood.com.

Blogging

A blog (short for *web log*) is a dynamic online journal where you can post new articles, informational pieces, recaps on events, or just random thoughts. Entries on a blog are usually displayed in reverse chronological order, with the more recent articles posted on top. Entries can be divided by date, subject, or author. If the feature is enabled, readers can post responses to blog entries, creating an actual dialogue between blogger and blog reader.

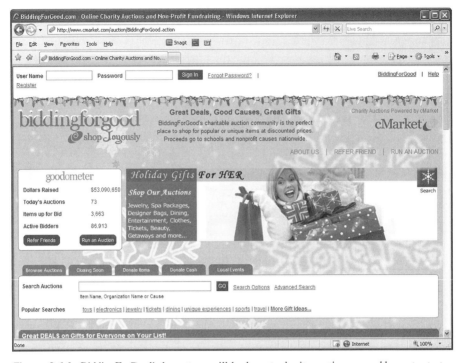

Figure 9.14 *BiddingForGood's home page will lead you to charity auctions or enable you to start one yourself.*

Getting Your CEO to Blog

Your CEO should blog regularly. Use these blog entries to energize your base of donors, and always offer an option to donate on the blog. Monitor the blog continually and ensure that it is updated often.

Your CEO, president, or executive director should have a blog. This blog should be prominently displayed on your website, and new entries should be posted to the blog regularly, preferably daily or weekly.

Getting your CEO to blog might be challenging, and if you have a technology-averse chief executive, the blog should be written or edited by someone on the development staff. Readers of the blog will not know that the CEO isn't actually posting the blogs because the staffer will be drafting material in the CEO's voice, and the CEO will need to review and edit anything that is uploaded.

When your CEO blogs, this will create a dialogue between prospective donors, donors, and others in the community. It would be nearly impossible to create this online dialogue without a blog, so it is important that the head of your organization has one of these sites.

If your CEO starts up a blog, it is important to keep it current. Never start a blog and then forget about maintaining it daily or weekly. See Figure 9.15 for an example of how the Washington, DC Humane Society features its CEO prominently on its blog.

Figure 9.15 *Sample webpage showing blog link for nonprofit CEO.*

Understanding RSS and Atom

Many people check their RSS readers as frequently as they check e-mail. RSS feeds provide at-a-glance news from relevant blogs and websites.

Most people familiar with blogs have some sort of RSS or Atom reader. Blog entries can be syndicated using either RSS or Atom and distributed to people in your community automatically. These reader programs can subscribe to a specific blog. Then, when an entry is made to a blog, it will be pushed automatically to the RSS or Atom reader. Open the RSS reader, and you will see all of the blog entries you've subscribed to. See Figure 9.16 to see how easy it is to sign up for a blog reader on Google.

Figure 9.16 *Page from Google website to sign up for a free blog reader service.*

Finding a Blog Host

Blogger, WordPress, and TypePad are the top blogging hosts. Commercial blog hosts are easier if you don't have in-house web design expertise.

Most blog hosts provide the same core functionality. Some are free, and some charge a nominal fee. Most offer the ability to use a customized domain name as the main site for your blog.

You can use a commercially available blog site or you could have your web designer or ISP create a custom-built blog on your website. Either deployment method for blogs will give the same basic functionality, so it is a good idea to look around at a few blogging options before deciding on one. Check these out:

- **Blogger.com.** This site is owned by Google and is the world's largest blog-hosting site (see Figure 9.17). Blogs are free. Keep in mind that free blog sites have advertising, so your competitors could have an advertisement on your blog.

- **WordPress.com.** This site is an open-source blog project and has a large number of add-on widgets that can make your blog sizzle.

- **TypePad.com.** This site offers robust hosting at a nominal fee. No free sites are available here, but there also isn't any advertising.

Figure 9.17 *Go to Google's blogger.com to sign up for a free blog.*

In addition to these sites, there are thousands of other blog-hosting companies.

Webinars

Webinars (web seminars) can be an economical way to have a meeting. Using a webinar service, you can gather multiple people in an online forum. Everyone dials into a conference-call number, and you can share your computer screen with the group. That screen might include a PowerPoint presentation or a live demonstration on your computer.

WebEx, GoToWebinar, and Microsoft Office Live Meeting all offer the ability to create online webinars for a low monthly fee.

Choosing a Webinar Service

The three major web-conferencing services offer the same base functionality. All offer the ability to have up to 1,000 users on a webinar for a low monthly fee.

The service you choose should be based on a number of factors, including cost and ease of use. All of these services offer free trials, so it might be a good idea to sign up for a trial and do a webinar on each before committing.

The three major webinar services are:

- WebEx: www.webex.com
- Citrix GoToWebinar (see Figure 9.18): www.gotowebinar.com
- Microsoft Office Live Meeting: office.microsoft.com/ livemeeting

Figure 9.18 *GoToWebinar's home page offers a variety of web conferencing options.*

Your Website

First things first: You need a website. If you are working for a medium- or large-sized organization, you probably already have a web presence. Many small organizations, however, still have weak websites that are vintage Web 1.0 examples.

As part of your role as a development officer, you should advocate within your organization for a strong and feature-rich website. This website should contain continually updated information, because it will serve as a primary method of communication with your donors.

If a prospective donor goes to your site in January, visits the pages, and then comes back in March, there should be enough new information on the site to keep him or her engaged.

Search Engine Optimization

After investing in a website, you will want prospective donors, volunteers, activists, and others in your community to be able to find you on the web. Search engine optimization is a key part of this.

Search engine optimization is the process of taking your existing website and improving its rank in search engine results. If your organization is a cancer-research foundation, you are likely to be competing with many other similar organizations for exposure on the web. A search for "cancer research" on Google ideally should bring up a listing for your organization.

There are many companies on the web that specialize in search engine optimization, and you should consider hiring one. Search engines are constantly updating the algorithms used to rank sites, so a search engine optimization strategy that works today might not work tomorrow.

The simplest thing you can do to optimize your website for search engines is to make sure that each page within your website contains description and keyword meta tags. The following is an example of what the code on your web page would look like:

```
<META NAME="keywords" CONTENT="cancer, research, non-profit, colon
    cancer, XYZ Foundation, cancer treatment">
<META NAME="description" CONTENT="The XYZ Foundation provides support
    for research for a cure for cancer.">
<META NAME="robots" CONTENT="FOLLOW,INDEX">
```

If you do not understand that last paragraph, do not panic. Just make sure you hire a search engine optimization company to help out.

Asking for Contributions

Your website should always offer the option to donate online. If your organization is small and does not have an extensive web-based payment processing system in place, you can integrate with PayPal, Convio, or other online services that make it easy to process payments online.

Search engine optimization can increase traffic to your website and can raise your site in search engine results.

Be sure it is easy for anyone to donate money to your organization from your website. A "Donate Now" option should appear on every page.

Take a moment and go to the main page of your website. Within 10 seconds, can the average viewer figure out how to donate money to your organization online? If not, you should re-engineer your site. Create a "Donate Now" or "Make a Contribution" button on the front page, make it red, and make sure it stands out. See Figure 9.19 for an example of how the American Red Cross makes it easy for donors to find services and donate to disaster fundraising campaigns.

Figure 9.19 *Sample American Red Cross home page showing options for giving.*

90-Day Web 2.0 Checklist

✓ You can explain to your colleagues the differences between Web 1.0 and Web 2.0.

✓ You have evaluated the potential that social networking has for your fundraising activities this year.

✓ You have convinced your CEO to start a blog, if she does not yet have one. If she has a blog, you have begun to monitor it daily to ensure that there are new posts.

✓ You have inventoried your digital media hardware and have practiced with still and moving pictures.

✓ You have engaged your webmaster to help you upload still and moving pictures on your organization's website.

✓ You have evaluated two online fundraising tools for improving or increasing your fundraising capabilities this year.

Index